Southern Workers and the Search for Community

The Working Class in American History

Editorial Advisors
David Brody
Alice Kessler-Harris
David Montgomery
Sean Wilentz

A list of books in the series appears at the end of this book.

Southern Workers and the Search for Community

Spartanburg County, South Carolina

G. C. Waldrep III

UNIVERSITY OF ILLINOIS PRESS

URBANA AND CHICAGO

Library of Congress Cataloging-in-Publication Data
Waldrep, George Calvin, 1968–
Southern workers and the search for community: Spartan-
burg County, South Carolina / G. C. Waldrep III.
p.   cm. — (The working class in American history)
Includes bibliographical references and index.
ISBN 0-252-02587-3 (cloth: alk. paper)
ISBN 0-252-06901-3 (pbk.: alk. paper)
1. Spartanburg County (S.C.)
2. Textile workers—South Carolina—Spartanburg
County—History.
3. Textile workers—South Carolina—Spartanburg
County—Social life and customs.
4. Textile workers—Labor unions—South Carolina—
Spartanburg County—History.
I. Title.
II. Series.
HD9857.S65   2000
331.7'677'00975729—dc21   99-050611

1 2 3 4 5 C P 5 4 3 2 1

For Beatrice Norton,
in memory of Annie Laura West Bryant,
and in memory of
Margaret Elizabeth Sheck Waldrep (1913–68)

But something more is involved that is even harder to talk about because it is only slightly understandable, and that is the part that suffering plays in the economy of the spirit. It seems plain that the voice of our despair defines our hope exactly; it seems, indeed, that we cannot know of hope without knowledge of despair, just as we know joy precisely to the extent that we know sorrow.

—Wendell Berry

Now I urge those who read this book not to be discouraged by such calamaties, but to recognize that these punishments were designed not to destroy but to discipline our people. Let what we have said serve as a reminder; we must go on briefly with the story.

—2 Maccabees 6:12, 17

Contents

Acknowledgments

This project began as a series of fairly well-contained case studies of a handful of southern industrial communities. In each, I encountered a single individual ready with suggestions, background information, and (most important) connections. In Spartanburg, this individual was Clifton resident and historian Michael Hembree, whose own work provided crucial foundational material and whose personal assistance guided me into dozens of Clifton homes. I also thank the Phillips Fibers Corporation (in the former Saxon mill village) and Spartan Mills (under the late Walter Montgomery, Sr.) for their corporate assistance. Bob Dinwiddie of the Southern Labor Archives of Georgia State University, Harry Miller of the Wisconsin Historical Society, Bob Erwin of Perkins Library at Duke University, Michael Kohl of Clemson University's Special Collections Department, and Tab Lewis and Jim Cassidy of the National Archives all provided prompt and creative support. My greatest debt, of course, goes to the dozens of men and women who invited me into their homes and allowed themselves to be interviewed. Their voices echo throughout this book; their names appear in the bibliography.

As the story of Spartanburg's textile workers grew, I was forced—with much regret—to sideline my work in other southern towns, including hundreds of additional interviews from North Carolina, Alabama, Arkansas, Louisiana, and east Texas. This material, wide-ranging as it is, I hope to fit into subsequent studies. Particular thanks, and apologies, to the United Rubber Workers and United Steelworkers locals in Gadsden, Alabama; Percy Rogers and the OCAW of Lake Charles, Louisiana; Floyd Richard and the ICWU of New Iberia, Louisiana; the residents of Huttig, Arkansas; and the town of Elizabeth, Louisiana, together with the surviving former employees—both union and non-union— of the Calcasieu Paper Company there.

Shirley and Mack Makara provided housing during my forays into Spartanburg. Mark Olencki assisted with photographic reproductions. Yonni Chapman, Hannah Joyner, Paul Ortiz, Molly Rozum, Janet Irons, Timothy

Minchin, and Jennifer Ritterhouse offered encouragement and advice. Grant Wacker, Sydney Nathans, John H. Thompson, Jacquelyn Dowd Hall, Nancy Hewitt, Douglas Flamming, Peter Rachleff, David Zercher, and especially Lawrence Goodwyn all read drafts of this narrative at various stages in its production. From start to finish, Mary Wingerd has offered intensive collegial criticism and support. Friendships like this remind us to seek out those infrequent affirming moments that make the study of human history worthwhile.

Southern Workers and the Search for Community

Introduction

In the town eight miles from where I write this, on a reasonably fair Monday toward the end of the twentieth century, the last textile mill has closed—a victim, its owners publicly explained, of imported fabrics and exported jobs. The forty remaining workers cashed their final paychecks during Christmas week. Built in the 1920s, the Yanceyville mill gave southern expression to the American dream of economic salvation through industrial development. The company-owned stucco bungalows constructed in the factory's shadow nearly doubled the town's size. Through the years this mill remained the county's primary industrial employer. Hundreds lived and worked here; literally thousands of their neighbors from across the county commuted to textile jobs at other mills in Danville, Greensboro, and Burlington. For close to a century, textiles influenced every facet of life in the southern Piedmont.

The world of southern textiles—both as industry and as regional subculture—is vanishing rapidly. This vanishing is not new: The ravages of deindustrialization have been with America for some time now. Images from the carnage have filtered down into popular consciousness: abandoned steel mills in Pittsburgh and Youngstown, the disillusionment of Flint, and the poverty of Lowell. The withdrawal of heavy industry from the American landscape has proceeded region by region; after all, it was New England's prior deindustrialization that fueled the South's own textile boom between 1880 and 1930.

Like industrialization, deindustrialization—the voiding of factory America, both culturally and economically—has always carried a social cost. Some forms of social life are buried and others fostered, however distorted or complex. Neither of these consequences is a historical novelty: Books abound on these wrenching transitions, continent to continent, century to century.

What is new is the lack of a social vocabulary with which to describe and thus help comprehend pain. When we talk about the travails of a nineteenth-century steel worker, the hardscrabble lives of depression-era farmers, or the hopelessness pervading inner-city America in the 1990s, what we are really talking about is pain. Anguish, like all human emotions, seeks a language of expression. This is the way we, as human beings, apprehend our predicaments, explain ourselves to one another.

At other periods in history, vocabularies and syntax of suffering have been more readily available. Sometimes these arose directly from experience; more often they were appropriated from received aspects of the surrounding culture—ideological, historical, and religious. But one after another the West's guiding psychological and intellectual frameworks have frayed: the Judeo-Christian narrative tradition, capitalism, Marxism, and American democracy (if not as achieved social reality, then at least as widely shared aspiration). One result has been the effective lessening of the power and even the availability of inherited social vocabularies. "In the America where I'm writing now," poet Adrienne Rich observed in 1996, "suffering is diagnosed relentlessly as personal, individual, maybe familial, and at most to be 'shared' with a group specific to the suffering, in the hope of 'recovery.'"[1]

In this kind of vacuum even language is affected. Even the most compassionate scholars find themselves talking of "alterity" and "marginalization" rather than pain, of "solidarity" and "coalition-building" rather than hope, and of "hegemony" and "quiescence" rather than fear. The absence of a strain within the historical tradition that incorporates human suffering betrays a fundamental weakness in that tradition. And yet this is not solely an academic problem. The loss of language appropriate to the expression of human need is a cultural loss and therefore a social loss as well. The reason is by no means self-evident. Like pain, hope and fear are no longer part of the historical discourse, the language in which we tell ourselves where we've been and where we're going.

The problem with not having a language for suffering—of which pain, hope, and fear are all components—is that it prevents us from understanding human struggle. As Wendell Berry implies, aspiration is rooted in pain. If genuine human aspiration is dependent upon the invention of language in which that aspiration may be voiced, then the lack of a vocabulary for talking and thinking about pain as communal, as public, is grave indeed. Nowhere is this poverty of expression more obvious in America than in our appraisals of struggle.

When Americans talk about struggle—the more apparent phases of human striving—they do so with certain ingrained understandings. "Struggle" is contest and produces "winners" and "losers." We have been further conditioned to expect an interpretation of struggle as either uplifting, morally imperative, and fated to triumph (if a cause is "legitimate") or quixotic, self-serving, and doomed (otherwise). In Hollywood's reduction, it's either *Norma Rae* or the Teamsters, innocence or corruption.

Neither of these neat narrative lines permits much ambiguity. Protest and reform, among other human activities, rarely lend themselves to such neat interpretations. Emphasizing resolution, both frameworks contribute to a false perception of struggle as essentially episodic: usually unpredictable, often inexplicable, and therefore ahistorical. Through this process of forcing life into simplistic and even fictional narratives, we dismiss conditions basic to shared humanity, including hope and fear. Over time, of course, the price of euphemism—both linguistic and otherwise—has been the effacing of entire events, movements, and people from the annals of what we know as history.

What is needed above all is specificity. This book deals with one of those historical movements: the attempt by one group of southern textile workers during the 1930s and 1940s to redefine what human community could mean for them, within and without the constraints of their company-town world. Scholars have rediscovered these workers, in their most public moment, as participants in what is now known as the General Textile Strike of 1934. Yet it seems we are no closer to understanding the breadth and depth of the activity generated during the Roosevelt years than we are to comprehending the "quiescence" of the 1920s or the 1950s. The historiographical tendency to isolate heightened moments of assertion—strikes, marches, or boycotts—does violence to the fabric of industrial life. Action is severed from context. Happenings in remote places—Harlan County, Watsonville, Flint—become apocalyptic moments of working-class rage explainable neither in terms of what preceded nor what followed.

Context is everything. The events of these years, however breathtaking to historians and however exceptional to the regional rule, did not arise in a social vacuum. Southern workers did not lack for words. They inherited a social lexicography, a storehouse of received and experientially acquired knowledge about the world in which they lived. In this they were no different from Slavic coal miners or Yankee shoe craftsmen, although their peculiar milieu conditioned their responses in ways alien to much of the industrial North or Midwest. The union defeats of the 1930s and 1940s cast long historical shadows precisely because of the intense associations and multiple levels of meaning and import attached by workers to the union they joined. Southern textile workers re-created organized labor in images specific to their needs. The textile insurgency between 1933 and 1936 represented the crystallization of a social vision rooted in decades of life and work in cotton mills across the South. It cannot be understood apart from this experience.

~

The reforms of the early Roosevelt administration encouraged southern workers to assess the basic conditions of textile life and work—collectively, publicly, and on an unprecedented scale. To that task they brought their own understanding of what community could and should mean, one rooted in the mutuality of the company-town, mill-village world. Courage did not come easily. Only when workers perceived a window of opportunity sufficiently large enough to transform their entire worlds, not just wages and hours, did they risk the pain of overt struggle. They drew on the rhetoric of American democracy, the ideological ruminations of industrial unionism, deeply held religious beliefs, and (most important) the fabric of their own lives. And they did indeed manage to create something new: an alternative script for industrial life in the benighted South, underwritten by what we may call a culture of aspiration. This culture of aspiration was grounded in concrete hopes, predicated upon rejection made possible by the public posturing of the Roosevelt administration, of the immobilizing fear that had previously prevented serious challenges to the exigencies of industrial life. For a time, southern textile workers found the language they needed to assert both their dignity and their humanity.

But this assertion came with a cost. The vast majority of southern textile workers saw their vision crushed in the stark aftermath of their General Strike in 1934. Others—perhaps most in Spartanburg County—survived the General Strike with both their hopes and their union intact only to see both exterminated in the late 1930s following a series of violent, bitter wildcat strikes and bureaucratic wrangling in Washington. A few managed to hold onto their local unions (and sometimes even the social vision those unions had represented) into the 1940s and beyond—but very, very few. Felicitous circumstances had helped southern workers find the language they needed to challenge their anguish at its source. No such combination came to their aid later. The pain was excruciating, but the words with which to express it were missing.[2]

The story that unfolds here represents a certain high-water mark for self-conscious action in the modern industrial South. But the story itself is not provincial. The circumstances of Spartanburg's workers in the early twentieth century varied little from those in other recently industrialized sectors of the West. The protracted and agonizing defeat of their aspirations at the hands of their employers did indeed seem out of place in the 1940s and 1950s, organized labor's apparent zenith in America. It looks less so now.

Spartanburg offers a chance to understand what one group of working

Americans, in one place and over a finite period, would have done with their lives. In the face of enormous odds, they chose to make a public stand on behalf of their comprehension of what "community" could mean—their own social vision. To be sure, their vision was flawed, perhaps even parochial. It excluded black workers and remained bound within the cultural constraints of mill-village life. Yet one fact endures: At the base of a highly stratified, industrialized society, these workers somehow found the impetus, the will, the courage, and finally the vehicle to challenge the grinding world in which they lived.

~

The story of Spartanburg's textile workers during the 1930s is in part the story of their struggle toward language—of aspiration and of pain. It is therefore appropriate to consider the more recent descriptive difficulties historians of working people have faced. Several decades of "social history," devoted to rescuing traditionally obscure groups from scholarly invisibility, have succeeded in demolishing some of the more unhelpful phrases and conceits that disfigured the historical literature. Presumptions of working-class "docility" or "contentment" went early. Condescension masked by the prescriptive concern of sociological inquiry lost its intellectual cachet during the 1960s. Groups repeatedly labeled as "inarticulate" by well-intentioned observers have turned out to be surprisingly articulate when approached on their own terms and merits.

Perhaps the most problematic concept embedded in the literature of laboring people today is that of "autonomy." Taken loosely, the word *autonomy* has come to stand for an individual's or group's capacity for self-activity or self-expression beyond external constraints: A worker able to face a boss with the protection of a strong union is presumed to be "autonomous" in ways a worker without such protection could not. That worker and that worker's family, benefiting from high, dependable wages and owning their own home, could be expected to enjoy more autonomy than could the destitute denizens of rigidly controlled company towns. Obviously, the question of autonomy achieves central importance when members of a relatively weak and powerless group work in concert to challenge authority. One question recurs with remarkable persistence throughout historiographical debates since the 1960s, Was a given group of workers autonomous or was it not?

For a historian, this difficulty creates first and foremost a problem of description. One scholar might emphasize the political defeats of a given group of workers, thus implying a lack of autonomy and possibly the presence of its antonym, "hegemony." Rigid analysis along such lines easily displaces the interior lives of workers, both as individuals and as a potential collective. Another scholar might study the neighborhood dynamics of the same group of workers and find them to be vibrant and geared toward aspiration ("empowering"). But rich descriptions of an apparently self-created and self-sustaining culture often cause powerful structural constraints to recede from view, thus leaving the illusion of autonomy. In short, historians face the difficult task of describing how degrees of autonomy are achieved. That can be done neither by focusing entirely on constraints nor by emphasizing the self-created culture of work.

Received cultural traditions do not make it easy to differentiate between what we wish to suggest appropriately via the word *autonomy* and the complex ways in which human life is lived and defined. True autonomy is a historical and social phantom. Very little in daily life is fully autonomous. We relate to friends and loved ones, neighbors and enemies, employers, employees, and government through a nest of contingencies and constraints. Some are self-created and self-enforced, others are willed from outside one's immediate sphere. All aspiration emerges from structures of confinement and constraint but never entirely leaves the enclosure of contingency. Even under the most favorable circumstances, men and women never achieve the pristine state that autonomy presumes.

In this structural sense, southern textile workers were never really autonomous. Their poverty, their lack of real political power, and their overwhelming residence in company-owned towns prevented the same kinds of self-activity found in New York or Boston or even Lowell. On such agonizing terrain, however, they were indeed able to construct their own world—the interior social life of the mill village. It was a real world, and one not without power; the folklore of subtle and not-so-subtle challenges to employer authority in southern mill towns is as old as the mills themselves. What loyalty southern mill owners extracted from workers was indeed negotiated, even if workers were negotiating from a position of decided, and often extreme, weakness. In unbearable circumstances, workers could strike, which they did sporadically, throughout the textile South from the 1880s onward. If striking seemed an impossibility, they could always flee—a reality that manufacturers, complaining of a chronic "labor shortage," knew all too well. The challenges of the 1930s proceeded directly from this mixed fabric: immense cultural energy on the one hand and an equally strong element of structural constraint on the other. In this context, autonomy is an essentially unhelpful term. Quite simply, the word obscures the social reality it purports to describe.

This brings into view a second descriptive problem, symptomatic of a deeper conceptual difficulty. Southern textile workers could indeed function as internally unified collectives, at least in moments of overt conflict. That fact begs the question of "community," especially from the vantage point of the late twentieth century when the word itself had become an ideological battleground. Prudence dictates pausing again to consider what the word *community* meant and what it means.

For southern textile workers before World War II, the most meaningful unit of community was the mill village itself, a socially coherent, residentially segregated, and spatially distinct entity in the shadow of any mill. So strong were the social and cultural associations of mill-village life that workers never referred to themselves as living "in" a particular village; they consistently spoke of living "on" or "off." In larger towns, many of the more "stable" textile families prided themselves on "living off." To be "on the village" not only implied a certain level of dependency—but it also afforded round-the-clock participation in village life. Southern townspeople ritually excluded mill villagers from their institutions: Virtually all mill villages had their own business districts, baseball teams, police departments, schools, and churches. But southern textile workers just as ritualistically excluded townspeople, drawing together in surprising ways within the village's company-controlled bounds.

As a rule, the collectivity represented by mill-village culture included all resident white workers and their families, regardless of sex or age. Traditionally, textile work involved children as young as six or seven; even after the passage of child labor laws early in the twentieth century, twelve- and thirteen-year-olds continued to work in the mills. Entering the factory on or just after one's fourteenth birthday (according to law) was a boy or girl's principal rite of passage in South Carolina mill villages before 1933. Children were thus inducted into working-class culture—that is to say, the collective life of the factory and mill village—at early ages. Nor was sex a barrier to textile work. By the late nineteenth century, mill owners had come to associate women and children with certain tasks inside the factory—spinning, for instance. Although jobs such as fixing and carding were reserved exclusively for men, others, such as weaving, were allocated without regard to sex. Like mill-village men, women began factory careers as children. Marriage and childbearing could relieve a woman from mill work for a while, but most continued to work, at least part time. Men, women, and children all experienced southern textile life primarily as workers.

The very idea of community is a way to describe a basic human longing: a vision of possibility that can last long after a particular engendering moment or institution (a strike, a union) has passed. Community is not, however, necessarily egalitarian. For these particular workers, the key limiting factor was not age or sex but race. Southern textile workers were overwhelmingly white during a period in which white supremacy remained an organic part of the American experience. Black workers—who generally labored as janitors or at various maintenance tasks on the villages—were occupationally segregated from the white-defined rhythms of textile work. Nor did the vast majority of mill villages include housing for blacks, who were expected to find their own quarters in the adjacent town or countryside. Because white workers experienced such a high degree of spatial identification with the mill village itself, the exclusion of black workers reinforced the racial alienation white southern workers already felt. Black workers were sometimes able to form their own mill-village community ties—but independent of whites and only in the handful of villages with black housing. To most whites, blacks remained a marginal component of textile life. They were excluded from the prevailing white understanding of what community meant and largely, therefore, from the movements and events made possible by that understanding. Although the aspirations voiced by white workers were universal, mill-village community remained, for them, symbolically and effectively white. The culture of white supremacy has historically imposed a colossal constraint on the range of egalitarian possibilities Americans have intermittently envisioned.

One final linguistic hurdle remains, and it concerns the enormous range of human effort capable of being subsumed beneath the descriptive word *politics*. I regard hope and fear as politically charged emotions. One can go beyond this: Human emotions are, perforce, fundamentally political. At the heart of any political process are deep-seated fears and enabling hopes for everyone, rich and poor, powerful and powerless.

The ultimate meaning of politics cannot be approached without the incorporation of such terms as *hope* and *fear.* Often observers become distracted by the surface level of politics, certain ritualized forms such as the election or the choreography of legislation. But of course "politics" in a human sense is more than that. The General Textile Strike of 1934 and the myriad local conflicts associated with it were not only challenges to southern manufacturers but also to the established conceits of southern society on every level. At its peak, the southern union movement did include an electoral component, but that bid for formal power was only one of many avenues southern workers pursued. The post–1934 battle between southern textile workers and the federal government in Washington was nothing if not political. This book is about not only the appearance and manifestations of what we may call "community unionism" but also the extended interplay between community unionism and the various corporate and governmental actors ultimately responsible for its destruction.

~

These scholarly debates, although necessary and perhaps even illuminating, risk drawing attention away from the actual workers in question—their plight, their struggle, their fate, and the implications of their story for the postindustrial West. In the wake of institutional failure—the destruction of their unions—southern workers returned to their own private lives marked by feelings and experiences they could not easily discuss. Their world had changed forever. The scars from that transformation outlasted even the mills. But as deindustrialization proceeds at dizzying speeds, America's predicament enlarges upon their prior plight. We grope for a new language of description specifically appropriate to the postindustrial landscape. Without it, we cannot render our lives intelligibly or invest even the most basic words—like *hope*—with real meaning. At its best, this language, when and if we find it, will perhaps resemble the one that southern textile workers spoke, briefly, in the 1930s. At worst, we will, like most of them, be left in silence.

1 Shared Lives: The Textile Communities of Spartanburg County, South Carolina

It was a time of spindles. It was a time when a man or a woman could speak of doffing warp twisters, drawing-in as a quarter-hand, or taking down flags on a set of X-2's and be universally understood in a chain of territory stretching from Danville, Virginia, to Huntsville, Alabama. The southern textile world that developed in the late nineteenth century, and which enjoyed its heyday during the first half of the twentieth, was the proverbial prodigal son of southern culture. The industry had largely been scorned or ignored during its antebellum infancy, only to be embraced later with fanfare and hopes of regional economic salvation during the so-called cotton mill campaign of the 1880s and 1890s. By the early twentieth century, textiles had become *the* southern industry in the minds of both southerners and the nation.[1]

Nestled in the foothills of the Blue Ridge Mountains, Spartanburg County, South Carolina, approached the southern agricultural ideal: fertile and temperate, with a patchwork of family farms and mid-sized cotton plantations well-drained by the Reedy and Pacolet Rivers and their tributaries. In the hills of the Piedmont South, such streams meant water power, and water power, ultimately, could mean industrial development. Spartanburg County boasted an embryonic textile industry well before the Civil War. Small mills at Cedar Hill, Fingerville, Crawfordsville, Valley Falls, and Glendale—none except Glendale employing more than a few dozen operatives—spun yarn and wove cloth from the 1840s onward.[2]

The presence of these small-scale mills and their tiny villages did nothing to threaten the overwhelmingly agrarian cast of life in Spartanburg County. A few bales of local cotton may have wound up at Glendale instead of Lowell, and a few poor white families might have found extra—and often seasonal— employment as textile operatives. But Spartanburg County remained an archetypal example of more or less prosperous agriculture in the southern Pied-

Clifton No. 1 panorama, circa 1910, showing the streetcar line that once ran from Spartanburg to Glendale and the Cliftons. (Courtesy of Converse College)

mont. As county seat, the town of Spartanburg slowly evolved into an Up-country commercial hub, but even with the railroad its emergence as an urban center was initially uncertain. As late as 1880 it still only counted three thousand inhabitants.

All this began to change on 3 January 1880, when D. E. Converse and Company (owners of the Glendale cotton mill) purchased two hundred acres of land at Hurricane Shoals on the Pacolet River nine miles east of Spartanburg town. A Vermont native, Dexter Converse had resided at Glendale since 1856. He was, for all practical intents and purposes, just as southern as the men who joined him in his quest for a new factory that would rival any northern mill.[3] The Clifton Manufacturing Company began spinning cotton into yarn in the late spring of 1881. Lonely Hurricane Shoals was soon transformed into a population center rivaling Spartanburg itself as poorer families poured in from the surrounding countryside to take advantage of the new jobs. Some were recruited by company agents, others arrived on hearsay, all were drawn by the promise of cash work. Even before the first mill's machinery was completely installed, the village of Clifton contained a store, a school, sixty six-room tenant houses (intended for two families each), and about 350 inhabitants. By March 1882 Clifton's population had passed one thousand and was still climbing.[4]

From the outset, Clifton's world remained removed, and even estranged, from the rest of Spartanburg County. Even the wealthy Converse family became frustrated at how poorly Clifton integrated into the fabric of county life. As Dexter Converse's son and chief publicist complained in an open letter to the local press, "Do the people of Spartanburg County realize that within the last two years there has grown up in their midst a town of more than one thousand inhabitants? Do they realize the practical and financial advantages of such a town in any county? That in its cotton factory 550 men, women, and children can and do make their living. . . . Sir, do the editors of the SPARTAN and *Herald* realize that there is such a place?"[5]

The only ones who seemed to realize the full implications of industrialization were the men, women, and children who suddenly found themselves laboring inside the Clifton mills' red-brick walls. As an anonymous writer on behalf of Clifton's underfunded school put it in mid–1882, "The people of Clifton are poor and must of necessity work hard and to this general rule, the children who ought to be at school most of the time, are no exception."[6] The factory's twelve-hour work days left no room for traditional middle-class ideas of self-improvement, as a "Factory Girl" protested in early 1884: "You seem interested in the welfare of our sex, and often you have a word of encouragement for working, struggling women. Now can you give one who has to work ten to fourteen hours a day some hint as to the best plan for improving the mind. Sometimes I feel low-spirited and see nothing but work and drudgery ahead of me. I do not dislike the work, but I would like to improve my mind a little, and know something of what is going on in the world."[7]

Workers viewed their new lives at Clifton at best as an ambivalent improvement over their rural struggles and at worst as slavery. Thomas Barry, a Knights of Labor organizer, found Clifton typical of the southern Piedmont mill villages he visited in 1888: a classic company town with "the same overbearing spirit prevailing amongst the employers against the interests of labor," in which "it is as much . . . as a person's life is worth" to be known as a union member.[8] Segregated into company-owned villages and viewed with suspicion by townspeople and rural folk alike, mill workers quickly became known as a people apart.

Inman Mills, circa 1905. (Courtesy of Wofford College)

Their numbers grew with the industry. "To the building of cotton mills there seems to be no end," a Spartanburg editor noted in 1889.[9] In Spartanburg County, as elsewhere in the Piedmont South, the so-called cotton mill crusade went on and on. A few of the newer mills, like Glendale and Clifton, remained locally owned and operated, but most were either built outright by northern interests or ultimately controlled by northerners—especially the Milliken family and Boston's Lockwood-Greene engineering firm—under the guise of local management and incorporation.[10]

As at Clifton, the first generation of southern mills were generally located at strategic water-power sites, away from established population centers. As the scope of textile manufacturing grew, this isolation necessitated the construction of elaborate company-town settings populated exclusively by workers, managers, and their families, all segregated—by the rhythms and regulations of industrial life—from the surrounding countryside. Steam power and, later, the rise of regional electrical utilities brought mills to the edges of established cities and towns, but the mill village remained a nearly universal industrial instrument. Manufacturers saw the company-owned village as a necessity in order to retain a residentially captive labor force, while workers came to expect housing as a basic condition of employment. Either way, the persistence of the mill village only deepened the estrangement of the textile world from southern society at large.

By 1926, when Massachusetts-based Pacific Mills completed its mammoth Lyman finishing complex, Spartanburg County had thirty textile mills, each with its accompanying village: store, churches, school, fraternal lodges, residential neighborhoods, and baseball team—in short, its own unique little world. There were old mills like the Cliftons, with standard look-alike duplex housing, and new mills like Powell Knitting and Lyman, with tastefully terraced village streets and modern bungalow housing built on a variety of eye-catching plans. There were big mills like Victor of Greer and little mills like Fingerville. There were rural mills where the majority of workers continued to drift back and forth between farm and factory, and there were urban mills tied to the burgeoning city of Spartanburg. There were regular cotton mills (like Inman and Arcadia), and there were specialty operations (finishing at Clevedale, flax processing at Tucapau). There were mills renowned for the attention management lavished on employees: the nurseries and playgrounds at Pacolet or the educational opportunities afforded by Saxon. And there were mills that were not—places like Arkwright and Jackson Mill, where the housing was poor, the recreation nonexistent, and the work, it seemed, always ran mean (map 1).

There is, of course, truth in the idea that a more or less universal southern textile culture united mill villages from Virginia to Alabama.[11] Yet textile workers saw it differently. To them, the mill itself—the looms, the red-brick factory, the village streets and houses—was a given in much the same way as were countryside and plowed fields for cousins who stayed on the farms. A few considered the differences between mills and villages mere window-dressing.[12] Most, however, dwelt upon what distinguished one mill complex from another. The result was an informal hierarchy of mill-and-village rankings, a specialized language of place. If one desired to further one's education, one tried to get on at Saxon, where management encouraged workers to enroll in the neighboring Textile Industrial Institute's work-study program.[13] If one wanted a quiet place to raise children, one might choose Inman Mills, whose owners sought to cultivate a family atmosphere. If one wanted to retail moonshine, one might choose Fairmont, where governing strictures were notoriously lax. And if one wanted the best of all possible material conditions, one might leave Spartanburg entirely for a place like the Matthews mill village in Greenwood, of which mill workers across South Carolina spoke incredulously, "They have brick homes . . . and electric ranges in their kitchens!"[14]

The lives textile workers lived in Spartanburg's mill villages were intricately bound up with the infrastructure of the villages themselves.[15] The main pur-

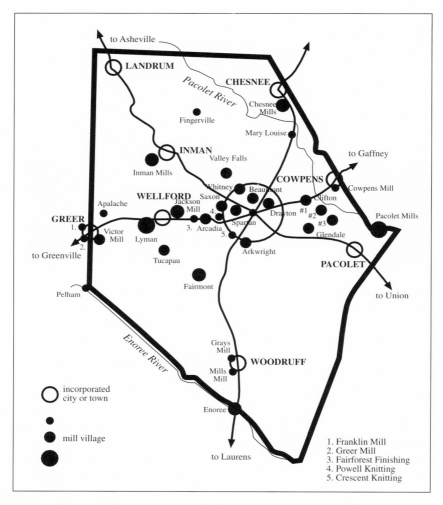

Map 1. Spartanburg County, circa 1930, showing towns and mill villages. (Courtesy of L. A. Waldrep)

pose of company housing, of course, was to engage and retain a maximum work force as close as possible to the plant itself. Heavily dependent on child labor and the family wage system well into the twentieth century, southern mill owners rejected Lowell-style apartments and boardinghouses. They preferred cheaply built "cottages" (small two-, three-, or four-room houses intended for single families) or duplexes (six to eight rooms that could be used

Saxon mill worker's house, circa 1913. (Courtesy of South Caroliniana Library, University of South Carolina, Columbia)

for either one or two families, depending upon family size and need). Separate neighborhoods were often constructed for supervisors and sometimes black workers as well. Although the last generation of mill villages benefited from the rising science of urban design and more closely reflected twentieth-century suburban sensibilities, places like Lyman, Powell Knitting, and the remodeled Pacolet Mills village remained exceptions to the rule. Company housing generally provided only the most basic needs of shelter, and the residential aesthetics of most mill villages were few. Aaron McConnell of Clifton No. 2 knew his home as "nothing but just a box house, whitewashed, boards straight up and down, beaverboard they called it on the inside," painted red and white just like the sharecroppers' shacks nearby.[16]

Inside the mill, the bewildering variety of textile jobs divided roughly into four departments: carding (the initial processing of cotton fibers), spinning, weaving, and finishing. Each department also had its own specialty jobs: opener, picker, slasher, and speeder in carding; spooler and doffer in spinning; doffer, battery-filler, drawing-in, and warp-tender in weaving; and inspector, stitcher, and folder in finishing. By long-standing southern custom, all production jobs were reserved for whites. Black workers held only a few menial positions, such as janitor or boiler fireman. "Fixers" topped the production ladder, skilled men who had become so familiar with the machinery over the years that they were eventually promoted to work as full-time mechanics. Because many workers conceded a status edge to weaver, loom-fixing became the most highly prized production job.

Mill villages operated in effect as small towns, so each company also employed dozens of "outside" workers: carpenters, painters, plumbers, electricians, sanitation crews, store clerks, and teamsters. The supervision strata included second hands (assistant foremen), section hands (foremen), overseers (department foremen), and, of course, company executives. Each village also had its small corps of professionals: preachers, teachers, police, and social workers, sometimes formally in the pay of the company, sometimes not. Except in the most urban settings, all of these men and women—from the lowliest production worker to the overseers and even some executives—lived together in the mill village.[17]

Mills initially recruited from surrounding territory. Company agents scoured rural neighborhoods, securing verbal—and sometimes written—promises from farm families, whose transportation to the mills they would then finance.[18] With the profusion of southern mills, however, company agents increasingly looked to Appalachia as their primary labor reservoir. By 1900, some Spartanburg mills were operating more or less exclusively with workers from a handful of western North Carolina counties, and when these sources failed, agents moved even further out, into the isolated valleys of southwestern Virginia and northeastern Tennessee. Southern textiles never seemed to get—or keep—a labor supply sufficient for its needs; at every point before the 1920s, as one worker noted, "They were begging people to come to the mill."[19] The ideal mill family had a maximum number of workable children and was destitute: "Back in those days those mills were tickled to death to find a widow woman . . . with a bunch of kids."[20] When Helen Cash's father came to Clifton from their exhausted farm in Greene County, Tennessee, "They just closed up their house, and they came to Clifton. He never did know what had happened to their stuff back there. They left it."[21]

Migrants to the mill villages came with certain expectations, many of which mill life met or exceeded. When J. H. Foster moved his family to Spartan mills from Union County, South Carolina, in 1890, he was initially pleased. In the words of Foster's grandson, "There were certain advantages: they had a better house here; there were schools (my dad went to about the fourth grade); churches were close by; you had a company store where you could buy groceries, even on credit." Low pay—if it was regular—was better than the exigencies of sharecropping. Over time, however, the Fosters came to view the mill-and-village system with less enthusiasm. First they abandoned the company store, later the mill village itself. "At that time . . . when children reached a certain age, if they needed help in the mill, the children were supposed to go to work in the mill," as Foster's children and grandchildren well knew. In 1924 a Foster boy was offered a more lucrative job in a downtown department store. As his brother later dryly explained, "Rather than go through all the hassle about why he didn't go to work in the mill, about that same time we moved." Eventually, the entire Foster family quietly asserted its independence by relocating to Spartanburg's West End, just across the tracks from the Spartan village.[22]

Once in the mill, men and women viewed textile work in diverse ways. Mill work "was just a way to make a living" for Aaron McConnell of Clifton. "I never did like it," explained one of his coworkers, "you know, I didn't have no choice: you was made to go to work." To Venie Elders, spooling "was the same old thing, over and over—you just go from one end to the other. You go down to this end, and you race back up to this end, catch the machine before it comes down, putting your bobbins in."[23] Some found it difficult to take pride in work that was being coerced from them regardless of their skill.[24] But others knew that no matter how the company classified them, or on what basis they were paid, they still possessed a measure of craftsmanship, which they cherished. Even though she was never considered anything more than a weaver, Beatrice Norton's mother Daisy McGaha "could put a design of roses, she could put a design of the stripe she wanted in it, and when it got through, that cloth looked beautiful." Saxon worker Ruby Beville recalled of her mother, "Daddy said she was one of the best weavers that ever walked in a cotton mill. He said when she left a loom, it was *fixed,* and you knew that it was right."[25] Textiles engendered a full sliding scale of responses. At Clifton, workers toiling in sight of each other would later aver that "I always just loved mill work anyway. . . . I loved every minute of it" and also that laboring in the regimented plant system was "like Hitler."[26]

When they chose to vote against the company, most mill workers did so in the only way they knew—with their feet. The nomadic qualities of the southern textile work force were proverbial.[27] "People used to move every time you turned around, years ago, you know. And they'd go so far, and then they'd come back, and then they'd go somewhere and come back. That was just a normal thing for this vicinity," Marie Coggins of Clifton recalled. "It wasn't nothing whatsoever to see somebody going down the road in a one-horse wagon or maybe an old pickup truck, with their belongings in it," an Arkwright worker agreed.[28] Sometimes wanderlust was a matter of anger, sometimes ambition, and sometimes whim. Sometimes relocation came unexpectedly, at the company's discretion, when a family's work or conduct was deemed unacceptable.[29]

Over time, each village developed two distinct classes of workers: those who stayed put (the settled cohort) and those who did not.[30] As the settled groups came more and more to define what community life meant in their respective villages, their itinerant neighbors became, to them, less and less visible. Statistically, Arkwright was one of the least-settled mill villages in Spartanburg County, yet lifelong resident Homer Lee Harrison recalled of it that "sometimes there'd be a family to move, then it might go for a long time, nobody else would move in or out either one." Elbert Stapleton lived only a few doors down from Marie Coggins at Clifton No. 2, but in his memory the No. 2 village was an island of stability: "Just about everybody that come to live here stayed here."[31]

If anything, textile workers moved even more often within mill villages than they did between them. As Ibera Holt of Converse explained, "If a house came open that you liked that was in a better location, and a nicer house than the one you was living in, all you'd do was ask them to let you change houses."[32] A family might move to be nearer friends or relatives, or to be closer to the plant, or to advance within the mill-village hierarchy. "We were just trying to better ourselves, from house to house," recalled Vessie Bagwell, who moved eight times at Clifton No. 2 during the first twelve years of his marriage.[33] Mill promotion automatically meant relocation, because fixers, clerical workers, and supervisors were all accorded better-than-average housing.[34] Even when it exposed class divisions, however, intravillage jockeying tended to reinforce community life rather than disrupt it, allowing residents to associate with old friends and new families alike within the existing village framework.

Before the rise of textile managerial programs in state universities, promotion inside a mill—at least into the lower levels of supervision—came from the ranks of self-taught textile workers. For white men with ambition and skill, the possibilities were real. Everyone knew the story of Smith Crowe, who worked his way up from illiterate child labor at Arkwright to the superintendency of Milliken's vast Drayton plant. Many men planned mill careers as children. "My ambition was to go all the way through and make a textile superintendent—that's what my aim was," recalled J. Luther Campbell of Arcadia.[35] Clifton's Paul Dearybury was a third-generation mill worker when he began in 1936, two days after his sixteenth birthday. His father, a loom-fixer, "did everything there was to do in the weave room" and was eventually promoted into supervision. For young Paul, the lesson was clear: Hard work and on-the-job training could pay off handsomely. "I wanted to go as far as I could, but I wanted to learn everything in the weave room that I could before," including warp handling, weaving, doffing, tying-in, quill skinning, filling batteries, and spare work. In 1952, with only a ninth-grade education, he was appointed overseer of weaving at Clifton No. 3. By 1960, when he left textiles, Paul Deary-bury served as No. 3's night superintendent.[36] At other mills, possibilities for promotion were more limited.[37] The fact remained, however, that most of the middling rungs on the ladder of supervision were occupied by men co-resident with, and frequently related to, the workers they supervised.[38]

Even if kinship sometimes blurred the class divide, the divide remained. Mill villages had social fault lines. Given the organization of the village system, these were most frequently expressed—when they surfaced at all—in terms of neighborhood. "The old 500, that's where they went out in the woods . . . and gambled and played poker and everything, and had chicken fights," recalled Jasper DeYoung of Tucapau's Hickory Street neighborhood. "It was rough customers that lived over there."[39] No doubt Hickory Street residents would have viewed matters differently. At Saxon, "it was kind of a prestige thing" whether one lived in the old village or in "New Town," the stylish bungalows built on the west side of the mill in the 1920s: "All that beautiful homes over there—nothing but big shots, nothing but the stiff shirts. We wasn't allowed over in that section. We wasn't allowed to hardly even walk up that street," an old-side resident later claimed.[40] At Clifton No. 2, those in the "classier" Main Street section (mainly supervisors) sometimes looked down on Cedar and Valley Street residents, some of whom in turn held themselves a hair's breadth above the denizens of Tram Street and Cow-pens Line across the river.[41] Such were the internal complexities of mill-village life, but only rarely did they threaten the greater whole. As Georgia Seals concluded, "They'd call it the No. 1 mill, No. 2 mill hill, and Converse. But we all knowed we all was from Clifton."[42]

The dominant institution of mill life remained the mill. Work defined life in the textile South. Mill and village were indivisible. Yet within the mill system, textile workers did create their own institutions, their private arenas for social interaction. Given the drain of time and energy and the material poverty that accompanied mill work, much of this activity was necessarily informal. The "Factory Girl" of Clifton's youth had been advised by a Spartanburg newspaper editor that she "first . . . make it a point to do better work than any other girl in the factory" and then form a community reading club in her spare time.[43] The reading club never materialized; other efforts at "self-improvement"—

science clubs, school booster clubs, musical bands, debating societies, and polit-ical auxiliaries—appeared only sporadically and were consistently short-lived. The institutional practices that dominated human exchange in the textile mill villages of Spartanburg were visiting, fraternalism, textile league baseball, and, most important, religion.

Inside the mill, textile workers labored every day side by side on the com-pany's terms; outside the mill, they used their off-times as a chance to invest their co-residency with a degree of meaning impossible on the shop floor. Organized social activity was rare: "Didn't have no recreation," Spartanburg workers later recalled bluntly.[44] Into this vacuum, mill workers poured the only ingredients at ready hand: themselves. To underestimate the importance of visiting as ritual is to miss the social glue that held mill villages together.[45] Without cars or money, visiting became the most prevalent recreational form: "That's the only entertainment you had."[46] "You didn't have anything to do at home, you'd go to your neighbors', or somebody on the village, just sit and talk with 'em. My mama and daddy did it. We did it, the kids did it," every-one did it.[47] On weekends, visiting might flower into socials or parties, espe-cially for younger folks.[48] Or it might take on a religious hue, as at Saxon, where workers gathered for prayer meetings and front-porch hymn-sings.[49] Some-times the women would gather separately, sometimes the men; sometimes all would come together to hear a favorite radio program perhaps or for reassur-ance in threatening weather.[50] Regardless of circumstance, it was the sheer act of visiting that bound mill villagers together. The process of building and maintaining working-class communities began with visiting. It was incremen-tal, as Beatrice Norton of Saxon recognized: "We *visited* each other, we *talked* to each other, we were *concerned* about each other."[51] That closeness provided the necessary social medium in which other, more institutional expressions of community could germinate.

During the late nineteenth and early twentieth centuries, the fraternal-ist impulse surged in southern mill villages, nearly all of which simultaneous-ly boasted lodges of Masons, Odd Fellows, Woodmen of the World, and (pe-culiar to the textile South) the International Order of Red Men.[52] Some of these organizations, like the Masonic lodges, were established around more or less ancient mystical rites; others were little more than glorified insurance companies of recent vintage. All served larger purposes. Their meetings, rit-uals, and banquets brought mill people together in ways that simultaneous-ly ratified and strengthened preexisting bonds of community. They constitut-ed an institutional expression of prevailing hedgerow social relations, at least for a time and among the white adult males of the villages.[53]

Off-times: the Stapleton family and friends, Clifton No. 2, circa 1920. (Courtesy of Michael Hembree)

Textile league baseball, in contrast, provided mill villagers—*all* mill villagers—with a secular communion of sorts. The southern textile industry's origins were contemporary with that of American baseball, and in the textile South the two were inextricably intertwined as early as the 1880s.[54] By the 1920s, the southern textile belt supported hundreds of mill teams in dozens of privately operated leagues. Upcountry South Carolina alone launched some eighty mill players on professional careers—including the fabled "Shoeless Joe" Jackson—before textile ball's decline in the 1950s.[55] Team rivalries were fierce, and crowds were huge. Baseball was the only weekend entertainment going at Clifton No. 2, Pauline Bible remembered, "unless you'd go over there when they had that theater over at No. 1, or go to town," neither of which happened very often. The Cliftons were typical: "When you'd hear that music start on Saturday evening, everybody just about would go to the ball games," Abbie Lee Croxdale recalled. "We had a pretty good-sized stand,

One of Clifton's more popular fraternal orders: the Woodmen of the World Lodge, with a goat, circa 1910. (Courtesy of Michael Hembree)

and people would fill that thing up, every seat," according to player Herman Bagwell. "They were *crazy* about it!"[56] To some during the General Textile Strike of 1934, what distinguished bloody Honea Path, where company deputies shot and killed nine strikers on September 6, was not the violence but the fact that the resulting funerals caused Honea Path's Chiquola Mill team to forfeit the Anderson County championship series to archrival Gluck.[57]

As its historian has noted, "Textile baseball was a way of life. It gave a sense of legitimacy in a society content to see the 'lintheads' remain invisible citizens somewhere far away on the wrong side of the tracks."[58] In the humbler words of a participant, textile league baseball found its niche among southern workers "because they *believed* in it."[59] Ironically, mill officials allowed textile ball to thrive, perhaps because it, like fraternalism, in no way threatened existing power relationships. In one sense it even reinforced them: While providing beleaguered workers with opportunities for release and achievement, textile ball ultimately immersed all its communicants even more strongly into the mill system. The reason that thousands of fans cheered for Tucapau against

Clifton baseball team, 1922. (Courtesy of Michael Hembree)

Clifton was necessarily complex. At root, textile ball not only encouraged workers to identify with mill companies but also provided workers with provocative, new, and even ritualistic levels on which to do so. Company officials realized this and sponsored teams and rewarded players generously.[60] Most of the time, workers ignored the darker side of textile ball and enjoyed the spectacle. "Baseball was the biggest thing"—next to churches.[61]

Outside of the mills themselves, churches provided the most advanced institutional framework that most mill villagers ever experienced. Southern textile executives soon overcame their initial indifference regarding employees' religious instruction. Whether or not they had the goal of social control in conscious view, by the turn of the century Baptist and Methodist congregations stood in the shadow of every southern mill.[62] As late as the 1910s, rural southerners—especially mountain southerners—were still known more for institutional skittishness than for piety. But mill villages were a new environment, and workers and their families responded in new ways. At Tucapau, "People went to church then. . . . *Everybody* did." At Clifton No. 2, "My mother and daddy would take us to church every Sunday morning and every Sunday night, and every Wednesday night." And at Saxon, "Hardly ever did that church bell ring . . . without the people was ready to walk in."[63]

Little other than tradition and polity separated Baptists from Methodists, and while more sectarian groups also took root in mill towns, their numbers remained comparatively insignificant outside metropolitan centers.[64] Mill workers visited in each others' churches and even scheduled summer Bible schools so that all children, regardless of denominational affiliation, could attend.[65]

Although "churches" existed, "church" was the social reality, uncontested at the institutional center of mill-village life. As a lifelong Arcadia resident simply declared, "It was first."[66] By the 1930s, most mill-village residents appear to have been churchgoers of one kind or another, but levels of spiritual commitment remained wildly uneven. Mill people were religious, but only "to a certain extent."[67] Church was as much a social institution as it was a spiritual one. As a Tucapauan wryly observed, revivals were "always" huge events, "somewhere to go, for one thing."[68] For another, mill-village churches existed only at company sufferance and always remained answerable, directly or indirectly, to mill officials.[69]

The coercive side of mill-village religion cannot be denied, and textile workers certainly knew who was responsible for their pastors' salaries. Yet something of the ethic of love, humility, and interdependency did reach out from company-town churches. As Beatrice Norton of Saxon recalled, "The preachers would talk about unity—not brother against brother, but brother helping brother. . . . And I think that kind of got people's minds off of that job, which took them away from everything."[70] These were complex lessons mill workers took to heart in their own ways and for their own purposes, as the events of the 1930s revealed.

Church, ball games, visiting, and the occasional movie or lodge function, such were the off-time rhythms of Spartanburg's textile worlds. At Arcadia as elsewhere, "People knew everybody: people worked together, and they went to church together, and they played ball together, and they associated with each other."[71] The price for this closeness was the mill system. Did Clifton residents like the uniform color scheme applied to their houses? "Well, they didn't have no other choice, because you see the houses didn't belong to the people—they belonged to the Clifton Manufacturing Company." Did Tucapauans approve when Spartan Mills bought the mill and changed the town's name to Startex? "There wasn't nothing they could do about it." Did workers at Arcadia relate well to the mill-owning Ligon family? "They were very nice people when you met them and talked to them and everything, but they owned the mill, and people

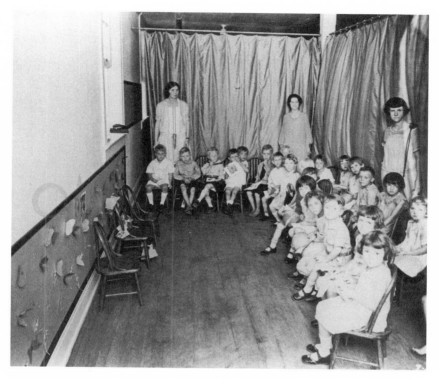

Sunday school class, Arcadia, 1927. (Courtesy of Wofford College)

had to do what they said." In short, "You was just raised with textiles as a way of life, and that's all it was."[72]

Rules were hard, but the worlds textile workers created for themselves were very real. They had a power that company officials could not dislodge. This power was rooted in a culture of mutuality, a sense of the collective that implied social obligation. The only thing in personal experience to which textile workers could compare this ethos was the extended family, and it was most often to family metaphors that they turned to describe their lives together. Testimony from mills across the South is united on this point.[73] When textile workers said that their worlds were "like a family," they had in mind a very specific set of social relations that built upon rural traditions of neighborliness.[74] Sometimes they actually meant consanguinity.[75] More often, however, the social contract that bound mill villagers was predicated on a reciprocity of compassion. This is how it worked: "If you got down sick or anything, they'd

Converse Baptist Church, Clifton No. 3, circa 1930. (Courtesy of Michael Hembree)

help you any way they could. If you needed to go over to the doctor, if they had a car, they'd carry you. If you were sick at home and had to have somebody to stay up at night with you, they'd come and stay with you."[76] If you were short of money or food, your neighbors pooled their meager resources to help.[77] In short, "If you needed anything, your neighbors were there. . . . All mill villages were like that," a Tucapau resident declared.[78]

Few actual families ever operated so systematically; as more perceptive observers understood, "family" was a well-worn metonomy for a much more complex aggregate of social relations. Family did not fully encompass the enormity of obligation and association that governed mill-village life: "You worked
together, and you worshipped together. It was just a shared life amongst us."[79]
    Sharing was at the heart of the community ethos because textile workers

simply had so little. Mill-village mutuality was rooted in poverty. At the Cliftons, "We was all in the same boat. One didn't have any more than the other." At Tucapau, workers shared because "they didn't have anything else."[80] Those that did have something else—the overseers and the executives—were part of this network of exchange only if they so chose. "Ever since I can remember, the people . . . always helped out," explained Zelia Ann Mabry of Clifton. "Now management didn't—the people you worked for didn't help you. . . . It was the people in the community." And the community, according to Mabry, was composed of workers like herself who understood the relationship between love and need.[81] Everywhere, as at Spartan, textile workers "found out they needed one another."[82] Ultimately, what prevailed—as a worker from a neighboring county later put it—"was not exactly communal living, but certainly the matter of the spirit of sharing."[83] Later, after the passing of the mill-village era, it was this sense of the collective that textile workers mourned: "the knittedness, the closeness of the people, and . . . the compassion people had for one another."[84]

What mill villagers shared—on the factory floor, on village streets, in church, at the baseball diamond, and on the wide porches of their company-owned homes—was a common life. As a people, this was the source of their resilience, the key characteristic that made textile workers, as they themselves so often claimed, "the best people in the world." At its best, under pressures economic, social, or spiritual, this commonality could become refined into an even more potent social phenomenon: community. At its worst, mill-village commonality circumscribed the very parameters of what textile workers, as communities, could achieve on their own behalf.[85]

It was a life, and mill people made the most of it. By the 1920s, generations of southern mill workers had, by and large, reached an accommodation within the existing system.[86] This accommodation, however, was fragile, grounded in the tenuous respect that mill officials offered workers and, perhaps even more important, in the traditionally relaxed nature of mill work. Hours were hard and wages low, but discipline was such that mill workers had considerable freedom in their jobs.[87] Workers were often allowed to set their own pace, with plenty of time for rest, meals, conversation, and even play. "Work run so good, you could go home and stay an hour and come back and maybe you'd have one loom stopped," Mae DeYoung of Tucapau recalled. "Back in those days . . . you had long hours, but you were always passing somebody and talking, and if you were a good worker, you could stand and talk, maybe have fifteen minutes that you could stand and pass the day with each other."[88] Some mill workers undoubtedly had a later tendency to romanticize a golden age of textile work that never actually existed, but to ignore their testimony is perilous.

Mill people knew they had made a bargain when they signed on for textile work. Up through the 1920s the bargain seemed worth the deal, at least for most workers, most of the time.[89] "A cotton mill used to be a good place to work, when you could keep your head above the water," according to Furman Mabry of Clifton.[90] Then came the stretch-out, and the tenuous compromises upon which textile workers had learned to pin their lives began to unravel.

2 Hope Rising: The National Industrial Recovery
Act and Textile Unionism in Spartanburg County

During the late 1920s and the 1930s, the combination of a plummeting economy, intense competition in the decentralized textile industry, and the apparently inevitable march of technology all worked together to rob southern textile workers of whatever accommodations they had reached with the forces
of industrialization. The most obvious manifestation was the so-called stretch-
out: In virtually every southern mill, workers claimed that management had
embarked on an insidious plan to maintain or increase profits by gradually
speeding up machinery and expanding individual work assignments. The
result was a mushrooming sense of desperation in mill villages. When textile
workers overwhelmingly supported Franklin D. Roosevelt's presidential campaign in 1932, they sensed in him an unprecedented moral and political ally.
When the details of Roosevelt's National Industrial Recovery Act (NIRA) became known across the region in mid–1933, workers seized upon them with
the hope that they would ensure steady employment and alleviate the prevailing conditions of labor. For workers such as Ibera Holt of Clifton, Roosevelt
came to represent their last chance, as the textile world they thought they
knew deteriorated at an ever-accelerating pace. "Roosevelt was a godsend for
us," Holt later recalled. Or, as one of her neighbors put it even more succinctly, "Roosevelt, he was our king."[1]

   To be sure, southern textile workers had never been as consistently doc-
ile as manufacturers would have liked. Wildcat strikes, brief in duration and
grounded in specifically local concerns, had been a headache for mill owners and managers since the industry's infancy.[2] The Knights of Labor, America's first nationwide industrial union movement, made considerable—if
ephemeral—headway among southern textile workers between 1886 and
1888. After an even more promising start, the American Federation of Labor's
National Union of Textile Workers (NUTW) was driven from southern mills

after protracted strikes and lockouts in Augusta, Georgia, and South Carolina's Horse Creek Valley in 1898 and 1899; North Carolina's Alamance County in 1900; Danville, Virginia, and Columbia, South Carolina, in 1901; and again in Augusta in 1902. Isolated strikes—some of them major, as at Anderson, South Carolina, in 1915—peppered the next several years, culminating in a massive regional strike wave between 1919 and 1921.[3]

To workers, "stretch-out" meant a comprehensive management-sponsored program of alterations in work pace and load, all designed to obtain ever more production during the same hours of work. To management, stretch-out was an excuse workers used to resist all changes in work assignment, job classification, or technology, whether real or imagined.[4] Both sides held the controversy over stretch-out as a threat to their very survival. Workers considered their dignity, livelihoods, and physical health to be on the line, while mill owners—driven increasingly by market glut—viewed their continued existence as absolutely dependent on their ability to experiment with new, more efficient ways of producing yarn and cloth. Some companies began hiring "minute men" and acting on the recommendations of so-called scientific management in the immediate wake of World War I, while others maintained traditional work rhythms through the early 1930s.

Whenever it came, however, textile workers remembered the stretch-out's advent for the rest of their lives.[5] Here is how it went at Spartanburg's Drayton mill in the words of J. Luther Campbell, who had once dreamed of working his way from the spinning room to the superintendent's office:

> When I went to Drayton, it wasn't too long after I went that they put these minute men on, timing the time it took you to do anything. They checked you, they checked you out: checked all the spinners. They come around with a time clock. They timed you. If you went to the bathroom, you was timed how long you was in there. They timed you putting up an end. They timed you setting in a stick of roving. They just timed you, *period.*
>
> We knew what was happening. We knew they was going to add more to you—we could see what they was doing. . . . They could see how much you was doing in eight hours. Why, it wasn't long when they come around that if you was running ten sides, you run twelve: stretch-out system, that was it.
>
> When they checked the speed of the spinning frames, they speeded those frames up. . . . You had a lot of bad ends and things come down, and they kept changing and changing and all that kind of stuff. Then they got the word that they was going to stretch the doffers out. . . . It just affected the whole mill.

When I first went to Drayton, I went on eleven hours a night, and I slept half of it. And my spinning job ran so good that I had some on fifty-four boil that run over eighteen hours to the doff. And sometimes it wouldn't even doff. I carried my lunch with me, and I'd go around and get my eighteen sides, all the ends up on 'em, and lay down on the floor or set up against the wall and go to sleep. Nobody never come in and say nothing to you about it. It was a perfect job, that's what you might say, but it lacked a lot of being a perfect job when I left there.[6]

Indeed. The stretch-out was an affront to nearly every aspect of textile life. Before, workers had been able to preserve some level of control over their labor. They saw that slipping from their grasp, even as they were blamed for the declining quality of their work. Textile workers knew how much their machines could and could not stand. "They didn't have the machinery to take that speed," Furman Mabry of Clifton recalled bitterly. "Those little old E-model looms they had out here in the weave room, 157 picks a minute is all they were supposed to run. Why, they had them things up to 200! It was all belt drives—the belt slipping and squeaking and everything else. That's what kept the jobs tore up."[7]

More important, the stretch-out devastated what patterns of mutual aid had managed to penetrate the red-brick walls of the mills. At the Cliftons,

Drayton spinning room employees, April 1931, on the eve of the stretch-out. (Courtesy of Barbee Moore)

workers traditionally took time away from their own jobs to help co-workers, especially when someone was sick or was having trouble. "We worked as a family," an Arcadia worker declared.[8] That ended with the stretch-out. To J. Luther Campbell, helping other workers in time of need was not only the traditional way of coping with textile work but also the honorable way and his Christian duty as well. Not so at Drayton. If he was caught surreptitiously helping a spinner, "I'd catch the dickens for it, because my job was *fixing.*"[9]

As the machinery ran faster and faster, life inside the mills became more and more unbearable. Precisely when the breaking point came varied from mill to mill. Stretch-out and accompanying wage-cutting were the chief issues behind the southern strike wave of 1929 through 1930, the worst the region had ever witnessed, including the widely publicized struggles at Gastonia, Marion, Elizabethton, and Danville.[10] Without a doubt, the overall conditions of life and labor were eroding rapidly. Textile workers had learned through the years to deal with mistreatment and discontent privately for fear of dismissal; they either kept their anguish to themselves or voted against it with their feet. The spreading implementation of the stretch-out system, however, cou-

A Tucapau "Practical Loom Fixing" class, circa 1933. G. Walter Moore, who later led Tucapau workers through the union conflicts of the 1930s, is second from right. (Courtesy of George W. Moore, Jr.)

pled with unpredictable wages and layoffs at the onset of the Great Depression, added new urgency to their plight. Although the stretch-out did not change time-honored ways of coping immediately, the advent of Franklin Delano Roosevelt's New Deal did.

The policies of the National Recovery Administration (NRA)—coupled with Roosevelt's personal endorsement of industrial unionism—legitimized the space textile workers thought they needed to challenge the inequities of the world in which they lived, especially the stretch-out. "You have done so many many things to relieve the poor and depressed of the U.S.," a Spartanburg woman wrote to the president in early 1934. "We as a party of overworked textile operatives beleave you are the only one who will sympathize and can abolish the stretchout system in our cotton mills."[11] Ending the stretch-out was at the very heart of southern workers' loyalty to the Roosevelt administration. Their faith in Roosevelt as man and president translated into an unswerving belief in his National Industrial Recovery Act, designed in 1933 to resuscitate the American economy through regulation of the nation's major industries.[12]

Textiles was one of the NRA's earliest targets. Through the Cotton Textile Code, New Deal architects attempted to regulate the basic rhythms of the industry. For manufacturers, the code set out standard rules for operation and competition; for workers, the code mandated a forty-hour work week and a guaranteed minimum wage. Mindful of the periodic wildcat strikes that had afflicted textiles since 1929, NRA architects also set up a Cotton Textile Labor Relations Board (CTLRB) designed to investigate alleged code violations and, when necessary, mediate industrial conflict. Like so many of the NRA's component boards, however, the CTLRB held no ultimate power to enforce its recommendations. With its administration placed squarely in the hands of industry, the code itself soon became a fiction as hundreds of companies began to circumvent or violate its provisions with apparent impunity.[13]

Historians have noted the inefficiency and cavalier ineptitude of the CTLRB and its investigators, "a story of mind-numbing business-dominated bureaucratic boards and empty hopes."[14] Yet throughout the NRA's brief life, southern textile workers clung to the code (or at least their understanding of it) with the same fervor and trust that they lavished on Roosevelt. It would be difficult to overstate the confidence they placed in the NRA; as Janet Irons has noted, "They were among Roosevelt's most enthusiastic recruits."[15] Spartanburg's textile workers were no different. They listened to Roosevelt's weekly addresses on their radios. They insisted on viewing him (along with NRA administrator Gen. Hugh S. Johnson) as—in the words of a Pelham worker—"the fixer if any thing should go wrong."[16]

And things did go wrong from the start. Whatever their public postures, southern mill owners and managers were not about to relinquish what profits they were still making in the early years of the Great Depression. The question was not so much how to abide by the code as it was how to do so without sacrificing production. The answer was brutally obvious: With fewer hours and higher wages mandated by the government, mill owners raised individual production quotas up to or beyond pre-NRA levels. This was, of course, the reasoning behind the odious stretch-out. Although the stretch-out was already something of a fixture in southern industrial life by 1933, the passage of the NIRA provoked a regionwide offensive on the part of manufacturers: myriad changes in workloads and working conditions that, for workers, virtually negated the positive effects of the act. As an Apalache worker correctly noted, under the NRA the stretch-out was "now . . . the only way the mill company has of fighting back."[17]

The NIRA went into effect across the nation on 17 July 1933. Within a matter of days the CTLRB began to receive its first complaints from Spartanburg County. Doffer W. H. Fowler of Apalache explained that on 17 July he and his fellow doffers were handling nineteen frames; a week later the number was twenty-three. Workers in the carding and spooling rooms also found their workloads increased without warning, but the worst changes came in the spinning department, where all workers not able to keep up with a new eight-side minimum were discharged on the spot. A month later the minimum was raised to ten sides, with another round of discharges.[18]

This pattern repeated across the South. Jubilation changed to horror as workers began to comprehend the industry's united response to NIRA rules.[19] Unable to make a living on their hardscrabble farm, one Spartanburg woman with her two daughters had sought employment at the Enoree mill, where all three worked six weeks filling batteries. Ten days after the NRA went into effect the woman explained the situation to her member of Congress:

It was very hard for us, we worked eleven hours at night and only received pay for seven hours work. They paid us $1.05 a night. We went to work at 6 o'clock, stopped at eleven for lunch, started back to work at 11:20 and worked until 5:20 in the morning. We kept up with the work they put on us. . . .

We did our best, thinking when the eight-hour law came on we would be fixed but on the seventeenth of July we went into work as usual and the second boss came around and told me they were going to put so much on us that he wouldn't need us any longer. We feel sorry that the change was made, as it was we were making $5.25 a week and as it is we are not making a penny.[20]

The gulf between the Textile Code's promises and its actual results left workers dazed. "I have been reading all the Papers about the new textile code and was greatly pleased with it for I understood that hands were not to be put on more work," an Arkwright worker noted five days after the code went into effect, but in fact, "it has caused these mills to almost double work."[21]

The pace of production was something textile workers could measure in terms of human sweat, but the fluctuations in their wages were more complex. More work at the same pay meant a reduction in real wages, but manufacturers rarely stopped there. Textile workers routinely mailed charges to Washington of being paid less than the code's weekly $12 minimum.[22] Not only were workers who had made less than $12 a week still receiving low pay, but those who had previously made more also found wages sliding backward as mill management came to view the code minimum as a new standard against which all workers' wages could be measured.[23] Some mills maintained a uniform $12 weekly wage by allowing those who "underproduced" in any given week to "float": "In case the piece weaver does not make $12.00 they are loaned enough to make the $12.00 minimum," explained a Drayton worker. Of course, at some point the weaver was expected to "overproduce," whereupon the difference (or "loan") would be deducted.[24] At other mills, weavers were actually required to buy back damaged or substandard cloth at their own expense.[25] Finally, dozens of mill jobs—primarily maintenance—were not covered by the code. Workers were excluded from its wage or hours provisions, and those whose jobs were covered often found themselves "reclassified" into less remunerative positions while performing the same work.[26]

Because wage and hour provisions would ideally limit the amount of work the already-employed were legally able to perform, Spartanburg's workers expected code provisions to create job opportunities and reduce unemployment. In fact, the aggressive implementation of the stretch-out did the opposite. Complaints of layoffs as a result of the stretch-out were endemic—three hundred in Spartanburg alone within two weeks of the code's passage.[27] At Powell Knitting, one woman reported, "The Superintendent of the mill tells the hands when laid off that it was 'Uncle Sam's' doing, not him."[28]

With layoffs, of course, came evictions. Writing three weeks after the code went into effect, Clyde Rogers of Saxon Mills reported that the company had sent police to evict him the day after his discharge:

> Mr. Johnson they haven't gave me no chance to get a house ore a Job and further more you can't get a job because they are laying off hands every were around here. I thought they was to put more peoples to work but they

are [more] people out of Jobs at Spartanburg now than they was and peoples are on starvation. Saxon Mill is laying off hands every day and then send the constable that they must be out of the houses in three days. . . . How can we get out when we can't get a house or a Job. I want to know if they can throw us out in the road with no place to go no job and no house.[29]

As workers soon learned, the code did not cover evictions from company-owned housing.

To workers, the most objectionable part of the stretch-out was the insidious way in which management implemented it. Some mill managers surreptitiously replaced the pullies on main drift shafts with larger models to speed the machinery.[30] Others illegally ordered workers to begin five, ten, or even more minutes before the announced starting time. At Fairmont, exhausted workers secretly subcontracted out their maintenance tasks in order to make production, while at Valley Falls, workers became so confused that they "never know when they are to start working or when they are to stop."[31] "They keep streaching out on a small scale in differant parts of the mill affecting a few hands at a time," a Pacolet worker reported, thus lessening chances that an entire mill's work force would rally at any given moment.[32]

In reading so many individual complaints, CTLRB officials undoubtedly missed what, to workers, was the key characteristic of the stretch-out: the systematic way in which it was applied. That is why southern workers frequently referred to the phenomenon as "the stretch-out system" rather than just "stretch-out." In the spring of 1934, Annie Laura West of Saxon Mills sought to impress this crucial understanding on the leadership of both the United Textile Workers of America and the CTLRB when she filed some twenty specific examples of stretch-out at Saxon since the code's advent.[33] At their deepest levels, southern workers perceived the stretch-out as an insult aimed at well-meaning, hard-working textile people who could never live up to its demands. As a worker from Clifton noted, "You will find very few people at the mill who are not willing to do all they can do. You will find plenty of people working so hard doing their *very very best* to run the work that is put upon them. . . . Why a race horse would not be allowed to go as fast as he could go for eight hours."[34]

In the company-town world of the textile South, most aspects of existence were linked to one's relationship with the mill company. Under the New Deal, southern textile workers finally gave themselves permission to voice their anguish over changes in their work. In the process, they necessarily opened the floodgates on every other objectionable fact of mill life: isolation, unsanitary living and working conditions, and high prices at the ubiquitous company stores. "You [k]no[w] when you get started at a company store they will keep you behind," a Cowpens worker reminded the board.[35]

The standard insensitivities and inequities of mill-village life were suddenly thrown into sharp relief. Mills frequently used the discharge of an individual, for instance, as an excuse to repossess an entire family's house.[36] When Mrs. N. R. Wheatley, a long-term resident of Saxon mills, sent her daughter's pay tickets to Washington in December 1933 to prove a charge of substandard wages, she made clear that housing was her primary concern. The Wheatleys lived in a six-room house, for which the company charged $2 a week in rent. Not only were comparable houses in the village renting for 90 cents a week, Mrs. Wheatley reported, but it was also the case that hers wasn't "fit to live in. Also I have to furnish a hot water tank and bath tub if I have one. The overseers' houses have all of these conveniences and pay no more rent than I do." As for the long-standing industry policy of allotting housing according to the number of workers per family, the Wheatleys were in a difficult bind. Mr. Wheatley was an alcoholic and had left his wife with eight children, only one of working age. "Now right after Xmas when it is very cold and jobs hard to get they have ask for our house, because there is only one working in the mill. They will not work me because of ill health they say."[37] To families like the Wheatleys, short pay tickets were only one inextricable cog in the machinery of mill-town oppression. But like so many other aspects of textile life, neither company stores nor company housing fell within the CTLRB's jurisdiction.

For the CTLRB, stretch-out was at best an inescapable part of textile life and at worst a fiction concocted by edgy textile workers. CTLRB investigators may even have been instructed to ignore stretch-out complaints. One investigator made special mention in a report on Fairmont that he had checked into stretch-out allegations, but "I understand that the so-called 'stretch-outs' do not involve violation of any provision of the Cotton Textile Code."[38] When Sen. James F. Byrnes of South Carolina—then a public crusader against the stretch-out—expressed hope "that as the result of the establishment of the Board . . . there would be no further extension of the so-called stretch-out system," an incensed Robert W. Bruere of the national board replied. "When you consider that every introduction of improved machinery or technical methods is likely to be interpreted as stretchout you will appreciate the optimism of your hope," Bruere wrote. "The protest of the workers in the textile industry against the stretchout is as old as the introduction of the power loom, and will, I fear, continue so long as the inventive genius of man is applied to textile production."[39] Southern workers had no ally in Bruere.

Taking their cue from Bruere, CTLRB investigators routinely found no actual code violations in the mills they visited. Some were industry men, others career bureaucrats; all appear to have been predisposed to believe courteous, well-dressed managers over bedraggled, ignorant mill workers. After a warp-doffer at Saxon complained in early 1934 that his weekly wages had dropped since the code had gone into effect, investigator R. F. Howell evaluated him as "not very familiar with the true situation at this plant." Passing over the possibility that an actual worker would be more familiar with the "true situation" in a plant than would an itinerant investigator, Howell observed from his own study of the company's books that warp-doffers had in fact made $12 a week or less before the code went into effect. "Perhaps they were earning $16.60 at some time prior to the Code, but not within recent years," he concluded.[40] Running from mill to mill tracing literally hundreds of worker complaints, the CTLRB agents frequently limited their "investigations" to stopping by a plant office, consulting with the superintendent, determining that a certain complaint conflicted with "company policy" or was contradicted by the company's time sheets, and dismissing the complaint without further ado.[41] In this fashion, mill managers were free to solve their code problems by denying that they existed.

All of these dynamics—stretch-out, desperate workers, obstructionist mill managers, and, above all, the failure of the CTLRB—crystallized in the case of Saxon Mills.[42] Very few worker complaints ever resulted in hearings before the state CTLRB boards, largely because very few state boards ever functioned, but South Carolina was an exception. Its board did meet, hold hearings, and issue reports. In late 1933 and early 1934, the unusual number of complaints emanating from Saxon Mills led the South Carolina CTLRB to schedule a hearing. Workers alleged that the mill was stretching workers beyond endurance, cutting wages, and firing anyone who protested. Nine discharged workers testified before the three-person state panel: Prof. H. H. Willis of Clemson College (for the "public"), state labor federation leader Furman B. Rogers (for "labor"), and Greenville industrialist J. E. Sirrine (for "industry"). Testimony also came from the mill's president, a supervisor, and Annie Laura West, a battery-filler at the Saxon plant and a local crusader against the stretch-out.[43]

Over protests from Saxon workers, the state board held its hearing in the office of Saxon Mills president John A. Law and then waited more than three months before rendering a verdict. The board dismissed all nine discharge complaints, although it did suggest "that management had not handled cases tactfully" and timidly recommended that two of the nine be offered reemployment.[44] In response to the more general stretch-out charges, the board ordered that a time study be made of the entire mill. It later found that Saxon's workloads were generally within "acceptable" limits, with the exceptions of slubber hands ("somewhat overloaded"), frame hands ("a slight decrease should be made"), and filling doffers in the spinning room. The board suggested that the mill hire one additional worker per shift to doff and lay up roving for the slubbers; a similar recommendation covered filling doffers. The board noted that the work in the spinning and weaving departments was running very poorly; under normal circumstances, the board concluded, these workloads would also be acceptable. The sum of the board's decision was this: the hiring of six new employees coupled with rather vague orders that the company improve work or readjust workloads in its spinning and weaving departments.

According to the men who designed and staffed the CTLRB, that should have ended the matter; representatives from the company and the workers should have met subsequently to iron out specific matters arising from the board's decision. Yet they did not. On the day that worker spokesman G. E. Henderson received the board's decision—21 May 1934—he and his committee "immediately presented it to the mill management." According to the telegram Henderson sent later that day, "Management refused to recognize [the] Committee and the recommendations of the State Board."[45] A week later, H. H. Willis replied to Henderson, assuring him that the mill was indeed trying to remedy the situation and advising "patience" on the part of the workers. Henderson and the others tried having patience and then informed the board on 11 June that nothing had been done.

Henderson also appealed to the national CTLRB. On 13 June, the national board sent R. F. Howell to investigate—the same R. F. Howell who had investigated, and summarily dismissed, dozens of workers' complaints (including at least three at Saxon) earlier in 1934. Howell reported that he had a long conversation with owner John A. Law, who explained the workload changes his mill was undertaking. Law adamantly refused to rehire either of the two workers recommended by the state board and furthermore attacked G. E. Henderson on the grounds that he "was exceeding his rights under Section 17 in continuing as present chairman [of the CTLRB-sponsored workers' committee] and that he possibly exceeds his authority by demanding hearings and issuing ultimatums—frequently and at any place."[46]

Clearly, by this point G. E. Henderson had been outmaneuvered by the mill, which had convinced the CTLRB's investigator—and therefore the CTLRB—that Henderson was irresponsible. Annie Laura West, however, had not been so outmaneuvered. While the hearing was under consideration by the board, West continued to bombard everyone she could think of—Robert W. Bruere, Secretary of Labor Frances Perkins, her congressional representatives, various state and federal representatives of the CTLRB, and Thomas McMahon of the United Textile Workers of America—with correspondence. Nothing helped. Rep. J. J. Swain and Sen. James F. Byrnes took enough interest to pass along inquiries to the national CTLRB. Writing to Byrnes on 12 July, Robert W. Bruere formally washed his hands of the matter: "Many of the problems that have been in controversy at the Saxon Mill have been adjusted. Some of the problems to which the letter [West's] refers will probably never be adjusted to the complete satisfaction of . . . certain of the workers. . . . Everything within our power, however, has been and is being done to assure substantial justice."[47]

Bruere's tone revealed more than his actual words; the CTLRB did little more with the Saxon case. In August, the national board repeatedly attempted to get either Saxon's management or its own state board to provide more information for a general review. Neither complied. At the end of the month, Annie West telegrammed Frances Perkins that Saxon had just fired all the weave-room workers that the mill had hired in compliance with that portion of the state board's decision. Saxon had also laid off two regular weavers. Those who remained had been raised to fifty to sixty-two looms from forty to forty-six and given new maintenance tasks as well.[48] The national board tried to contact John A. Law again on 10 September to no avail, but by that time the General Strike was on and matters had, of course, spiraled far beyond the control of the CTLRB.

If the Saxon case indicates both the breadth and depth of the CTLRB's failures in southern textiles during 1933 and 1934, it is sobering to discover that, from the workers' standpoint, this was a best-case scenario. Hundreds of complaints from textile workers in South Carolina were never even investigated. Most that were investigated were dismissed. Only a handful of hearings were ever held, and in each case the essential features of the board's recommendations went unheeded by mill management. Annie Laura West wrote a blunt letter to Robert W. Bruere in May 1934, concluding, "If Saxon Mill has not broken the Code repeatedly there is no Code."[49] Judging by the CTLRB's handling of the Saxon case and numerous others like it, she was correct.

Worker frustration with the NRA's inability to address their concerns grew exponentially in 1933 and 1934. "We the members of the N.R.A. are in the dark on the N.R.A. program," declared Pacolet Mills activist R. S. Kirby in the fall of 1933, "and we want you to explain it to us," particularly what portion of the code allowed Pacolet's management to announce without warning that the mill was about to shut down for a week.[50] Informed that the code did not specifically cover stretch-out, a worker from Apalache mill demanded one that would.[51] Back at Pacolet, management had completely ignored suggestions made by the state CTLRB in December 1933; workers' attempts to receive satisfaction through either the state or national boards had proven futile. Mill superintendent D. W. Anderson had publicly stated of the NRA that "'he would fight it to the last ditch.'"[52]

Spurred by the stretch-out's new virulence and by growing disenchantment with the CTLRB, Spartanburg County's textile workers joined the tide into the United Textile Workers of America (UTWA), a venerable AFL affiliate. Not only did the NIRA offer a clear yardstick against which conditions in individual factories could be evaluated, but the act also contained the talismanic section 7(a), which guaranteed workers the right "to organize and bargain collectively through representatives of their own choosing." Roosevelt's often-quoted words recommending union membership further encouraged southern textile workers to assert themselves in new ways under the NIRA. Section 7(a)—which many textile worker activists could recite by heart—looked, and ultimately turned out to be, a vague and flimsy sort of protection.[53] It was more, however, than either the UTWA or southern textile workers had ever had before, and both attempted to take advantage of it. It was this combination of the stretch-out, NIRA-inspired hope, section 7(a), and President Roosevelt's personal endorsement of unionism that paved the way for the most successful union organizing drive in southern history.

The UTWA had been in the South before, during the strike waves of 1919 through 1921 and 1929–30.[54] After the defeats of Marion, Danville, Gastonia, and Elizabethton, the UTWA's viability in the South—like the defeated Knights of Labor and NUTW before it—seemed tenuous at best. Spartanburg County's work force was less scarred by earlier defeats than workers elsewhere. Although the UTWA chartered at least five locals in the county between 1919 and 1921, no crushing conflicts followed.[55] The union had maintained an itinerant presence in Spartanburg since 1929, primarily through the person of John Peel, the UTWA's southern vice president and chief organizer for South Carolina. Peel's initial efforts at organizing Spartanburg workers evaporated in the wake of ill-fated strikes at Woodruff in 1929 and Arcadia in 1932. Not until late 1933, with the implementation of the NIRA and the simultaneous worsening of conditions in the mills, did textile workers once again begin to flock to the UTWA banner.

The work of organizing Spartanburg County began in earnest in August 1933 and continued up until the General Strike a year later.[56] Knowing full well the power mill officials had over both the social and the physical terrains of mill villages, the UTWA pursued the initial phases of its campaign on the margins,

Off-village businesses, south Glendale, circa 1930, including the "community hall" used for union meetings in 1933–34. (Courtesy of Michael Hembree)

at such places as Cudd's Pool Room just off the Chesnee Mill village or McClure's general store between Clifton No. 1 and No. 2. The peripheries of virtually all southern mill villages were surrounded by constellations of independently run groceries, saloons, and other businesses, and it was in such locations that the early union movement necessarily took shape.[57]

Once an organizer had secured a core group of interested workers and convinced each to pay the mandatory one dollar initiation fee, the UTWA would charter a local union. The first of these came at Clifton No. 2, where Local 1780 was established in the early fall of 1933. As workers discovered how unresponsive CTLRB officials were to individual complaints, they increasingly opted for the UTWA as the appropriate agency through which to obtain government-promised relief and redress. Over the next twelve months, twenty-seven other locals were chartered or revived in Spartanburg County. By mid–1934 the union boasted functioning organizations at twenty-four of the county's thirty-two operating mills (table 1). At the time of the General Strike, only eight plants in the county lacked UTWA locals (map 2), all either miniscule operations or mills in communities where worker activism had been recently suppressed.[58]

A brief history of the Tucapau union—Local 2070—gives some idea of a strong local's development during 1933 and 1934. Pressed by the stretch-out,

Table 1. UTWA Loals in Spartanburg County, S.C., 1933–34

1705	Beaumont (originally organized 1929)
1780	Clifton #2
1834	Clifton #1
1835	Drayton
1836	Valley Falls
1881	Spartan Mills
1882	Saxon
1883	Converse
1884	Clifton (black workers)
1934	Cowpens Mill
1935	Inman Mills
1936	Powell Knitting
1994	Pacolet Mills
2017	Whitney
2070	Tucapau
2119	Arkwright
2135	Fairmont
2145	Spartanburg (black workers)
2186	Jackson Mill
2189	Glendale
2190	Victor Mill
2191	Lyman
2218	Apalache
2219	Spartanburg (black workers, 2d local)
2232	Woodruff
2236	Enoree
2266	Pacolet Mills (black workers, organized July 1934)
2275	Fairmont (black workers)
2298	Franklin Mill

Note: Mill charters were issued sequentially by the parent union.

encouraged by section 7(a), and aware of the UTWA's local presence, a handful of Tucapau workers began meeting together in the early fall of 1933 to discuss the possibility of forming a union. A few months later they contacted the UTWA. On 11 December 1933 organizer J. W. Nates officially established Local 2070 with fifty-two charter members, including the men who would become its three most prominent leaders: Cloyd L. Gibson, B. C. Comer, and S. P. Caldwell. Initial growth was slow, with seventeen more joining in the last week of December and twelve and fourteen, respectively, in the first two weeks of January. This provided a critical mass, a core group of some ninety-five union members inside the plant.

Directed and sustained by this core group, the real work of organizing Tucapau began in earnest: fifty more workers joined Local 2070 in the last week of January, eighty-eight the first week of February, eighty-three the second,

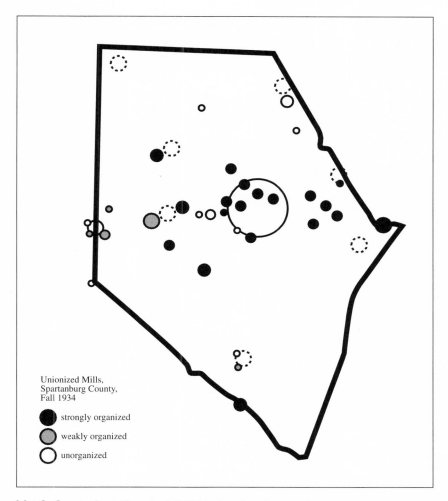

Map 2. Spartanburg County, fall 1934, showing degree of unionization at all mills and villages. (Courtesy of L. A. Waldrep)

forty-four the third, and 116 the fourth week—bringing total union membership up to 446, a majority, by the end of the month. Unionists spent the next two months consolidating its position in the plant, bringing in 141 more members in dribbles and spurts.

In mid–April, Local 2070 joined the Spartanburg County Textile Council and the South Carolina Federation of Labor. The real work of organizing Tucapau was now complete; new members would thereafter come in only as a

Clifton weave room, during the 1930s. (Courtesy of Converse College)

result of shifting personnel inside the mill.[59] Virtually all of this organizing was done by Local 2070 members themselves: The UTWA's full-time staff were kept busy enough chartering new locals during these months to spend much time aiding established ones.[60]

Perhaps the best gauge of Local 2070's priorities during 1933 and 1934 comes from its financial records. The pattern of disbursements indicates much about what Tucapau's unionized workers considered important—that is, worth spending their hard-earned money on in times of extreme economic distress. The local's first public event—held on 27 January 1934—was a "birthday ball" in honor of its patron saint, Franklin D. Roosevelt. Beyond such social events, Local 2070's greatest expenses were in assisting other southern textile locals already out on strike in the spring and summer of 1934. In April, the local sent $25.15—almost half its monthly budget—to striking workers at Spindale, N.C. In May and June, they sent $24.80 to aid strikers at Cowpens Mill (along with Local 2070 president Cloyd Gibson to give an inspirational talk). In August, they sent $10 to locked-out and destitute workers at Gaffney's Musgrove Mill. Local 2070 also occasionally spent small amounts of money to defray emergencies in the lives of its members. The priorities of Local 2070 were clear: loyalty to President Roosevelt and his New Deal, solidarity with other textile workers in communities across the Piedmont, and service to the critically needy in their own midst.[61]

Although the UTWA was able to charter hundreds of locals with amazing rapidity during 1933 and 1934, the task of transforming those paper charters into meaningful organizations was complex and daunting. Some manufacturers fought the UTWA from the beginning, harassing organizers and firing workers who joined.[62] Others turned a blind eye to the union's activities; a few Spartanburg mills even allowed local unions to meet on company property. Either way, the most critical element in the building of a strong local union was time. It took precisely six months—from mid–October to mid–April—for prounion sentiment at Tucapau to metamorphose from informal meetings of disgruntled workers into a fully operational local union. About half of Spartanburg County's local unions ultimately had this time before the General Strike permanently disrupted union activity in the region. The rest, organized in the spring and summer of 1934, did not.[63]

For the most part, UTWA organizers attempted to sidestep the thorny question of race as they signed up white textile workers. Southern textile mills universally denied production jobs to African Americans, but black men and women did labor for the mills in opening rooms, warehouses, and laundries as well as on village maintenance crews. Black workers were also caught up in the excitement of the New Deal. They, too, wrote desperate letters to President Roosevelt, although their jobs were all among those excluded from the wage and hour provisions of the code. With even more to gain and (perhaps) less to lose, black workers began to approach union organizers almost as soon as the UTWA sent staff members back into the South.

"We didn't organize them," white activist Robert Donnahoo later recalled, "they came to us." Organizers feared that signing black workers into white locals would alienate whites, but refusing to sign them up at all could easily transform them from allies to potential strikebreakers.[64] The union's white organizers made an on-the-spot decision to sign black workers when they approached and, if interest was sufficient, to set up separate black locals.

As Robert Donnahoo himself told black workers, "We've got a place for you. We'll *make* a place." Five segregated locals were set up at Spartanburg County mills, and membership cards were issued to blacks in at least two other plants. These locals, although small, did function. Local 2145 even advertised its meetings, which were held on Saturday mornings at the black Knights of Pythias hall on South Liberty Street in Spartanburg. The UTWA's African American policy was admittedly makeshift, partially because of the delicate politics of race and partially because of black workers' minuscule presence. As Donnahoo exclaimed, "What could we do with them? We could sign them up and give them a card," but that was all. "They came to us wanting in the union. So to hold them we said, 'Here, we'll give you a charter of your own,' to hold them until we got some contract here in the plant." The UTWA hoped to merge these black workers and locals into the white unions at some later date, or, failing that, to negotiate separate contracts for them. During 1933 and 1934, the unofficial policy was to "stash them away," to save them for later. Later never came.[65]

In the spring and summer of 1934, the UTWA's southern membership began to put pressure on union leaders to call a general strike to settle the question of stretch-out once and for all. As spring gave way to summer, scattered locals began to strike on their own, and by the time the UTWA actually called a general strike in September, virtually all the mills in northern Alabama were already out.[66] Workers at a few mills in South Carolina also struck on their own in mid–1934. In Spartanburg County, nowhere was the rising tide of worker frustration and impatience more evident than at Cowpens Mill, a small, locally owned plant that had been particularly hard-hit by the depression. Management had obligingly passed on its plight to workers via the stretch-out. When the workers at Cowpens Mill formed a union in late 1933, supervisors began to fire members, but neither the UTWA nor the CTLRB seemed able or willing to do anything about the situation. By 30 April 1934, members of Local 1934 had lost patience with their supervisors, their union officials, and, most important, the CTLRB.[67] They walked out.

Local 1934's shop committee met state CTLRB chair H. H. Willis with a detailed slate of demands covering every single job, wage, and workload in the mill. The shop committee also demanded that the company withdraw its recently posted curtailment notice, which Local 1934's members interpreted as a thinly disguised excuse to cover a massive (and final) layoff of union members. The management at Cowpens Mill maintained that workers were simply overreacting to the company's last-ditch efforts to restore profitability.[68]

After much negotiation, Willis and his panel were able to extract from the company a promise to reopen the mill "as soon as satisfactory orders can be secured," to reinstate all employees without discrimination, and to govern layoffs when and if they became necessary "by such factors as seniority and efficiency." Willis also reminded Cowpens Mill's management that unskilled workers employed on mixed jobs (such as sweepers with extra duties) were covered by the code. Beyond that, however, Willis would only refer the workers' specific complaints to CTLRB investigators; he flatly refused to grant the shop committee's request "that no further changes be made in speeds or organization of equipment." Willis and his panel urged the employees to return to the plant and go back onto whatever jobs the company demanded of them for a sixty-day trial period. "At the end of such period of time, if there is a disagreement as to machine load or wages, committees must be set up as outlined in Section 17 of the Cotton Textile Code," with further resort to the state and national boards as necessary. After Local 1934 received a promise of a CTLRB time study at the mill, the union provisionally agreed to end its strike, and on the morning of 15 May the workers voted to return to work.[69]

The settlement made no difference. Throughout the summer of 1934, Cowpens Mill's management continued to threaten and discharge union workers.[70] On 16 July, Furman Rogers—labor's representative on the state board and a signatory to the CTLRB's Saxon decision earlier in the year—finally lost patience. In a sharp letter to national CTLRB chair Robert W. Bruere, Rogers explained the situation at Cowpens: "Shortly after the mill resumed operations a number of employees were laid off, apparently upon allegations that they were not co-operating with the company in its efforts to get the mill running properly, for doing poor work, which in effect was a charge of sabotage." These discharges, which included most of Local 1934's officers as well as anyone else "who had been of any influence in the union," began the very first week the mill went back on production. At the time of his writing, Rogers reported that "more than forty" were out of work, "many on transparent pretexts . . . until the workers are greatly discouraged at the prospects of securing any compliance with the agreement or ruling." Eviction notices had been served despite promises from both board chair H. H. Willis and mill president H. W. Kirby that evictions would be postponed until the CTLRB had a chance to review the case.

Only Rogers's personal appearance in the courtroom prevented a number of families from being forcibly put on the street. From the state board's standpoint, the net result was "a condition under which the members of the union could not secure the necessary action to set up the machinery whereby the terms of the agreement and the ruling might be enforced."[71] In other words, the CTLRB's involvement in the Cowpens Mill situation had become an open farce.[72]

The CTLRB attempted to save face and scheduled a hearing on 25 July at which the union presented fifty-eight cases of discriminatory discharge. H. W. Kirby testified that his company had investigated all but one of the cases and that all were for due cause. Kirby offered to reinstate only a handful of the discharged workers, claiming that the company's precarious financial condition barely allowed him to "run the mill and take care of about three hundred of our operatives and their families that are interested in cooperating with us," much less an additional fifty-eight troublesome union members. In its decision of 2 August, the state CTLRB recommended that only ten of the fifty-eight be rehired—and then only if and when jobs came open at the plant. A few days later, Local 1934's shop committee sent formal notice to Robert W. Bruere that they could not accept the state board's decision. Upon H. H. Willis's recommendation, the shop committee dutifully resubmitted all fifty-eight cases to the national board for reconsideration.[73] Before the national board could act, however, Cowpens Mill—along with the rest of Spartanburg County and the textile South—was swept up in the General Strike.

3   "It's Now or Never": The General Textile Strike of 1934, Part 1

When Roosevelt shut down all the plants and called everybody out on a strike, and he put that New Deal into effect, that's when it started. . . . The people organized, and they demanded some rights then, and were able to get them, because they had strength in unity.

—Ibera Holt, Clifton, S.C., 1993

By the summer of 1934, the UTWA was having trouble everywhere keeping its members on their jobs. No longer concerned solely with issues of workload, pay, and shopfloor mistreatment, southern textile workers' trust in the NRA and in all that President Roosevelt's New Deal represented was turning swiftly into outrage. As James Hodges has written, "After a year of the code, mill owners and mill management still ruled supreme on the mill floors. For the cotton textile workers section 7(a) had been only an invitation to a fancy dress ball they were too poor to attend, and their resentment at their exclusion had grown."[1] Or, as the beleaguered workers of Cowpens Mill put it, "The government give us the Board to give us a chance to get a square deal, and we signed the agreement to depend on the board, and we believe that the Board meant to give us and the company a square deal without having to strike again. . . . Don't ask us to set still and get our throats cut while we wait on a fair deal." In short, "We signed the agreement and meant to keep it—but we don't intend to let the company violate the agreement and not do anything about it."[2]

The sequence of events termed the "General Textile Strike of 1934" had its roots in the stretch-out and its vehicle in the United Textile Workers of America—that much is clear. Yet precisely what constituted the strike—what it did and, ultimately, what it meant—differed from community to community. As Janet Irons has shown, the "strike" was in fact a crazy-quilt of disparate activity. Striking workers in Rhode Island had little or no communication with their northern Alabama counterparts; even in the South, worker response to the strike call could vary enormously over a few square miles of Piedmont terrain. Union locals at some mills survived not only the strike but also the vicissitudes of succeeding decades, a few down to the present day. In other textile communities, the UTWA was beaten so decisively that no union would ever again succeed in gaining a foothold. To understand the strike's course in a single county of locations—in Spartanburg—is to begin at last to excavate its complex, and sometimes self-contradictory, legacies.

At Cowpens as in countless other mills, workers were on the verge of taking matters into their own hands in mid–1934, leaving the UTWA with a difficult choice. The union could call a general strike—as it nearly did in June—and ride the crest of worker discontent to wherever it might lead, realizing the immense risk such a course of action would entail. Or the UTWA could remain still and watch, for a third time, as its southern membership melted away. It was an unpalatable dilemma, but, from an organizational standpoint, one with a single solution: The union would have to go on strike with its members or else be repudiated entirely in the South.[3]

In South Carolina, the decisive threshold was passed in late July, when the UTWA's state body—the South Carolina Federation of Textile Workers—met for three days in Spartanburg. Frank Walsh of the United Garment Workers of America opened the convention and set its tone by declaring, "Slavery has not been abolished in the South; the color of the slaves has only been changed." Reporting from strike-bound northern Alabama, UTWA representative John Dean told the assembly, "This is not alone a strike. It is a revolt against the stretch-out system. Low wages and an increased machine load have made conditions for workers intolerable. They may as well starve on the outside as on the inside of the mills." Next to the stretch-out, the convention's principal target was the NRA and its profusion of useless boards. As John Dean noted, however, the New Deal's failure was only one facet of textile workers' overall problem. "This is not a strike against the NRA, or against any group," he told the convention. "It is a strike against the entire system in the state of Alabama" and the textile South as a whole.[4]

On the afternoon of its last formal session, the South Carolina Federation of Textile Workers took the step that workers, manufacturers, and observers had been expecting for some time. The convention "went on record as giving its support to Thomas F. McMahon, national president of the U.T.W.A., 'whenever it might be necessary to call a general strike.'" The convention also endorsed resolutions calling for a sixty-hour work week, a 33 percent wage hike, elimination of the stretch-out, a general reduction of machinery speed, recognition of the UTWA, and reemployment of workers fired because of discrimination.[5] Spartanburg County's own locals were well represented at the convention, with three delegates in particular serving in active roles: H. C. God-frey and Paul Stephens from Spartan Mills and H. M. Branch from Clifton. Late Saturday afternoon, the delegates began their journeys back to the dozens of textile communities they claimed to represent. The stage was set.

Even before the strike was officially called, Spartanburg County's textile workers planned a protest of their own. On 6 August, the county's Central Labor Union urged that all county mill workers honor Labor Day (Monday, 3 September), with or without the cooperation of mill owners.[6] Less than two weeks later the UTWA formally set its strike date for Saturday, 1 September.[7] The idea that Spartanburg County would be at the heart of whatever occurred received a boost on 19 August, when Charles W. McAbee of Inman Mills was named to the UTWA's national executive board.[8] From then until the day of the strike, the *Spartanburg Herald* and *Journal* kept county residents abreast of strike plans on both national and local levels.

As the deadline approached, both the UTWA and various companies began holding mass meetings; the *Journal* dutifully published reports from across the state as each mill's work force went on record as for or against the strike.[9] (The only Spartanburg County mill whose workers publicly opposed the strike was, predictably, Arcadia, where workers still smarted from their own defeated strike of 1932.) Each of the county's textile locals met on either Friday or Saturday, 23 or 24 August, to take strike votes. On Saturday night, three hundred delegates to the Spartanburg County Textile Council voted overwhelmingly to support the strike.[10]

Outside the mill villages, responses to the strike threat varied greatly. Ignoring more than a year of inaction and incompetence from the CTLRB and the Code Authority, the *Spartanburg Journal* opined that

> Just what could be accomplished by hundreds of thousands of regular workers in one of the greatest industries marching out without first exhausting every means to prevent it, is a subject of gravest speculation.
>
> The textile industry was the first to adopt a code and put it into practice under the NRA. Under its workings the employes have fared better than those of any other major industry, and they have been given regular employment.[11]

The *Journal* even belatedly tried to play the race card by noting on the day before the strike that a "negro local" had been organized at Fairmont.[12]

Already under attack by the SCFTW, Gov. Ibra Blackwood bluntly termed the strike "an expression of impatience and ingratitude toward the administration which has already accomplished so much good." Mindful of their electoral base, politicians from Spartanburg County took a more conciliatory approach. Statehouse representative T. Wright Cox of Woodruff even telegrammed President Roosevelt, advising him to "get all textile mills to agree to abolish stretch-out system." This, Cox added without any apparent sense of irony, "might accomplish compromise."[13]

Nor did Spartanburg's industrialists present a clear or united front. Some mills did take preemptive measures. As early as June, company officials at Beaumont began threatening permanent discharge for anyone involved in any strike that the UTWA might call. Pacolet Mills reportedly broke the code by raising work hours "to get cloth out before strike."[14] Management at most mills, however, took no such precautions. As the strike loomed, a few mills that had been running on curtailed schedules made a joint announcement that they would soon resume forty-hour weeks, perhaps hoping that the promise of full-time work would convince workers not to strike. Officials at three mills—Saxon, Chesnee, and Tucapau—announced they would not take the Labor Day holiday, whereas officials at two others—Drayton and Arkwright—announced that they would. The rest remained silent, apparently waiting out events.[15]

In fact, the situation in Spartanburg County was confused, with claims and counterclaims flying between mill owners and the UTWA. Nowhere was this more evident than at Pacolet Mills. On Saturday, 1 September, D. W. Anderson— treasurer of the Pacolet Manufacturing Company and bane of Local 1994— issued a public statement to the effect that "approximately 950 of the 1,100 operatives had signed a petition urging the company to continue operations as usual." Anderson even staged a "mass meeting" of Pacolet's workers to dramatize the petition. "We have not heard of a single mill employe who is in favor of the strike," Anderson told the *Spartanburg Journal;* "The whole sentiment of the meeting . . . was that the workers wanted to continue on their jobs and to keep up the reputation of Pacolet Mills as being one of the highest type of mills in the country and one of the most law-abiding communities to be found anywhere." In a burst of paternalistic benevolence (and lest anyone think Pacolet's management felt seriously threatened), Anderson concluded his public statement by noting, "From the standpoint of the mill it would be better for us to close down for a month or ninety days, but we are going to remain open at the request of the mill operatives themselves, because we are anxious to do so as they desire in this matter."[16]

On the union side, County Textile Council president John W. Pollard of Spartan Mills labeled Anderson's entire story preposterous, noting that all but four of Local 1994's four hundred–odd members had voted in favor of the strike a few days earlier.[17] Pollard's statement was intended to reassure textile unionists across the county that support for the strike was solid at Pacolet, but his inadvertent admission that the UTWA had only four hundred dues-paying members out of a potential membership of 1,100 indicated otherwise. The statement about closing down "for a month or ninety days" was also ominous. The simple truth was that no one—not the mill owners, not the UTWA, not the press, and not even local union activists—could be sure what would happen on Monday, 3 September 1934.

The strike was set to begin at midnight on Saturday, 1 September. The *Journal* noted that "the zero hour . . . passed at 11:30 o'clock last night apparently without incident in the Spartanburg County industrial section," although pickets were reported at Beaumont on Sunday. The real test came on Monday morning. The *Journal* estimated that two-thirds of the county's fourteen thousand textile workers stayed away from the mills, leaving sixteen plants idle and thirteen running.[18] During the early days of the strike, that tally would mutate on a daily, sometimes hourly, basis. By Wednesday, roving bands of union pickets—known as "flying squadrons"—had successfully closed all but four of the county's textile plants, and even those four closed early for the weekend. In Spartanburg County, at least, the General Strike seemed to be a success.

The reactions of local manufacturers in the opening days of the strike continued to indicate anything but unity. Of the mills closed on Monday, three—Drayton, Valley Falls, and Inman—"announced that they plan to open as usual Tuesday morning." Spartan Mills president Walter Montgomery reported his mill "closed . . . until people want to return to work." An official at Whitney stated, "We're closed for Labor Day, beyond that I am not sure just now." The Clifton company reported that they were officially taking the holiday, but "we can't say about Tuesday. It hasn't been decided whether we will open or not." John Law tersely reported his Saxon plant "closed indefinitely." Only Arkwright's officials publicly acknowledged that their mill was closed on account of the strike. Management at Beaumont probably summed up the situation best in a uniquely elliptical statement: "We're closed today, on Labor Day, and unless the people come back to work on Tuesday, we will remain closed until further notice."[19]

If mill owners' public statements were inconclusive, the actions of state and local governments were not. Strike opposition in its most irreducible form came from county sheriff Sam M. Henry. Henry, whose deputies had been used to break the Arcadia strike in 1932, swore in nearly fifty "special deputies" on Labor Day.[20] During the course of the next seven years, Henry and his deputies would become the scourge of Spartanburg County unionists, but during the General Strike itself the deployment of the National Guard was of much greater importance in intimidating workers. The first such deployments in Spartanburg County occurred on Tuesday at Lyman and Victor, two large mills at which the UTWA had only marginal support. The earliest Guardsmen were mostly local men, assisted at Victor by "three carloads of officers armed with riot guns" sent in by Sheriff Henry. Later, both Guardsmen and Sheriff Henry's deputies were also sent to guard the two Woodruff mills and Cowpens Mill.[21]

The Guard's function in the General Strike was twofold. Ostensibly, it allowed mills to run unimpeded where the union was either particularly weak (at Victor, Lyman, and Woodruff) or the management was particularly vicious (at Cowpens Mill). Too, Governor Blackwood's blanket use of the National Guard constituted an obvious reminder about who held military power in South Carolina and who did not. Yet the psychological importance of using the Guard ran much deeper than simple intimidation, both on individual and community levels. Just as fraternal societies like the Masons had enjoyed great popularity in South Carolina's textile mill villages for decades, so did military companies; large numbers of young men from Spartanburg County's mill villages were Guardsmen. Before the strike, the National Guard had functioned as yet another social institution for binding the community together, a patriotic forum for male bonding and a source of pride and entertainment in communities where both were often lacking. All that changed when the Guard was called to "defend" textile mills from strikers. Frequently union members from one community would be called to stand guard by mills at another, and they would sometimes face off against their neighbors as flying squadrons attempted to close those plants.[22]

Guard units from Spartanburg were called to guard the Poe, Monaghan, and Dunean mills at Greenville; some were also used at Honea Path and witnessed the shooting of nine strikers by company deputies there on 6 September.[23] The use of textile workers—many of them union members—to "guard" mills and intimidate strikers became one of the most symbolic issues of the strike. At Arkwright, for instance, mill overseer and Guard officer Mark Shook literally walked down the union picket line, calling out his unit's members for duty in Greenville. A witness to that event later testified to its trauma: "It was hard to go, too, off the picket line when they thought they was doing the right thing."[24] For some, the tension between Guard duty and loyalty to the union became unbearable. A few Spartanburg workers—including Conway Gault, an officer in the Saxon local—were jailed for refusing to report for Guard duty.[25]

The disruptive use of the National Guard stood in stark contrast to the abstinence of the American Legion during the strike. Like the Guard, the Legion functioned more as an expression of community solidarity than as the paramilitary organization it ostensibly was. The primary difference between the Guard and the Legion was the degree of local autonomy individual posts possessed. In the early days of the strike, state commander William D. Schwartz, Jr., of Charleston ordered all local units in strike areas to offer their services to local sheriffs. In Spartanburg County, where Sheriff Henry's character and the example of the National Guard were both becoming infamous, Schwartz's intention to use the Legion as yet another strikebreaking force was obvious. Reactions of local posts to Schwartz's command varied precisely according to those posts' memberships. The post at Woodruff—at this time the most antiunion stronghold in the county—endorsed it "unanimously." The posts at Spartanburg and Greer—composed of volatile mixes of unionized textile workers, nonunion textile workers, and townspeople from outside the mill communities—opted for neutrality. They met, voted to receive Schwartz's urgent telegram as "information only," and disbanded for the remainder of the strike. The post at Pacolet, however, was headed by a union member, and twenty-nine of its thirty-two members were mill workers. In a carefully worded statement, Pacolet commander A. E. Phillips would say only, "I believe that the legion should offer its services in their respective communities, but should not be called upon to go into any other section of the state." Phillips thus indirectly blasted the National Guard leaders who had sent Spartanburg County textile workers to guard mills in Greenville and elsewhere. He also affirmed that his post's loyalty was to its home community, not the sheriff, and its primary role was to support and defend that community, not tear it asunder.[26]

With little direction from the UTWA's national leadership, the Spartanburg County Textile Council attempted to coordinate local manifestations of the strike and scheduled "special open air meetings" throughout the event.[27] It also made a few rudimentary efforts toward providing economic relief for strikers, a task primarily left to the cash-poor union locals.[28] Picketing, left to local union leaders, ranged from the anemic to the highly organized, especially at Drayton, where some four hundred men and women worked four shifts of one hundred each during the early days of the strike.[29] At mills like the Cliftons, where management had stated its intention to keep its mills closed for the duration of the strike, picketing was a formality; at other places, however, it was a serious matter. During the early days of the strike the small, preexisting union cadres at Victor and Lyman both picketed but were unable to shut down those mills on their own.[30]

To most southern textile workers, however, what distinguished the General Strike from all other conflicts before or since was the use of the flying squadrons. It is, perhaps, impossible to understand much about the General Strike without probing its key feature. The flying squadron was to the General Strike what the sit-down was to Flint: not only the strike's principal innovation but also a key organizing tool and, ultimately, a rallying point for all who participated.

The idea behind a flying squadron was simple. Sometimes on the spur of the moment, sometimes according to careful plan, textile workers from the more solidly organized mills would pile into whatever motor vehicles were available and head for whatever mills were still running. Also known as "roving pickets," squadrons were first used in Spartanburg County on late Tuesday afternoon at Arcadia, which they failed to close. Although the attempt at Arcadia was apparently uncoordinated, the convoy of textile workers that left Spartanburg County for Greenville on Wednesday morning was obviously under tight direction. According to an Associated Press reporter who witnessed its assault on Dunean Mill in Greenville, the squadron consisted of about 625 textile workers in a motorcade of 105 cars and 3 trucks. The lead vehicle flew an immense American flag. The Greenville mills—all still in operation, some with reduced forces—were under National Guard protection when the squadron arrived. Although the Guardsmen were armed with weapons ranging from fire hoses to bayonets, a hurried consultation among mill managers resulted in a decision to close the mills temporarily rather than risk almost certain bloodshed at the plant gates.[31]

Dunean Mill closed within minutes of the Spartanburg squad's arrival, and neighboring Judson Mills shortly thereafter. After spending the rest of the morning in Greenville, the squadron headed back toward Spartanburg, closing mills as it went. Greer was its first target on the return trip. With its American flag still flying, the squadron "reinforced local pickets at Victor Mill," with the result that Victor's afternoon shift refused to enter the plant at 4 P.M. Across town, Greer Mill's work force walked out on its own at precisely the same moment. Fifteen minutes later, the squadron closed neighboring Franklin Mill, and at 4:55 P.M. it successfully disrupted work at Apalache. From Greer the squadron moved on to Lyman, where it lined up in front of the mill and "evacuated" the work force, and Arcadia, where managers also decided to close the mills rather than risk trouble. At some point Fairforest Finishing and Fingerville also closed rather than face the squadron, which apparently broke up in Spartanburg around dinnertime. Its work for the day was not quite done, however. At 10:30 P.M., Chesnee Mill—twelve miles north-

Spartanburg flying squadron leaving Apalache mill on its way to Greenville. (Courtesy of UPI/Corbis-Bettmann)

east of the city—dismissed its night shift when it began receiving reports that a reconstituted squadron was coming its way.[32]

Spartanburg's flying squadron returned to Greenville on Thursday morning. After "demonstrations" in front of several mills there, it "disintegrated into scattered groups" according to press accounts. Meanwhile, the National Guard attempted to counter the squadron by sending out four companies to "trail" various bands of strikers as they headed back toward Spartanburg by different routes. On Friday, the squadron's coordinator, J. O. Blum of Drayton, announced that it would "rest up" for a few days while plans were hatched for the coming week.[33]

What were Spartanburg's textile locals trying to accomplish with the flying squadron? To many, the object seemed obvious: intimidation of nonunion workers. In this view, the union hoped to accomplish by coercion and threat what it had not earlier succeeded in doing through organization. J. O. Blum, however, portrayed the squadron in very different light. Responding to criticism after the first day of activity, he explained, "What we are attempting to do now is to organize every mill in South Carolina and the nation." For Blum, the flying squadron was not a force for intimidation or coercion but rather a shock troop responsible for laying critical groundwork for further organizing. Following the squadron's visit to Greer, Blum emphasized not that it had been successful in closing the town's four mills but rather that squadron members had succeeded in organizing embryonic local unions at plants such as Franklin Mill that previously had none. The following day, Blum described how the squadron successfully established a local at Greenville's Woodside Mill. Responding to criticism that the squadron fomented violence, Blum reminded the public that "not a member of the flying squadron is armed and not a man carries a weapon," in sharp contrast to the National Guardsmen they faced. "Our sole weapon is moral persuasion, and we are simply asking our brother workers for their cooperation in this effort to get justice, and to show them the numerical strength of our union."[34]

The squadron's purpose, then, was dual. On the one hand, it amounted to an invitation—a forceful one, to be sure, but from the point of view of its participants a joyful one—to become part of the strike movement. On the other hand, it was a show of strength, not in order to intimidate but rather, as Blum implied, in order to break down the walls of fear that surrounded so many mill communities.[35] With the squadron's hundreds of members at a plant's gates, workers inside no longer had reason to feel isolated, afraid, or paralyzed. They could, the squadron's leaders and participants hoped, feel free enough to shake off their fears and act independently of mill owners and bosses.

J. O. Blum called off the squadron Thursday night to plan a strategy for eluding the National Guard; according to his public statement, he fully intended for the squadron to return to Greenville on the following Monday. By this time, however, the use of flying squadrons had apparently become controversial among the UTWA's top leadership. On Monday, several smaller squadrons emanating from Spartanburg spread out across the region, a tactical switch to confuse the Guard. Later that morning, however, John Peel—the UTWA's southern vice president—issued a statement to all local unions: Flying squadrons would henceforth be prohibited. Unionists were shocked. One of the Spartanburg sub-squadrons had left at 2 A.M. to make the ninety-mile trip to Ware Shoals, South Carolina, and arrived only to be handed Peel's proclamation by a National Guardsman. They disbanded and left.

Neither Peel nor his superiors ever adequately explained why they chose to discontinue the squadrons. Closer to the ground, a downcast J. O. Blum could only state that "steps are now being taken to determine just what are the rights of pickets" and that the squadron would remain disbanded until such time as its legal standing was decided.[36]

Spartanburg's flying squadron—described by the press as the largest in South Carolina—operated for only four days during the first week of the General Strike.[37] Yet it, more than anything else, held the memories of those who lived through the strike, regardless of which side they took in the conflict. For those who stood against the union or opted for neutrality while trying to remain on their jobs, the squadron was perceived as a direct physical threat. For decades thereafter, hundreds of workers at places like Judson Mills remembered the fear it engendered. But with its American flag flying, its cavalcade of vehicles moving across the textile landscape, and its members urging workers at other mills to come out and join the struggle, the squadron became etched in the memories of unionists as a grand and joyous moment. Part parade, part picket line, and part charivari, the flying squadron was, at root, an attempt to define "community" in broader ways than its participants had ever known.

Formed of workers from an array of organized mills in Spartanburg County, flying squadrons were attempts to answer a very simple question: Could the community ethos that so closely knit together individual mill villages be ex-

Flying squadron outside Judson Mills, Greenville, 9 September 1934. (Courtesy of UPI/Corbis-Bettmann)

tended beyond the bounds of kin or place to cover the entire textile culture of the Piedmont South? For a culture that looked so homogeneous—so clearly "like a family," as Jacquelyn Hall and others have noted—that seems possible. The degree to which the UTWA was able to organize workers and strike mills across the South in 1934 indicates the remarkable coherence of the South's textile villages as a separate and distinct subculture.

Yet the textile South's homogeneity holds up only when viewed from the outside. Underneath the endless streets of look-alike company houses and mill stereotypes lay a surprising variety of factories, managers, villages, and workers. Clifton differed from Judson in hundreds of objective and subjective ways. By September of 1934, Clifton workers possessed a year of experience in trying to build a local union. Judson workers had no such experience. When strikers from Clifton confronted Judson workers on Greenville's Easley Bridge Road on Wednesday, 5 September 1934, they discovered they were speaking two very different languages of community. As at other unorganized mills, the Judson workers refused the squadron's offer of a broader understanding of what community could mean. They opted for their own version, one defined by the more traditional bounds of kinship and geography.[38]

In this sense, the flying squadron represented the high point of the General Strike in the South and its failure the beginning of the end. John Peel's command that all strikers return to picket duty in their home communities affirmed the primacy of geography over class in the construction of community identity in South Carolina. In the broadest sense, the *General* Strike was over. Whatever happened after 10 September 1934 would occur locally, village by village, mill by mill.

4 "Getting Our Throats Cut": The General Textile Strike of 1934, Part 2

By 10 September the textile communities in Spartanburg County had fallen cleanly into one of three categories. First were the more or less solidly organized; in most cases, company officials had made tacit or even public promises that these mills would remain closed for the duration of the strike. Into this category fell Spartan, Beaumont, the Cliftons, Drayton, Whitney, Arkwright, Valley Falls, Tucapau, Fairmont, Jackson Mill, Inman Mills, Saxon, Pacolet Mills, Glendale, and Enoree. Second were plants in which the UTWA's presence was negligible: Mills and Brandon Mills of Woodruff, Crescent Knitting, Fairforest Finishing, Fingerville, Arcadia, and Chesnee. The third category was the smallest but also the most strategically important: mills at which the union had achieved a foothold but nothing more before the strike.

Across the South, these mills served as lightning rods.[1] Mills that were solidly organized stayed closed without interference; mills that were unorganized remained open; but mills where union and nonunion workers were pitted against each other were potentially explosive, especially when management attempted to keep such mills running. The architects of the flying squadron knew that these mills would provide the critical tests; at their best, the squadrons provided workers at wavering mills with precious moments of space and time in which to organize. What the squadrons could have accomplished along such lines in places like Greenville had they been allowed to continue must remain conjectural. After the squadron's demise, however, the strike situation in Spartanburg County coalesced around three communities where the UTWA, although functional, was feeble: Greer, Cowpens Mill, and Lyman.

Of the four Greer mills, Victor was the flagship; its sprawling, unincorporated village—one of the largest in Spartanburg County—covered the town's entire southeastern quadrant. The UTWA had chartered a local at Victor in the late spring of 1934 but had apparently not been very successful in attracting members. During the first week of the strike, Victor had operated on Monday and Tuesday under the protection of National Guardsmen before being closed by the flying squadron on Wednesday afternoon.

The union situation at Victor was complicated. According to the later testimony of Local 2190 officer L. L. Smith, the union had 104 members in good standing before the strike, but at the critical moment a key officer of the local lost his nerve. Smith described what happened: "L. E. Broom . . . the Secretary, could not get it into his head they could pull a strike. They found the car of the President of the local union in front of the Superintendent's house. He signed a paper that he had quit the local union and gave up everything connected with it. . . . They elected another President and carried on." But the damage had been done. Victor's workers did not obey the initial strike call, although they emptied the mill readily enough when Spartanburg's flying squadron arrived.[2]

Over the weekend, the union apparently gained strength at Victor. By Monday the UTWA claimed some seven hundred members out of a possible nine hundred. Although that was surely an exaggeration, the union was able to parlay its existing support into a brief sit-down strike on the company's railroad siding, preventing the mill from unloading coal at its own boilers. The show of power apparently frightened Victor's management, who sent for the National Guard again. This time the Guard assigned a unit from Florence, South Carolina, far removed from textile country. Perhaps feeling that the earlier deployment of local Guardsmen had sapped the strikers' fear, the Guard also sent along three machine guns. Victor's unionized workers took the machine guns—pointed directly at them—as an affront. They staged a rally of their own across the street from the mill, and although the press reported that some of the pickets had armed themselves with homemade clubs, no violence resulted. Neither, however, did the union gain any new converts. On Wednesday, the Victor, Greer, and Franklin mills at Greer successfully reopened under the Guard's auspices. All three were only able to muster substantially curtailed work forces; the strike at Greer was clearly crumbling.[3] The UTWA held out some hope at Apalache, however, which did not reopen until Thursday morning. The union chartered a local there two days later, and for a time there even seemed some possibility that Apalache's workers might rejoin the strike.[4] Yet without the six to twelve months of organizing experience that sustained other unionized mills in the county, or the protection of flying squadrons, the skeleton locals at Victor and Apalache were unable to withstand the combined pressure of community leaders, mill owners, and National Guardsmen.

Across the county, Cowpens Mill was a very different story. There, union

forces had been fighting for recognition since the spring and had already endured a brief but nasty strike of their own. Since that time, company president
H. W. Kirby and superintendent D. G. Floyd had whittled away at Local 1934's
strength through an orchestrated campaign of harrassment, intimidation,
and discriminatory discharge. Local 1934 clung to life, but by the time of the
General Strike some of its members and most of its officers were no longer
actually working in the mill.

Immediately before and during the strike, Cowpens Mill's management—
in keeping with its earlier conduct—tried every conceivable tactic to intimidate
or discredit the union. On 31 August, two company supervisors went through
the mill village with a petition for workers, declaring "that they [the workers]
didn't want to strike"; when Cleo Linder, who belonged to the union, refused
to sign, its bearer told her that she was "a gonner."[5] On the first day of the strike,
only some forty persons reported for work.[6] Kirby sent them home and kept the
mill closed for a week. On Monday, 10 September, however, he quietly reopened
the mill; the *Journal* reported that a motorized National Guard unit was been
"rushed" from Greenville to the mill early that morning as a "precautionary
measure."[7] That same day Kirby issued an open letter to his employees, pulling
out all stops in his effort to convince workers to abandon the strike:

> What you do here, when compared to the thousands involved, will not
> amount to a drop in the bucket in settling the strike. You have already lost
> five weeks time—you have done your part. Many mills throughout this
> section of the country are running and have lost no time.
>
> This is a very serious question—it may last for a long time.
>
> We are facing winter—you will need clothing, shoes, food, books for
> your children and coal for yourselves and families.
>
> We know most of you want to work.
>
> It makes no difference what organization you may or may not belong to.
>
> We are going to run the mill and give you a chance to make a living for
> yourselves and families.
>
> The Governor of South Carolina, the Sheriff of Spartanburg County, the
> Mayor of Cowpens, together with their strong forces will protect you.
>
> This is your opportunity to come in and claim your job. . . . If you do not
> come in on or before Wednesday September 12th, we will take it for grant-
> ed you do not want your job, and it will be our idea to give it to someone
> else. We hope you will not force us to do that.[8]

Over the preceding weekend Superintendent Floyd had even gone through
the village, offering wavering employees dollar bills and clandestine whiskey if

they would report to work.[9] Kirby claimed that by late Monday he had attract-
ed a full shift, although the union claimed the mill's operations were substantially curtailed.[10]

During the second and third week of the strike, Kirby's supervisors stepped
up efforts to bully workers into returning to work. One supervisor tried to in-
duce a picket to accept illegal whiskey so the company could have him arrested; another repeatedly cursed pickets and even threw one of them bodily off
the picket line.[11] This was unbearable. On Wednesday of the strike's second
week, Local 1934's shop committee wrote to Lawrence W. Pinkney of the NRA,
demanding that NRA remove the Blue Eagle from the Cowpens plant. "They
have violated the cotton textile code with out allowing us the rite to strike and
peacefuly picketing our jobs," the enraged committee wrote, "and have put
other hands in the mill them being non union[.] They have armed gards over
us at all times." According to the committee, Superintendent Floyd was offering $10 to anyone who would reveal the names of those guilty of encourag-
ing working personnel to join the strike. "We dont think that he has any rite
to do any thing like," the committee concluded, "as the supreme court give
us [the] rite to ask them and to picket our jobs."[12] That evening, the mill's
operations were interrupted briefly when its power plant failed. Someone had
thrown a chain over the high-voltage line from Gaffney, shorting it out.[13] Such
tactics, however, could only close the mill temporarily. H. W. Kirby had already
been able to pick and choose his nonunion work force over the course of the
summer. However fiercely the remaining members of Local 1934 fought to
save their local, the strike at Cowpens devolved into a selective lockout more
than anything else.

If the reopening of the Greer Mills and the Cowpens stalemate were major blows for the UTWA, the reopening of Pacific Mills's sprawling Lyman
complex on Monday, 17 September, was a disaster. The UTWA had about two
hundred members at Lyman before the strike but had been unable to bring
out the entire plant; later the mills were closed by the flying squadron. On
17 September, the National Guard moved two companies with some one
hundred infantrymen and a pair of machine guns into Lyman before sun-
rise. Guardsmen barricaded Lyman's main street, questioning anyone they
encountered either on foot or in automobiles and forcibly disarming both
pickets and company deputies. The military occupation of Lyman was the
most thorough of any textile community in Spartanburg County; throughout the day, crowds gathered and dispersed across the street from the mill
to witness the spectacle. According to the company, 800 of the plant's 1,700
workers reported for work on Monday morning, the total approaching 1,200

by late afternoon. The union, however, claimed that only 275 had reported for work in the morning, with only "a small number" trickling back later in the day.[14] The union continued to picket, and union stalwarts even erected blockades of their own to keep the company from bringing in strikebreakers from the country. Although the blockades were able to keep a few dozen strikebreakers away on Wednesday morning, some twenty-three strikers were ultimately arrested for their part in the blockading. The effort failed. The Lyman complex continued to operate, gaining workers by the day.[15]

Even though the majority of Spartanburg's mill workers remained on strike, the highly publicized losses at Greer, Cowpens Mill, and Lyman were demoralizing for the union. Encouraged by the stalemate, Spartanburg County's non-union mills cautiously began to resume production. Fingerville reopened on Monday morning, 10 September. Arcadia, Apalache, and Fairforest Finishing reopened on the thirteenth. With National Guardsmen present, Lyman and Crescent Knitting reopened on the seventeenth.[16] The more firmly established UTWA locals continued to operate as if nothing were amiss, but a dangerous sense of drift was evident, both locally and nationally.[17] It became obvious during the second week of the strike that the union would be unable to continue what food distribution it had undertaken, and on 13 September the Federal Emergency Relief Administration (FERA) announced that it would open eight food distributions stations in the county.[18] And with the absence of flying squadrons or any other newsworthy events on the local level, attention turned to the ongoing negotiations on the national level. The shift was enervating to the local union movement, even at mills where the UTWA was strong. As the *Spartanburg Journal* noted on 16 September, "With eyes of both mill directors and employes turned on the national leaders representing both sides of the textile strike situation, Spartanburg County's thermometer of activity in the textile communities recorded zero yesterday."[19]

The UTWA formally ended its General Strike on Monday, 24 September 1934. The proposed settlement, brokered by President Roosevelt, had circulated in Spartanburg County on the previous Thursday and Friday. Roosevelt's "personal appeal," as the *Spartanburg Journal* called it, became the topic of "widespread discussion" as soon as it became known. Known as the Winant settlement (for the Winant Commission, the three-member board Roosevelt appointed to mediate the conflict), the settlement recommended that the president ask workers to end the strike and that manufacturers take back strikers without discrimination; that the Bruere Board system be abolished and replaced by a new "Textile Labor Relations Board" to handle worker grievances; and that no further machine load changes be made by manufacturers until a federal commission could be appointed specifically to investigate the stretch-out. Despite the fact that the report provided not a single concrete redress of any of the myriad grievances going into the strike, the UTWA's leaders accepted it in good faith.[20]

With unswerving faith that Roosevelt would never betray them, Spartanburg's textile workers also seem to have accepted the settlement gladly. The *Journal* reported hearing one striker comment, "We'll do anything for the president," and a picket at Lyman promised that "the president is going to play fair with us."[21] Even on the local level, their euphoria was understandable. While the strike was on, Spartanburg's own Olin D. Johnston had defeated lowcountry blueblood Wyndham Manning and the aging Cole Blease in the state's Democratic gubernatorial primary (equivalent to election). Johnston, who had labored in textile mills as a child and then worked his way through college and law school, had already established himself as a friend to workers and an adamant foe of the stretch-out.[22]

On Saturday night, Francis Gorman telegraphed every local in the country with news of the union's "complete victory." That night, Spartanburg's workers organized their largest demonstration yet. With pickets removed from area plants, strikers from all over the county gathered at 8 P.M. at Morgan Square downtown. They marched behind an American flag to the Central Labor Union Hall, where a mass meeting was held to celebrate the moment; several carloads then departed for celebrations in other communities. Just before midnight, a second impromptu parade, with "blaring horns and happy faces," passed along Main Street. At the CLU's mass meeting, L. E. Brookshire of Greenville captured the general optimism: "Since the response to the call has been so marvelous it is my opinion that it is going to instill into these workers a new confidence and a new sense of their importance as the major element of society in South Carolina and the South. From this time on, organization is going to be the stabilizing factor in handling the affairs of the workers and in all forms of negotiations with their employers. . . . The union movement has come into southern mills, and it has come into them to stay."[23] In the words of the UTWA's Special Strike Committee, southern textile workers had at last won "an end to the stretch-out." "We have taken every trench," the committee's final report concluded. "Our strike has torn apart the whole unjust structure of the NRA, lifting a load from all labor as well as from ourselves."[24]

Yet southern UTWA representatives at the committee's 22 September meeting were not so sure. Reporting for North Carolina, a tight-lipped H. I. Adams said only that his workers "wanted to return to work." J. A. Frier of Columbia, representing the South Carolina Federation of Textile Workers, also chose his words carefully. Frier "believed sentiment of his people will be to follow those that were chosen to lead us in the strike and in the termination of the strike." Only partially masking disagreement with acquiescence, Frier added that he was sure the national strike committee would know more about what kind of settlement was possible than would "those in the field." The feeling of the "majority" of workers, he concluded, "was to leave it to the strike committee." From Georgia, W. P. Bolick was more blunt. He told Thomas McMahon that the "report was not what southern people are looking for" and "asked the Executive Council to tell them how to handle [the] situation."[25]

What southern people were looking for was a settlement that guaranteed not only the rather vague right to organize but also the very specific right to return to individual jobs. That distinction cannot be overemphasized. Reemployment without discrimination had been a keystone of the Winant settlement. The settlement, however, contained no enforcement procedures. Even if it had, southern textile manufacturers by this time had accumulated some fifteen months of experience at circumventing the existing enforcement procedures of the CTLRB. With will and verve, mill managers began weeding out active unionists. On Monday, 23 September 1934, thousands of textile workers across the South returned to mill gates only to find themselves locked out or fired.[26]

Discrimination cases began to pour in. At Lyman, Local 2191 president J. H. Stone reported that some four hundred workers had reported for work Monday morning but had been turned back. A Pacific Mills spokesman declared that his company was "employing former employes as fast as positions are available," but Stone asserted otherwise: "They let in the non-union people but not the union workers. We were forced back across the street at the point of bayonets, men and women being treated alike in this respect."[27] Even as Spartanburg's mills gradually reopened, the growing number of discrimination cases indicated the path that subsequent events would take.[28] Within a month of the strike's conclusion, the UTWA had tallied discrimination cases from 363 mills (237 of them in the South) and estimated that some fifteen thousand textile workers were still without jobs on account of their participation in the strike.[29]

By late November, the southern situation had become so dire that the UTWA convened a special meeting in Greenville to survey the field. Delegations from throughout the textile South attended. Their complaints were uniform: post-strike discrimination in open violation of the Winant settlement. Spartanburg County was well represented. A Converse weaver reported that he had been fired after the strike "on account of low production but his envelope showed over-production." From Cowpens, Local 1934 reported that only fourteen or eighteen of some one hundred workers who had applied for reinstatement had been taken back, and H. W. Kirby was exercising his local influence to prevent blacklisted strikers from obtaining government relief supplies. Similar reports came from Glendale, Spartan, Saxon, Apalache, and Victor Mills. In addition to being out of a job, L. L. Smith of Victor had even had a "fiery cross" burned on his lawn. Local 1836 at Valley Falls tersely reported that its members were "stretched out in every way possible." Local 1936 reported that Powell Knitting's management was pressing eviction cases against strikers. Lyman's J. H. Stone declared that "before he went on strike, he was a weak union man—now he would go to 'the gates of Hell' with 'Tom McMahon and Frankie Gorman.'" Yet Stone, too, was a victim of post-strike discrimination. Before the strike he had been making $20 a week as a hooker man at the plant, but the company had rehired him at only $8 a week to help landscape a new baseball field. Stone closed his report on an ominous note: The new baseball diamond, where virtually all of Local 2191's active members were now laboring, had been christened by other workers as the "Gorman Ball-Field." Francis Gorman patiently explained to everyone present that the proper recourse was to file formal complaints via the CTLRB in Washington, even though many delegates, including those from Saxon and Powell Knitting, reported that CTLRB investigators had already visited their communities to no avail.[30]

If southern textile workers' faith in the CTLRB, the Code Authority, and the New Deal had been shaken by their experiences before the strike, that faith was demolished by the CTLRB's performance afterward. Again complaints poured into Washington, and again CTLRB investigators began making the rounds of southern mill communities. This time, however, they met stiffened resolve from mill owners and managers. Where before they had received vague promises to improve working conditions and enforce code minimums, this time they received blanket refusals to rehire anyone deemed unworthy of post-strike reemployment, regardless of what the CTLRB recommended.[31] As with the CTLRB's performance before the strike, Spartanburg County provides a model laboratory in which to evaluate the government's role in enforcing the provisions of the NRA, the code, and the Winant settlement in the wake of the strike.

In hundreds of southern mills, the stretch-out continued as if neither the strike nor the Winant settlement had ever existed.[32] The Clifton case is representative. The three Clifton mills had already been the subject of an extended stretch-out investigation, complete with a state CTLRB hearing, in the spring of 1934, with indeterminate results. On 17 November 1934, H. M. Branch of

Local 1780 reported to Francis Gorman that workers were still awaiting the comprehensive stretch-out investigation they felt they had been promised as part of the Winant settlement. "We have been trying consistently since December, 1933," Branch noted, "to have our work load investigated by the old State and National Board[s], the two agencies in effect at that time." According to Branch, the recommendations of the state board had never been complied with, while the local's appeal to the national board had never been addressed.[33] In January, Branch reported that "the management . . . has increased the machine load since the national strike . . . which we understand is a plain violation of President Roosevelt's executive order."[34]

By mid-March, Clifton's desperate workers were on the verge of striking again.[35] UTWA vice president John Peel, in a last-ditch attempt to obtain some kind of help from the post-strike board, went so far as to remind the board's new administrator of his predecessor's record: "You are perhaps conversant with the lack of activity of the former Board, and should know that absolutely nothing was accomplished by the Bruere Board. The case, in so far as we are concerned, is not closed."[36] Yet the CTLRB took no further action at the Cliftons before dissolving in mid-1935.

Breaking pattern with manufacturers elsewhere in the South, some Spartanburg mill owners chose not to purge their plants of unionists. In mid-December, strike leader John Pollard would declare relations between Local 1881 and Spartan Mills "most satisfactory," while unionists from Jackson Mill reported that "all is quiet with our management here at the mill so far as discrimination is concerned."[37] Other mills took a harder line. From Fairmont, Local 2145 reported that "all were taken back and then they begun to fire them." Before the CTLRB could launch an investigation, half of the mill went back out on strike in protest.[38] At Powell Knitting, the company used armed deputies to block union members from reentering the plant and began eviction proceedings against local union leaders.[39] At Pacolet Mills, Local 1994 charged that management spent late 1934 slowly weeding out union activists by firing them under other pretexts. After two months of dickering with the CTLRB, Local 1994 president P. D. Hughes noted that "the cards seem to be stacked against us. The company has denied all discrimination and refuses to put any of these hands back to work," while the state CTLRB seemed either unwilling or powerless to take any further action.[40]

The continuation of the stretch-out and unresolved discrimination cases took more of a toll on worker morale and union spirit in Spartanburg County than the strike itself ever did. The General Strike left Spartanburg's unionized textile mills and workers in one of three categories. At plants like Spartan and the Cliftons, the post-strike situation approximated the pre-strike situation: Local unions continued to operate from positions of considerable strength. Elsewhere, as at Pacolet Mills, the failure of the government to halt the stretch-out or protect union members eviscerated what had been strong local unions. In at least two instances, the government's gross inability to live up to the promises of the Winant settlement killed local unions outright. Although the cases of Lyman and Cowpens Mill were extreme by Spartanburg County standards, they were in fact much more representative of the strike's aftermath elsewhere in the South. Taken in detail, they shed considerable light on how badly the UTWA and the Roosevelt administration failed southern textile workers in the wake of the General Strike.

About four hundred Lyman workers were left stranded and unemployed when the UTWA called off the strike.[41] According to CTLRB investigator Peter Carmichael, "This case is one primarily, or exclusively, of discrimination, according to both sides." The remaining members of Local 2191 were not charging stretch-out or even demanding that the company recognize their union. They simply wanted their old jobs back. Superintendent C. B. Hayes, however, steadfastly refused to discharge working employees to make room for former strikers.[42] Carmichael's impassioned appeals to the company's Massachusetts headquarters resulted only in continued assurances that Pacific Mills would rehire workers as positions became available in the plant.[43] Trying to put the best spin on the situation, B. M. Squires of the CTLRB termed this understanding an "agreement" and assumed that the Lyman crisis would be settled quickly.[44]

While Lyman's management bided its time and CTLRB officials hoped the case would solve itself, Lyman's former strikers did the only constructive thing President Roosevelt's administration had taught them to do: They wrote more letters to Washington—dozens of them. "We have been discriminated against more than any other mill I know in South Carolina," Bruce Sheriff declared.[45] J. O. Ivester told Secretary of Labor Frances Perkins that "the officials of this mill here at Lyman have made threats and said that neither you or Mr. Gorman, also Mr. Roosevelt, and the Winant Mediation Board was not running their plant. They told the help that are still out they were fired and said when somebody died, or quit they might give them a job."[46] H. A. Wooten was one of those lucky enough to be rehired, but on a window-washing job at only $10 per week—"and we can't buy wood and coal and pay our rent and live on that."[47] "They have country people on our jobs, and we have the jobs that they have been using the negroes on," Ralph Mullinax exclaimed. "I just want to quit and walk out, but keep thinking that something will be done about it."[48] Mrs. G. W. Lankford admitted, "It is just awful. . . . I am trying to keep a brave heart but some times it looks so blue. I cant even pay for my childrens school book[s] and I cant see no way of clothes and shoes for them this winter."[49] "Do you think there is any chance of us getting our jobs back?" pleaded Edna Atkins.[50] "The hands that are still out can't go to other places for jobs because the officials at Lyman tell the officials of other mills not to hire us," N. J. Sheriff explained. "It's all done to freeze out the union."[51] According to Annie Morgan, the plant superin-tendent "stated he will close the mill down for five years before he will per-mit his employes to have an organization of their own."[52] "We were given a free right to organize and if we can't organize and keep our jobs it doesn't seem like we are free to do so," wrote Clora Leonard.[53] "We don't think that the people here at Lyman has got a fair deal," A. L. Millwood summed up. "Now do you?"[54]

So long as the CTLRB let stand companies' policies of refusing to discharge employees hired during the strike in favor of those who remained out, the Lyman situation boiled down to a single question: Was the company in good faith hiring back the unemployed as positions arose? For the next three years, Lyman's workers, company officials, the UTWA, the CTLRB, agents of the Fed-eral Mediation and Conciliation Service, the newly constituted National La-bor Relations Board, and, ultimately, the civil courts debated the matter. J. M. Brown, a Lyman worker, explained. "We understand . . . that they have made a settlement with the board and are putting the strikers back to work as quick as possible, which they are not doing," Brown wrote. "The strikers they are re-employing are placed on the outside digging up trees, digging ditches, and washing windows on the inside of the mill at a reduced wage." At least fifty former employees were not working at all.[55] The wage cuts, according to Lo-cal 2191 officers J. H. Stone and Furman Garrett, amounted to between 10 and 30 percent, not considering the particularly onerous nature of the work that former strikers were being asked to perform. "Do you think this is Discrimi-nation?" they asked B. M. Squires. "We don't feel like we can take much more of this foolishness, peoples relief has been cut off and something must be done about it."[56]

The jobs created for former strikers were not permanent; C. B. Hayes and his associates obviously hoped they would pacify the CTLRB for the time it would take to wear down what was left of Local 2191. In November and De-cember the jobs began to run out. Clora Leonard, writing in mid-November, declared that the Lyman group had "been treated worse than negro slaves." The company had never rehired any of the female former strikers, while what outside work had been given the men—at ridiculously low wages—had just been cut to 2.5 days per week.[57] Wholesale discharges of these men began in January, along with the first eviction proceedings. In yet another letter to Washington, Clora Leonard and Annie Morgan reiterated the increasingly dire situation the remaining unionists faced: "It seems nothing is being done about our case here. Many of us are still out of work and the mill officials tell us that they can't give us work until there is an opening. We have waited almost five months and we think if any thing is going to be done about it that it should be done now. . . . Many of the people are actually suffering for food and clothing while the farmers are here on our jobs."[58]

The UTWA had filed a petition for a discrimination hearing in December, and in January even a CTLRB investigator admitted that "a hearing is absolutely necessary."[59] By the end of the month, John Peel termed the Lyman situation "critical."[60] The CTLRB finally ordered a hearing in the case, steeling itself for what a board attorney expected would be a real "fight." On 12 February, however—two days before the scheduled hearing—the company capitulated to a written agreement obligating itself to eventually rehire every man and woman on the union's list. Local 2191 accepted, and with an audible sigh of relief the CTLRB canceled the hearing. On 27 February 1935, CTLRB investigator J. L. Bernard reported that "the local union and the management are working out their problems together very satisfactorily" and recommended that the case be closed.[61]

That should have ended the matter. The agreement, however, proved to be just another element of Pacific Mills's overall plan of delay and intrigue. By mid-June, investigator Bernard was back in Lyman and reporting "a very bad feeling."[62] When the NIRA was declared unconstitutional, Lyman's management unilaterally abrogated all agreements, real or implied, that it had ever made with either the CTLRB or Local 2191. Thus released, the company abandoned all pretense of rehiring from the union pool and finally began wholesale eviction proceedings against former strikers. The situation became increasingly volatile. At a CTLRB-arranged conference between C. B. Hayes and Local 2191's shop committee in late August, union secretary Furman Garrett threatened that former strikers would forcibly resist evictions, while C. B. Hayes declared that "he has a perfect right to employ or discharge whoever he pleases" and described the old preferential hiring list prepared under the CTLRB as "expired."[63]

Hayes began to carry out his evictions in December 1935.[64] Meanwhile, the remaining members of Local 2191 gathered together all the correspondence, affidavits, and other documents that had thus far been generated in their case and resubmitted the entire package to the newly formed National Labor Relations Board (NLRB). In early 1936 the NLRB finally provided the Lyman strikers with their long-sought hearing, but due to various procedural delays the case was still in process more than a year later. On 11 June 1937, the exhausted unionists formally withdrew from the board's proceedings and filed civil cases in the state courts.[65] Four days later, the management of Pacific Mills came to terms. In the final settlement, Pacific Mills agreed to rehire twenty employees back on their former jobs, to pay forty-four former employees $320 each, and to pay nineteen more $105 each. Although the local labor press termed this "a great victory for labor in this section," the victory was Pyrrhic.[66] After the last of the former strikers had cashed their checks, what was left of Local 2191 disintegrated. Back in January 1935, Furman Garrett had captured the Lyman fiasco definitively in a letter to Franklin Roosevelt. "It has been awful here to live since the strike was settled," Garrett wrote, reviewing the case at length. "When the law gives us the right to organize, and if the law does not protect us, I am wondering what will become of us now?"[67] He never received an answer.

Across the county, workers at Cowpens Mill faced similar privation and discouragement. The basic facts at Cowpens were simple and undisputed: On Monday, 24 September, Local 1934's members had applied for reemployment and been turned away at the mill gate. According to union committeeman Jack Kirby, the company had assembled Superintendent Floyd, the complete corps of overseers, and a detachment of National Guardsmen. As each worker approached the gate, "The guard would ask the superintendent or overseer if it was all right for him to go in and if they said yes, they let him in." The others were left standing. On orders from the UTWA, those remaining returned to the gate the following Monday. They found the National Guard gone but the overseers present "and the gate fastened. Lewis Kirby had a tablet and pencil and wanted to take our names and said if they needed us they would send for us."[68] Three days later, George Garland of Local 1934's shop committee desperately demanded action:

> I ask you to please send the Board to Cowpens, S.C. to put us back to work. We came out on a strike when you ordered us out to strike and the Board has been all around Cowpens, S.C., but never has come to Cowpens, S.C. We are in need. Its getting cold weather and our children are barefooted and almost naked. We have no way of clothing them until we get to work. . . . .
>
> The company is suing us for our houses and they will evict us next week. . . . .
>
> There are 168 of us Union members that is barred from the Mill. We are starving and some sick. We want some action if it is for us.

Having had more prior experience with the CTLRB than any other union in Spartanburg County, Local 1934 was finally losing faith. "If the Board is not coming to Cowpens," Garland wrote, "please just tell us and we will not look for it no more." The situation at the Cowpens Mill village was bleak. As Garland observed by way of conclusion, "If that is all we get out of the strike, I don't suppose no more locals will strike in this country any more."[69]

Garland's letter so affected B. M. Squires that he telegrammed H. W. Kirby the following day, only to be told that "our help were all offered their jobs that they were on August 31st, unconditionally."[70] Kirby was lying. At this point the CTLRB probably suspected as much, for Squires immediately dispatched the woman who was his most conscientious investigator: Dudley Harmon. She arrived in Cowpens only just in time to prevent Kirby from evicting all of Local 1934's remaining members. Trying a new tack, Kirby told Harmon that according to his own private information, "only about nine in his mill had really voted to strike." The rest, he reasoned, "had not voted for it, hence were not strikers, hence had quit and were therefore not entitled to have their jobs." Harmon noted that she had seen the union's list of more than a hundred workers who had voted for the strike, supported it, and not been reemployed. Kirby replied that the list had been "invented" by union leaders, who, he opined, were "more or less scoundrels." Nonplussed, Harmon offered to interview all hundred-odd people on the union's list personally to ascertain whether they had voted for the strike. Kirby told her that this would take "several weeks" but grudgingly agreed to believe whatever Harmon reported back to him.[71]

With Local 1934's ready cooperation, Harmon found virtually all of the former strikers within a few hours. Unable to obtain another audience with Kirby that day, she left word at his office, reminding him of President Roosevelt's commitment to striker reemployment and emphasizing "that I was sure he was the kind who would wish to cooperate in the matter." Kirby later agreed to "take back most of the workers" but told Harmon that "there were some whom he did not wish to take back, because they were drunkards, people who made threats, etc. etc." Kirby declined to name names, however, as did union president M. E. Jackson, who admitted that the union contained a few persons of "bad character" but declared "that Mr. Kirby was only planning by this means to discriminate, and that as soon as [Harmon's] back was turned, he would continue the evictions." Jackson and Local 1934 wanted to hand the entire case back to the board for adjudication but were told by B. M. Squires to accept Kirby's proposals and then file complaints when and if Kirby failed to carry through. Local 1934's membership hotly resisted that course of action, saying they would contact Francis Gorman. Harmon reminded them, however, "that Gorman would only refer it again to the Board, that they had promised to abide by what the Board said, etc. etc." Indeed. Under pressure from all sides, Local 1934 gave in and agreed to go along with Kirby's proposals—at least for the moment.[72]

Given Kirby's performance earlier in the year, the outcome was predictable. Nine days after capitulating to Kirby and the board, Local 1934's shop committee found Harmon in Spartanburg and reported that of the 110 cases, Kirby had rehired only six. Harmon telephoned Kirby, who explained that such matters were delicate and had to be handled "in a 'polite' way." A week later, Kirby was more definite and told Harmon that "he will shut down his mill before he will take some of them back to work." Unionists continued to go back and forth to the mill to apply for work, and Kirby's staff continued to invent reasons why there were not rehired.[73] By 24 November, even Dudley Harmon's genteel patience had been exhausted. Reporting to the CTLRB office in Washington, she declared that "Mr. Kirby had failed to live up to an understanding he had reached with me, and I find him guilty of discrimination."[74] Even though Harmon strongly recommended that the CTLRB schedule an immediate hearing, the board stalled, first sending in another investigator to review Harmon's work and then reacting to a company threat that if a hearing were scheduled Kirby would close the plant for good.[75] In none of this did the CTLRB notify either the UTWA or the workers of Cowpens Mill; John Peel was finally forced to resubmit the entire case, which by now had been whittled down to some sixty-four remaining plaintiffs.[76] Unable to sidestep the case any longer, the CTLRB finally scheduled a hearing for 22 March 1935, some six months after the conclusion of the strike.[77]

Sixteen men and women appeared at the hearing itself. The wife of shop committeeman George Garland testified that the family had tried and failed to rent a farm, during which time she had been told by a company nurse that "you people need not be sitting around here to get back in the mill," because the company did indeed have a blacklist and the Garlands' names were on it. Annie Bell Barnett reported that although she had been rehired after the strike she had been fired the day after her unionist father was seen talking with a CTLRB investigator. The rest of the testimony was similar.[78] The company's chief response was that it had made a good-faith effort to return employees to their old jobs on 10 September, after which it was not liable. The company's attorney even argued that there could never have been any antiunion discrimination because "no effort was made to acquaint the management with the membership of the union."[79]

In his report, examiner Robert H. Wettach of the University of North Carolina School of Law dismissed the claims of union members who had returned to work before the end of the strike and subsequently lost their jobs. He agreed, however, that the company's hiring of at least forty-six new employees since the strike did amount to antiunion discrimination. Passing the case back to the CTLRB for a final decision, Wettach privately expressed the opinion that the entire matter was a fiasco. "The Cowpens Mill," he noted "was generally regarded as having a rather poor mill village, and the complainants seemed to be representative of a group of fairly poor, uneducated people who had been caught in the strike without any realization of what it was all about." (It apparently never occurred to Wettach, nor to many CTLRB officials, that the workers were in the best of positions to know "what it was all about.") "Anyone would sympathize with them as persons in need of some assistance," Wettach continued. "On the other hand, the mill seems to have been hard hit [financially], and there appeared to be a rather desperate effort on the part of those in charge to make a go of it." Wettach was unwilling to side completely against the mill for fear of a permanent shutdown in retaliation, even though he shared Dudley Harmon's visceral reaction to H. W. Kirby and his associates, who had refused to cooperate with Wettach in any way.[80] As for the union, AFL organizer Furman Rogers was no lawyer, and his difficulty in developing the union's case became "fairly embarrassing," at least to Wettach, as the hearing wore on. Washing his hands of the matter, Wettach concluded that "your examiner must confess to a certain feeling of futility in connection with this mill and its problems."[81]

In the summer of 1935, two events demolished whatever slim chances the workers at Cowpens Mill might still have had for reinstatement. First, the NIRA was declared unconstitutional, summarily ending the CTLRB's troubled existence. When John Peel inquired as to the case's status in late May, Samuel McClurd of the CTLRB replied only that "since all codes have been suspended as the result of the decision of the United States Supreme Court . . . we do not feel that it is proper to release any more decisions until the situation has been clarified by future developments."[82] And however given to prevarication H. W. Kirby may have been, he does not appear to have been lying when throughout 1934 and 1935 he cited Cowpens Mill's shaky financial status. On 27 August 1935, the mill closed "for an indefinite period."[83] It ran only sporadically for the remainder of the 1930s.

The final devolution of the Cowpens Mill situation is best left to the words of B. B. Fowler, the most articulate of Local 1934's committeemen. In June 1935, Fowler wrote to Roosevelt to remind him that "we still have quite a few people out from the general strike." Whatever the company might say, Fowler claimed, there had been "no disturbance what-so-ever" during the strike. As at Lyman, unionists had watched as their jobs were given to farmers "who have a good living at home, and have made their brags that they save all they make in the mill."[84] Local 1934's remaining members were "barely existing." Most were still living in company houses, although Fowler knew they would do so for only a matter of time. "The people out are blacklisted[;] it is impossible to get a job anywhere else."[85]

"As you know the direct relief has been cut off," Fowler reported a month later, and "many widows and children are facing starvation of course, all the unemployables are without food. The papers state that flour and such commodities are to be given but nothing but canned beef and a small amount of dry skimmed milk comes here." Evictions had finally begun. Fowler enclosed a list of thirty-eight who were still out of work and were, in his opinion, "unemployables," including him and his wife, George Garland, and other Local 1934 activists. He noted wearily that "Bernard the Commissioner came out here again recently," to no avail. Fowler's final comments are perhaps the most appropriate requiem for the Code Authority, the CTLRB, and the NRA itself: "He says as all the rest has, that we have the best discrimination case in the state but since the N.R.A. is dead there's nothing that can be done. They have had plenty of time before the N.R.A. was ruled unconstitutional to have the affair settled if there could have been anything done. Why wasn't there anything done? I don't know of a single case where the board helped any to amount to anything."[86] One by one, the remaining members of Local 1934 either drifted away or found other employment. A little less than a year later, on 4 June 1936, Local 1934 at Cowpens Mill was officially laid down by the UTWA.

In the wake of the General Strike, evaluations abounded. The *Spartanburg Journal* termed the three weeks of the strike "weeks of gloom and uneasiness to millions of persons."[87] From the manufacturers' point of view, the General Strike was a tremendously frightening vision of what might become the industry's future—but little more than that. Before the strike, few southern manufacturers seem to have perceived either the enormity of worker discontent or the growing strength and fervency of the UTWA. At Spartan Mills, Local 1881 was even allowed to meet in the company's community building.[88] The extent of the harassment, discharges, and evictions after the strike indicates how greatly the event changed manufacturers' perception of organized labor. More important, the post-strike pattern of wanton discrimination showed that manufacturers were still able to do pretty much as they pleased in the textile South.

In calling the strike when it did, the UTWA capitulated to the enormous pressure for direct action that emanated from its southern membership; the union's leaders well knew the danger of calling a "general" strike at a time when the union had little or no presence in many plants. The UTWA's leaders on both the local and national levels, however, also knew the breadth and depth of textile worker discontent; they clearly hoped that a massive display of force would encourage workers at ostensibly unorganized mills to join the struggle. The flying squadron was the principal tool used to extend the strike in this manner, but it ultimately proved little more than a temporary vehicle of mass coercion. The UTWA lost all the unorganized mills it had managed to close, as well as most of the mills in which it had been weak. At mills such as Drayton and Arkwright, union strength had been more illusory than actual; both locals disintegrated rapidly after the strike.[89] At other mills, however, the union's struggle continued unabated for several years. Decades later, it would be the products of these later struggles—at Tucapau, Saxon, Spartan, Clifton, Beaumont, Fairmont, and Inman Mills—that held workers' memories.[90]

Yet the General Strike did indeed fail—at least on the all-or-nothing terms the UTWA's leadership had set out. The primary reason for that was simple: The UTWA called off the strike, and workers, trusting Francis Gorman, the Winant settlement, and above all President Roosevelt, returned to the mills. Under pressure from the federal government and realizing that many strikers were facing extreme privation, Gorman and other UTWA leaders were faced with a difficult question, whether to continue the strike selectively at mills where the UTWA might have enough strength to hold out for a contract or whether to call it off entirely. Maintaining consistency with their previous pronouncements that this was an all-or-nothing affair, the UTWA chose the latter course. In Spartanburg, the union had already lost plants such as Victor and Lyman and was on the verge of losing others. But other locals—representing half of the county's mills and textile workers—were ready and willing, at least at the time the strike was terminated, to continue. Calling off the strike when it did, UTWA leadership admitted its overall failure and hamstrung the local efforts of these more resolute unionists, irreparably breaching the strained relations between southern workers and union leaders. "Having thrown its lot in with the government, the UTW no longer had the perspective or the credibility to engage the southern mill hand," the strike's chief historian has written. "Instead, UTW leaders watched, heartsick and dismayed, as the union's southern organization simply fell apart before their eyes."[91]

Thus, the strike left workers with deep scars that manifested themselves in a variety of ways in later years.[92] Some tried to dissociate themselves from it entirely. Homer Lee Harrison, once secretary of the Arkwright local, later stated, "I don't see what they ever got out of the strike—I never did see nothing accomplished out of it." Searching for the proper words, Jack Thornton of Clifton tried to sum up his version: "It was a lark, as well as I can remember, being a child. It was a lark—they'd never been in anything like that, and I think they enjoyed it to a certain extent." For Thornton and others, the strike should have been seen—by the national UTWA, by the public, and by the textile workers themselves—as the firing of a gun to signal the beginning of in-depth southern organization rather than its apocalyptic end. Thornton observed that the General Strike was "more of a protest" than anything else.[93]

Some workers even blamed the strike on the federal government or on President Roosevelt for his public (yet ultimately empty) endorsement of industrial unionism. Hoyt Jones, a Clifton worker who had joined the UTWA in 1933, recalled the feeling: "At that time, they thought Roosevelt approved the union. But what Roosevelt was doing really, he was trying to get [the] textile [industry] out of the [economic] doghouse."[94] The failure of the government to resolve the myriad discrimination cases arising out of the strike successfully not only substantiated Jones's claim but also raised the overall toll of the General Strike far beyond anything the UTWA could have dreamed in late September of 1934.

The cost of the General Strike was more immediately apparent in places such as Greenville where it had been more definitively crushed. In Spartanburg County, the situation was not nearly so conclusive in the late fall of 1934. Many locals claimed—with some justification—that they had come out of the strike as strong as they had gone into it. But with neither the union nor the government able to resolve the issues of post-strike discrimination, the UTWA in financial and organizational shambles, and the NRA declared unconstitutional by the Supreme Court, no one in 1935 made much effort to pick up the pieces of the textile workers' struggle. The national UTWA exacerbated the post-strike situation by insisting that the Winant settlement amounted to some kind of victory in the face of overwhelming evidence to the contrary, infuriating and demoralizing textile workers who knew that such rhetoric was false.[95]

"You seem to think we won something," a UTWA organizer wrote to a friend less than two weeks after the strike's end. "I just cannot see it. Things here are in a much worse condition than they were three months ago."[96] The post-strike landscape would be problematic, to say the least, for workers and government officials alike. According to one modern account of the event, "The General Strike, whatever else it may have been, was a moment in history that laid bare longings and antagonisms ordinarily silenced, distorted, or

THE
STRIKE
IS ON

THE UNITED TEXTILE
WORKERS OF AMERICA

Affiliated with the American Federation of Labor

★

DON'T SCAB
IT'S NOW or NEVER

STRIKE COMMITTEE HEADQUARTERS OF THE UNITED
TEXTILE WORKERS OF AMERICA, CARPENTERS BUILDING,
WASHINGTON, D. C.

FRANCIS J. GORMAN, Chairman

W. G. WATSON, Secretary

EMIL RIEVE   JOHN H. POWERS   ABRAHAM BINNS

An example of the flyers posted circa Greenville and Spartanburg during the General Strike. (Courtesy of the National Archives) repressed," in which "people broke through the restraints imposed by economic defenselessness and dropped the mask of resignation to make a mark on their times."[97] Perhaps—but such a breakthrough had its price. During the strike, union flyers posted around Spartanburg had informed workers in bold letters that "it's now or never." As time passed, the cost of that particular portrayal became tragically apparent.

5   Dealt Out: Spartanburg Workers and the Roosevelt Administration, 1934–39

My shoes are full of holes, and my clothes are all out-of-date and shabby, and yet I'm still the person who has almost lost her life, more than once, on picket lines and organizing.

My spirit has been crushed, and much as I love the organization, no one can blame me for not talking unionism, can they?

I'll never turn yellow, but I won't take time to tell you the humiliating things I have been subjected to. I'm not blaming you; I know you could not help it. I hope you will understand.

—Annie L. West to Francis J. Gorman, 1942

As the final touches of autumn gave way to winter in late 1934, southern textile workers came to grips with something so tragic, so psychologically massive, that many of them never recovered. The disillusionment, frustration, and, ultimately, fear spawned in the wake of the General Strike became so pervasive in the textile South that workers were able to pass on the package, like an inheritable disease, to their children and grandchildren. Ironically, this unintended legacy was a direct consequence of the multiple layers of meaning that textile workers had invested in the union movement. Union leaders orated nonsense about the "victory" embodied in the strike's "settlement," but southern workers knew that their cultural landscape had been forever changed.

In mills where the union had been weakest, it disappeared almost instantly. In mills where the union had been stronger, workers attempted to regroup with only minimal help from the prostrate UTWA. Each and every surviving local faced bitter subsequent battles, ending more often than not in defeats that merged seamlessly with the larger defeat of 1934. Annie West, once the dynamic secretary of Local 1882 at Saxon Mills, later found herself isolated, immisserated, and humiliated. "Mr. Gorman, some times it looks as if I am the forgotten one, in the whole set-up," she wrote in 1940. "I have tried to help all I could and do my best . . . for you know that my whole life is wrapped around the Labor Movement. . . . I have been through a lot of hard-ship that I would not have been subjected to had I not been fighting for an Ideal." The psychological trauma caused by these defeats amounted to "a common loss of faith": "From this perspective, the southern workers lost, not because they did not trust, but because they trusted too much."[1] What the events of 1933 and 1934 proved most abundantly is that hope is a dangerous thing.

The UTWA was forced to watch helplessly during 1935 and 1936 as its membership hemorrhaged nationwide. In Spartanburg County, however, the union's basic infrastructure remained surprisingly intact. Only nine of the county's twenty-eight locals had formally disbanded by early 1936.[2] In dozens of southern mills, core groups of workers continued to pay union dues for more than two years after the General Strike. The size of these core groups varied considerably. At various points in 1935, the Pacolet Mills local had only fourteen dues-paying members and the Powell Knitting local only eight. By early 1936, however, union support had begun to stabilize across the county: thirty members at Arkwright, thirty-five at Glendale, thirty-nine at Spartan, forty-eight at Clifton No. 2, fifty-five at Pacolet Mills, sixty-six at Fairmont, ninety-five at Saxon, 116 at Inman, 131 at Clifton No. 1, and 174 at Converse. All in all, just under 10 percent of Spartanburg County's textile workers remained union members in 1936.[3]

The UTWA's true strength, however, was considerably more than these numbers suggest. Under the circumstances, only the keenest unionists continued paying dues. They kept their channels of communication open, however, through the Una *News-Review,* the weekly prolabor newspaper published by former Saxon worker Judson Brooks. Some locals reported to the publication on a regular basis, declaring that they were "strong as ever." Others communicated more sporadically, assuring union members elsewhere that they were "still alive" or "still on the map."[4] "Don't get worried, folks, if a few of your members drop out," advised a unionist from Clifton No. 2. "They will come back because organized labor has come here to stay."[5]

But given the plain facts, such optimism was hard to sustain. A worker from Pacolet Mills bemoaned "how many opportunities we have allowed to slip thru our fingers, opportunities to say or do something for our Local and the great organization known as the UTWA," opportunities that, he presciently noted, were now "gone forever."[6] Yet he, like so many others, clung to the UTWA and to the social vision that the organizing drive had represented. "Being union," after all, was a state of mind to many southern workers, not a mere matter of signing or withdrawing membership in an organization.[7] For those who had decisively crossed the line of action in 1934, it became a question of principle, even honor. "We must not forget that in the past two years thirteen of our own members in this state have laid down their lives," cautioned a Saxon worker in 1936. "We must 'keep the faith.'"[8]

Hundreds of textile workers in Spartanburg County did indeed keep the faith, but without recognition from or power over mill owners the viability of surviving locals remained constantly in grave doubt.[9] Studious corporate disregard augmented by unspoken threats and continued economic uncertainty was enough to numb or kill the weaker locals. As it became clear during 1935 that some locals were more tenacious than manufacturers had hoped, however, mill owners fought back more aggressively. Workers at dozens of mills where local unions had survived the trauma of the General Strike found themselves playing out a deadly endgame. Managers continued—and even improved upon—the stretch-out system while weeding out union leadership. Avowed unionists worked under the constant hostile gazes of supervisors, knowing full well that any slip of decorum or production could mean instant discharge. In the meantime, they tried to convince other workers that organized labor was still worth supporting.

In plants where the union still had a functional presence, the resulting strains were unbearable, provoking a wave of wildcat strikes across South Carolina's textile belt during 1935 and 1936. As many workers had feared, the termination of the General Strike and the UTWA's subsequent collapse demoted the textile workers' struggle from a mass movement to a series of localized and disconnected insurgencies. Mill owners were only too happy to instigate conflicts in order to accomplish what the General Strike had not: the complete eradication of textile worker activism. It was this endgame—the struggles and conflicts of 1935 and 1936—that conflated with the events of September 1934 in most workers' minds, investing "1934" with the psychological and social baggage that many carried for the rest of their lives.

In Spartanburg County, unionists continued mailing code-related complaints to Washington for as long as the NIRA remained valid. Threatened strikes in the county during 1935 and 1936—averted only by direct federal intervention—included one at Powell Knitting in protest of the company's refusal to rehire a handful of General Strike veterans, one at Fairmont over a broad accumulation of grievances, two at Jackson Mill (where the stretch-out continued), and two at Arkwright over the discharge of a local union official and over stretch-out.[10] Fairmont workers staged a lengthy strike in late 1935.[11] Workers at the three Clifton plants doggedly fought the stretch-out through established channels and finally forced the issue with a sit-down strike of their own in late 1936.[12] Such conflicts (and others that simmered less visibly) kept the UTWA alive locally long after the national union had ceased to involve itself in any kind of meaningful way.

The union's fate in South Carolina, however, came to rest on a handful of strikes more bitter and violent than these. The National Recovery Administration and its boards, including the CTLRB, had been ruled unconstitutional in mid–1935.[13] In its place Roosevelt's allies quickly engineered the National Labor Relations Act, better known as the Wagner Act. Signed into law in July 1935, the Wagner Act was a bold attempt to resolve the legal issues surrounding organized labor, issues only partly clarified under the NIRA. Its chief instrument was the National Labor Relations Board, revitalized from its NRA days, which laid the groundwork for all future federal mediation in American industrial life.[14] Because the General Strike occurred before the Wagner Act's passage and was officially settled under the Winant Board, its aftermath was officially off-limits to the NLRB. Not so the post–1934 strike wave and the accompanying antiunion purges. Strike-related cases from Pelzer, Union, and Gaffney and from Spartanburg's own Saxon, Spartan, and Tucapau mills were among the first the new National Labor Relations Board heard.

Following so quickly on each other's heels and in the aftermath of the General Strike, the Saxon, Spartan, and Tucapau conflicts electrified Spartanburg County. In later years, they rather than the General Strike itself were the subjects of worker memories. The reconstitution of the NLRB as the enforcing arm of New Deal labor policy finally made the federal government a full third player at the table previously occupied by southern mill owners and unionists. Ultimately, what distinguished the years after the General Strike was not so much violent confrontation as it was the legal strangulation and bureaucratic marginalization of the remaining southern unions.

Back in October of 1934, Saxon's management had waited five or six additional days before reopening its mill, perhaps to underscore with dramatic flourish the basic power relationship between those who held the keys to the front gate and those who did not. During the course of the next six months nothing changed at Saxon, at least in the workers' view. John A. Law and his overseers continued to tinker with machinery and workloads in the mill, and Local 1882's shop committee continued to meet with Law over the attendant stretch-out, without effect.[15] By May, some workers were calling for a second strike against the company. The last straw came on 19 July 1935, when the shop committee met with Law to discuss a host of grievances, including the company's new policy of placing older workers on spare or part-time work in order to make room for newer workers (a tactic Local 1882 charged with diluting union strength). Law promised the committee "a personal investigation," but days passed with no further word from him or anyone else. On Tuesday, 30 July, a thoroughly aroused work force voted to strike. At 3 P.M., workers from other shifts entered the mill, seized control of the emergency lighting system, and shut down the plant.[16]

John A. Law had always viewed his style of mill management as enlightened paternalism in the most exacting sense of the phrase. His village was known for good housing, good water, excellent schools, recreational opportunities, and a family atmosphere—all available to any worker and his or her dependents who were willing to acknowledge Law as the sole proprietor of the community in which they lived. Law walked through the mill and village every day, he attended every major community event, and he personally choreographed the village's Christmas celebrations with the help of his personnel manager, Marjorie Potwin. Law even enforced his paternalism by residency: He was the only mill owner in Spartanburg County—indeed, one of the few in the textile South—who actually lived in his village. As he later noted to a government official, "I am very jealous about the good name of the Saxon Mills, which it has always enjoyed as fair treatment of its employees."[17] If "paternalism" ever had meaning in the textile South, then it was embodied in John A. Law at Saxon.[18]

Paternalism, however, provided only a thin veneer to cover Law's hostility toward the union. Inside the mill, Law's tactics in dealing with Local 1882 conformed to the paternalistic ideal. He received the shop committee with unfailing courtesy and willingly discussed every issue they raised, all the while asserting and retaining the ultimate right of total control over both village and factory. Even in the face of what instantly became a bitter labor-management conflict, Law kept his composure. Five days after the strike began, he met with Local 1882's shop committee and a CTLRB representative. The group candidly discussed a thirteen-point strike settlement proposed by Local 1882, and Law promised both the union and the CTLRB that he would "take the proposal under consideration and present it to his Board of Directors." "No direct refusal of the proposed settlement was ever made," a government agent later noted. That became Law's signature style in labor-management relations. At no time during the mid–1930s did he ever refuse to deal with union or government representatives. He simply met with them, behaved like the gentleman he felt himself to be, and then did nothing to address their suggestions, complaints, or demands.[19]

On 15 August the shop committee tried another strategy, proposing that Law and the union submit the dispute to an impartial arbitration committee selected jointly by Law, Local 1882, and the CTLRB. Four days later, Law rejected this plan on the grounds that "we cannot recognize that the Saxon Mills, and your group, are the only two parties at interest, and, hence, alone entitled to representation in any plan of arbitration."[20] Thus Law, holding the line with the majority of American industrialists, questioned the majoritarian foundations upon which the principles of collective bargaining were based. In his view, multiple constituencies held stakes in the Saxon strike: himself, his managers, unionized workers, nonunion workers, stockholders, and customers. In the union's view, the situation was a clear-cut case of labor versus management. A stalemate ensued. In October, Local 1882 took its case to the new National Labor Relations Board.

Created only a few months before, the NLRB was just beginning to define both the nature and extent of its powers. Although its role as a mediator of strikes was uncertain, its role in determining the proper parameters of collective bargaining had been clearly mandated by the Wagner Act. Accordingly, NLRB regional director Charles N. Feidelson ruled that the only hope of breaking the Saxon deadlock was "in securing the employees of the mill their right under the National Labor Relations Act to bargain collectively" through the holding of a representation election.[21] By the time of the strike, the Saxon struggle had already become a three-cornered affair involving Local 1882, John A. Law, and the CTLRB in Washington. From the moment the fledgling NLRB entered the picture, Saxon became even further entangled in the world of New Deal federal policymaking as one of the board's first major southern cases. Whether to hold a representation election at Saxon, and what the outcome of such an election would be, riveted the attention of both manufacturers and textile workers in Spartanburg County.

For John A. Law, two key elements of his control over the Saxon mill and community were at stake. First, Law argued, an election would not help end the strike but "on the contrary, through the apparent support of the Federal Government, would lend new impetus to the union's unreasonable assertion of rights, such as the right to keep other people from going to work." On a more fundamental level, Law candidly explained to an NLRB agent that electoral certification of the union "would be a preliminary step to an obligation on his part to bargain collectively on hours, wages and working conditions, with the organization as the exclusive collective bargaining agency for the mill."[22] This Law viewed as a direct assault on his traditional policy of bargaining with any employee or group of employees who personally came to him with grievances or concerns. In Law's opinion, the NLRB's very intervention in the Saxon case threatened to undermine the foundations of employer-employee relations, upon which the paternalistic world of Saxon Mills was built.

Local 1882 viewed the holding of an NLRB-sponsored election as an equally important, albeit symbolic, event in the life of both the community and the union. UTWA staff pressed forward even after an NLRB agent admitted that Law was so opposed to the proceedings that he might well turn the strike into a lockout the moment the union was formally certified. In the view of organizer John Peel and the Saxon strike committee, an election victory would "solidify their own position," legitimizing the union in the eyes of both the federal government and the surrounding community. Local 1882's leaders also hoped that some kind of federal intervention—even a mere representation election—would deter Law from having the most active unionists and their families evicted from company-owned houses. Local 1882 was certain that it would win any such election. It boasted a membership of 274 out of 484 production workers at the time of the strike and claimed to have added more members since the strike began.[23]

The holding of the election itself—on 22 January 1936—did nothing to settle the conflict. Only 260 of 482 eligible workers voted; the union emerged victorious by a count of 252-8. John A. Law and his lawyer, L. W. Perrin of Spartanburg, protested the election's results on numerous grounds: that it was necessarily invalid "in that the National Labor Relations Act is unconstitutional"; that the polling place had been set up more than a mile from the mill (even though it was the company that had refused to allow the election on mill property); that the election was viewed by non-union employees as an exclusively union affair; and that many workers who were "permitted to vote were minors." Although the NLRB sustained two of Law's twelve objections, it ruled that a majority of Saxon's workers had nevertheless ratified the union, making it the sole collective bargaining agent under the terms of the Wagner Act. On 11 February, the board certified Local 1882.[24]

John A. Law had no intention of settling with the union, certified or not. Earlier that year he had purchased the bankrupt Chesnee Mill, fifteen miles northeast of Spartanburg. The Chesnee plant had always been an enigma to the UTWA. Geographically isolated from the county's other mills, it had been the only sizable plant at which the union had been completely unable to establish a toehold before the General Strike. As such, it immediately became a valuable investment to Law. In late August, as the determination of the strikers became evident, Law transferred Saxon's orders, some of its machinery, and about 150 of its non-union workers to the Chesnee plant, which Law promptly began running around the clock. As UTWA organizer John Peel later noted, this was, of course, "in violation, if not of Federal Legislation, certainly of the 'Gentleman's Agreement' entered into between the manufacturers" under the old Code Authority. Law admitted to the CTLRB that he was getting all of the production he needed from Chesnee and that he fully intended to keep Saxon closed "for several weeks and maybe months" until either the market improved or Saxon's workers evinced what he termed "a better spirit of conciliation." As a CTLRB agent dejectedly noted, "As I see it, [Saxon] is just a closed mill, with no assurance of reopening any time soon."[25]

Back at Saxon, the early days of the strike had been marked with petty violence on both sides, including random gunshots in the village and at least one attempt to dynamite the mill. In late October an attempt by the company to move a boxcar of finished cloth from the Saxon siding resulted in an impromptu sit-down strike on the tracks, and a number of Saxonites—most of them women and girls—were arrested. In mid-November, Law informed the CTLRB that "acts of violence are being made most every day," although Local 1882's shop committee vigorously refuted the claim.[26] In the wake of the NLRB election, both the union and Law's stockholders seemed inclined to settle. From Law's viewpoint, however, settlement hinged on whether he still

Union parade down Front Street, Saxon Mills, during the strike of 1935. The company store is barely visible to the right. (Courtesy of South Caroliniana Library, University of South Carolina, Columbia)

retained enough authority over the Saxon mill and village to punish those he deemed responsible for strike-related violence and disorder.[27]

Throughout late February and March, Law, the shop committee, and CTLRB representatives attempted to define precisely what constituted strike-related violence, who should be considered guilty, and what disciplinary action would be appropriate. Originally, Law submitted a list of 151 individuals—half of the union's membership and a third of his old work force—whom he did not plan to rehire because of alleged strike-related misconduct. A series of CTLRB-sponsored conferences reduced the number to seventeen and then to eight. In a five-hour meeting with Law and the shop committee, South Carolina governor Olin Johnston promised to find WPA employment for these eight and to quash criminal indictments against four others if only Local 1882 would accept the rest of the settlement and end the strike. On the urging of John Peel, Local 1882's members reluctantly acceded to these demands. On Saturday, 28 March 1936, they voted to end the strike. The mill resumed full operations four days later.[28]

Although John A. Law did live up to the provisions of the strike settlement—at least in the immediate aftermath—Local 1882's problems continued as if neither the strike nor the settlement had ever occurred. In May, shop committee chair J. Monroe Mills reported to Francis Gorman that the stretch-out continued unabated. "It looks at the present the only way to stop this stretch-out is to close down the mill," he concluded, although he knew that Saxon's workers were too exhausted to risk another strike so soon.[29] In July, Mills reported that union activists were being discharged one by one on various pretenses and forced to leave the village. "It took about a year" for the process to take its course, a unionist later recalled.[30] Law's goal was to dismantle Local 1882 piecemeal. Mills's turn came in September. He and an overseer had gone to the boiler room to smoke a cigarette during a break, as had been customary for years even though smoking in the mill was officially against company rules. Upon finishing his cigarette, Mills's overseer reported him to Law, who promptly fired both Mills and his wife.[31]

By 1940 virtually all of the original union cadre at Saxon Mills had been displaced. Meeting sporadically, Local 1882 maintained an anemic existence for several years. For all practical purposes, however, Saxon's union was dead by Christmas of 1936. Although the settlement of the Saxon strike represented at least a partial victory for the union, it was the velvet-clad fist of John A. Law that ultimately prevailed. Caught between the forces of paternalism and oppression, Saxon's workers proved unable to sustain the institutional momentum necessary for continued struggle.

∽

Yet such was not the case all over Spartanburg County, where other locals held on even beyond 1936. The strongest of these was Local 2070, and it was the struggles of workers and managers over mastery of the Tucapau mill and village that ultimately became the UTWA's last bulwark against extinction in South Carolina. The violent and highly publicized Tucapau strike of 1935 resulted in South Carolina's only brief example of contractual bargaining relations in textiles during all of the 1930s. The lockout of 1936—part of the mill's new owners' housecleaning program that also included the changing of the company's name from "Tucapau" to "Startex"—became one of the most troublesome cases to beset the infant National Labor Relations Board.

Tucapau Local 2070 had been the product of an almost textbook-perfect process of internal worker-sponsored organizing. The local passed through the General Strike without harm except to its treasury, which was depleted for groceries in September 1934. Tucapauans returned to work in early October with, at best, an uneasy truce. Four months later, however, a seemingly minor event plunged the community into what would ultimately become the most protracted labor conflict in Spartanburg County's history.

On Tuesday, 20 February 1935, a supervisor in Tucapau's bleachery division discovered that someone had maliciously run a lead pencil across a bolt of fresh cloth, ruining it. Unable to determine precisely who had committed the deed, plant manager L. A. Hamer decided to suspend two men— Otis Emory and Boyce Lane—whose particular jobs made them the most obvious suspects. As even CTLRB investigator J. L. Bernard later admitted, there was "absolutely no evidence" against either Emory or Lane, who protested their innocence. Workers in the plant heard about the layoffs the next day and by evening had taken a strike vote, deciding that the time for a full-scale reckoning with the management of Tucapau had come. On Thursday evening, about a dozen men entered the mill and urged the second shift to join the first in a protest strike. Whether—as management charged—these men forcibly stopped the machines of workers who refused to cooperate with the union or—as the union claimed—the entire second shift voluntarily left the plant quickly became a moot point. As of Friday morning, 23 February 1935, the workers of Tucapau were on strike.[32]

In fact, the cloth-marking incident was only one element in a familiar accumulation of grievances. First and foremost was the stretch-out. In mid-January, Tucapau Mills had announced a general rearrangement of work. Fearing not so much the specific reassignments as what they seemed to portend for the future, Local 2070 had already staged a one-day strike in protest.[33] Second, the CTLRB had never resolved a handful of discrimination cases pending from the General Strike; the company had repeatedly broken its promise to reinstate some of these workers while adamantly refusing to rehire others.[34] Third, New England Southern Mills—the Boston holding company that owned Tucapau—was on the verge of bankruptcy. Both company president Alan McNab and L. A. Hamer candidly stated on several occasions that they did not care whether the plant ran. Among the indirect results of New England Southern's financial troubles were not only the stretch-out but also the wholesale deterioration of the Tucapau village.[35] Little wonder then that Tucapau's organized workers were ready for a show-down, even in the wake of the General Strike and even if they had to fight the battle with virtually no support from their international union.

Almost as soon as it began, the Tucapau strike commanded the attention of both state and federal officials. With close to a thousand employees, the Tucapau mill was considered a bellwether plant in a region where union-management conflicts simmered everywhere. Not only did CTLRB officials and Gov. Olin D. Johnston worry about the effects of the strike on neighboring mills, but they also worried about what might happen at Tucapau itself. Local 2070 had claimed more than eight hundred members at the time of the strike, and it was clear even to J. L. Bernard that its membership was committed to the conflict. On his first day in town, Bernard warned Hamer that any effort to reopen the mill would almost certainly result in bloodshed.[36] Initial attempts by the CTLRB to mediate a settlement were rebuffed by both sides. Local 2070 refused to consider anything whatsoever until it had extracted a promise to rehire Emory and Lane; New England Southern was just as committed to seeing them ousted and was, in McNab's words, "satisfied to close [the] mill indefinitely."[37] A proposed settlement worked out by the CTLRB was rejected on 7 March by the mill's management, then busy with the formation of a "Good Will Association"—a company union—to be used in the event of reopening.[38]

By early April J. L. Bernard characterized the atmosphere at Tucapau as "very bad," with minor violence, several arrests, and the bulk of the strikers surviving only with aid from a federal relief commissary and the Red Cross.[39] In mid-May the situation escalated when the company actively began to recruit potential strikebreakers from outside the village. On 2 June it announced that it intended to reopen the plant and invited all interested persons to register for jobs. Outsiders entering the village, however, found themselves stoned with rocks and bottles and, on occasion, forcibly ejected from Tucapau by angry residents. Tensions soared over the next several days, culminating on 5 June with a near-riot when a crowd of several hundred rushed the plant gates to retrieve a job applicant who had slipped through. During the melee, an African American worker attempted to cross the picket line, declaring that "he would blow the mill whistle here, or he would blow it in hell." He was gunned down on the spot.[40]

Hamer and McNab agreed to call off the registration process temporarily and meet anew with Local 2070's shop committee, but both sides remained unwilling to compromise on any of the earlier sticking points. Hamer and McNab even went so far as to visit Governor Johnston in his Columbia office and request state troops for the planned reopening. Johnston, incensed by the request, not only refused to supply troops but also embarked on a private investigation of the situation. The conflict seemed dangerously close to spreading to other plants. A week after the disturbance at the plant gates, the remaining UTWA locals in the county voted to call a countywide textile strike should McNab and Hamer attempt to open the plant again without an agreement with Local 2070.[41]

From the moment that Johnston became personally interested in the case, however, Hamer and McNab's days were numbered. In 1932 Johnston had parlayed his textile upbringing—in the mill villages of Anderson, sixty miles southwest of Spartanburg—into the South Carolina governorship, becoming in the process what many viewed as a consummate New Dealer. He was also a consummate politician and had kept a decided, if overtly principled, distance from earlier events across the state. Something about the Tucapau case, however, overcame his reserve—perhaps the plight and fierce determination of its workers, or perhaps the cavalier insouciance of New England Southern officials. The result was a rare rift between state power and textile interests, formalized on 19 June when Governor Johnston went to Tucapau and found himself refused an audience with management. Instead, he addressed a gathering of some six hundred cheering strikers and sympathizers. When a forced meeting between Johnston, McNab, and Hamer proved equally unavailing, Johnston let it be known that he was considering placing Tucapau under martial law so that only mill-village residents would be allowed to work when and if the mill started up. McNab and Hamer then let it be known that *they* were considering closing the mill permanently and moving its machinery to New England Southern's Pelzer plant. Johnston proceeded to apply pressure on the company with virtually every mechanism at his disposal. Outmaneuvered, McNab finally signed an agreement on 6 July institutionalizing CTLRB channels for determining workload and reinstating all but twelve employees (ten who had broken mill rules on the evening the strike was called plus the original two alleged cloth-markers, who had by this time filed a $75,000 civil suit against the company). At first, Local 2070's shop committee rejected this settlement; they knew all too well how little "approving of CTLRB channels in determining workload" really meant. Johnston thereupon applied pressure against them as well. On 15 July, they, too, capitulated. Local 2070 sponsored an impromptu parade through the village that afternoon, and on the following day Tucapau mills reopened for business.[42]

For the next ten months, New England Southern Mills operated the Tucapau plant under the rather vague—but official—document they had signed at the behest of Governor Johnston and the CTLRB. (Union officials referred to this as a "contract" and boasted that in Tucapau southern textile workers had achieved their first contractual victory.) The financial difficulties alluded to by McNab were in fact real, however, not just ploys in the labor game. New England Southern liquidated in the spring of 1936. The Tucapau plant was sold to Walter Montgomery, president of Spartan Mills.[43]

Montgomery had great plans for Tucapau; indeed, acquisition of the plant was his first step in transforming Spartan Mills from a single red-brick complex in downtown Spartanburg into a vertically integrated, multi-mill corporation.[44] Resuscitating Tucapau would be costly. The mill was dilapidated, its machinery was outdated and worn, and much of the village was in shambles. From the start, however, Local 2070's members were worried that Montgomery meant to clean out more than just old machinery. His reputation with respect to labor unions in Spartanburg and Gaffney preceded him.[45] During June and July, while the plant continued to operate, Montgomery began to remodel the renamed "Startex" complex. Local 2070 dutifully kept track of all workload changes and even filed a formal complaint on 18 July that Montgomery was making these changes without consulting Local 2070's shop committee. On 10 August 1936, Montgomery issued a memo to all employees stating that he would, as part of the ongoing renovations, soon be closing Tucapau's print cloth mill for six or eight weeks. He would also slightly reduce the capacity of the main mill; this, he warned, would eventually result in some discharges.[46]

Tucapauans receiving this letter were instantly alarmed. They became more so after Local 2070's shop committee requested, and was denied, a hearing with Montgomery. Tempers calmed briefly once Montgomery began repairs on the village and dissolved the old company union. A few days later, however, when he issued pink slips to the individuals and families whose positions he claimed were being eliminated, his true motives became clear. Twenty-one families were targeted for discharge and eviction, including Local 2070's four top officers and

Dilapidated housing, Tucapau, 1936, at the time of Walter Montgomery's purchase of the mill and village. (Courtesy of Jesse West, Jr.)

several of its more active shop stewards. This was bluntly characterized by Montgomery as "eliminating the undesirables."[47] In short, Montgomery had orchestrated a plan of selective discriminatory discharge, backed by a lockout masquerading as a mechanical facelift for the plant, in an all-out effort to rid Tucapau of the union.

On 28 September 1936, Local 2070 formally filed complaint against Montgomery through the NLRB in Washington, where it joined pending cases from Lyman, Spartan, and other upcountry South Carolina mills. In the legal drama that ensued, Local 2070 treasurer and strategist G. Walter Moore appealed to President Roosevelt, Secretary of Labor Frances Perkins, the Department of Labor's Federal Mediation and Conciliation Service, assorted members of Congress, the UTWA, and, later, the Congress of Industrial Organizations' Textile Workers Organizing Committee (TWOC). Once Startex workers handed their problems to the bureaucrats of the NLRB, however, their struggle became less a question of workers' rights in a southern mill village than it did a small part of a complex national ballet involving competing federal agencies as well as mill managers, unions, lawyers, and individual workers. The Tucapau case spent two and a half years before the NLRB before being summarily concluded in a decision that pleased no one. More fully than perhaps any other case from southern textiles, the internal record of *UTWA Local 2070 vs. Startex Mills* illustrates both fundamental flaws in the Wagner Act's definition of labor conflict and the moral bankruptcy of the key institution the Wagner Act created, the NLRB.

The bureaucratic dynamics surrounding the Startex case worked against the workers of Tucapau from the very beginning. First, the NLRB was already engaged in a battle of wills with Walter Montgomery, at the time also defending the Deering-Milliken textile chain in cases at Spartan Mills, Gaffney Manufacturing Company of Gaffney, and Monarch Mills of Union. In this climate, the Startex case became another unwanted pawn in a much larger game of legal chess. Second, the NLRB was engaged in a quest for legitimacy and authority among not only the public and the legal community but also among one of the constituencies it was created to regulate: industrial corporations. Unsure of its legal standing and public reputation, the NLRB allowed Walter Montgomery to dominate the proceedings at every turn. Third, the NLRB, like the CTLRB before it, was becoming notorious for relying on inertia and delay in solving its most troublesome cases. Finally, the Startex case foundered on the NLRB's narrow construction of what constituted labor conflict within its jurisdiction. The board would not admit that eviction from company housing was a grievable offense, thus legitimizing one of the oldest and most potent threats ever used in the company towns of industrial America.

Walter Montgomery set the tone for the Startex case on the day after Local 2070 filed it. When NLRB field agent E. C. Curtis attempted to see Montgomery at his Spartanburg office, he was refused an audience and curtly informed "that the Board could do what it wished." NLRB agents spent the next two months in and out of Tucapau, investigating. In his preliminary report of November 1936, Charles N. Feidelson laid out the board's case. Feidelson found—in part from personal investigations—that not only had Walter Montgomery singled out the most active Tucapau unionists for discharge and eviction in an effort to break the union but he had also "maintained a truculent and uncompromising attitude toward any discussion of the issues even with representatives of this Board." Yet Feidelson strained to find a way to dissociate the board from the problem itself, suggesting that "this case is definitely one of the weakest from the viewpoint of jurisdiction." Because the Wagner Act only covered cases directly affecting "interstate commerce," Feidelson chose to believe that at Tucapau there were "no facts to prove an intent to burden commerce, unless such intent be deemed implicit in the unfair labor practices in which the mill is engaging." By that tortuous logic, he was able to conclude that although "it is our opinion that the

Startex Mills is flagrantly violating the law, with potential dangerous consequences, . . . it is also [our] opinion that under the current decisions, the law is certainly not applicable here."[48]

At this juncture, the NLRB—through Feidelson—refused to issue a complaint, but it intimated that it might reconsider when the print cloth mill resumed full operations. Local 2070 also grudgingly agreed to hold off any strike action until that time. Walter Montgomery thereupon took a "nibbling approach" to reopening the main mill. On the one hand, he knew that the longer he delayed full production at the print cloth mill, the longer he could delay any further interference from the NLRB. On the other hand, he knew that by slowly hiring back only non-union workers, he might pressure Local 2070 into calling a strike, thus jeopardizing its side of the NLRB case. In the meantime, tensions again began to rise at Tucapau. In mid-December, Curtis reported to Washington that "the prospect is now that very serious trouble may develop. . . . Bitterness between excluded workers and the management has increased to a grave extent. Arrests of union men on various pretexts are the order of the day." Curtis, at least, felt that the gravity of the situation required immediate action: "Jurisdictionally we seem to be nowhere, but on every other ground, particularly the close tie-up between the management and the law enforcing agencies, it is time for us to be moving in on the situation."[49]

Nothing happened. NLRB paperwork in subsequent weeks stated only "awaiting reopening of print cloth mill." January passed. Local 2070 reported more cases of discrimination but, apparently thinking it was playing along with the NLRB, refused to file formal complaints on them until the complete reopening of the main mill. February passed, then March. In early April, Local 2070 president Cloyd L. Gibson called the NLRB's Washington office and protested against the obvious fiction that the reopening of the print cloth mill had become. According to Gibson, "Although this company still has a number of looms which have not been put into operation, it is now employing more people than formerly." The NLRB still refused to issue any kind of complaint.[50] The arrival of the CIO and its textile affiliate, the Textile Workers Organizing Committee, only confused matters further.[51] Whether the union was waiting on the NLRB or the NLRB was waiting on the union, through the remainder of 1937 and nearly all of 1938 the NLRB took no action in the Startex case.

This, of course, suited Walter Montgomery just fine. In the summer of 1938, union members at Tucapau began once again to bombard both Atlanta and Washington with letters protesting the lack of action in their case, this time to such an extent that the NLRB's administrative assistant sent a private note to Feidelson, demanding an explanation for the delays. The regional director's confidential reply of 18 August illustrates precisely how and why the NLRB failed the workers of Startex. First, Feidelson attempted to blame the delays on the union. In mid-1937, he said, he had offered Local 2070 president and (by then) union organizer Cloyd Gibson a choice: The NLRB would hold hearings and pursue either the Spartan Mills case or the Startex case but not both. Whether or not this was a moral, or even legal, choice to offer, Feidelson claimed that Gibson had chosen Spartan Mills. The subsequent Spartan Mills hearing had been so riven with procedural problems that it had not even produced an intermediate report by mid-1938. A resolution of the Spartan Mills case, Feidelson tentatively argued, "might soften Montgomery's heart and make him readier to settle in both the Startex and Gaffney cases." In any event, "Any hearing in the Startex case is bound to be enormously long-drawn-out," a situation the NLRB wanted to avoid at all costs. Above all else, Feidelson wrote, "We have thought it wise to avoid the appearance of persecuting Montgomery, and so have turned to the Monarch Mills case" (in spite of the fact that Feidelson had previously judged the Monarch case to be "quite hopeless"). Given Montgomery's paranoia, Feidelson felt sure that any immediate action on Startex would doom the NLRB's negotiations, such as they were, at Monarch, Spartan, and the Deering-Milliken Mills of Gaffney.[52]

Bureaucratic jostling also kept the workers of Tucapau from appealing in any kind of meaningful way to the Federal Mediation and Conciliation Service (a division of the Department of Labor and unrelated to the NLRB).[53] Unlike the NLRB or the old CTLRB, Federal Mediation had an excellent record of giving prompt and reliable attention to labor conflicts. Yet in the Tucapau ballet the agency could do little. Local 2070 secretary G. Walter Moore's letters to Roosevelt and Secretary of Labor Frances Perkins had specifically asked for assistance in preventing evictions, a matter the NLRB claimed was beyond its jurisdiction. Federal Mediation director J. R. Steelman, however, was unsure of his agency's position regarding evictions, or, for that matter, the NLRB. Steelman gingerly suggested that his agent "contact Moore and then visit Montgomery, telling him we possibly do not have any jurisdiction in this matter, but in the interest of endeavoring to promote harmony and prevent any possible disputes, the matter was being brought to his attention purely from the point of our wanting to advise him of the unrest at the Startex Mills; and if he felt inclined to reconsider employing any of the twenty-one families it would be appreciated." Privately, Steelman concluded that the situation "appears hopeless." He did not, however, advise either Moore or Local 2070 of how hopeless their case now seemed. He even closed his field instructions with a note: "You had better tear this up."[54]

A week later, agent Henry Baker returned the Tucapau case to the Washington office for reassignment. Together with another conciliator, Baker visited Montgomery seeking more information and reported that Montgomery had "turned us down flat." Montgomery argued that if he gave out information it would almost certainly end up in the hands of the NLRB, where the Startex case was pending. Montgomery also warned Baker that if Federal Mediation issued any kind of complaint he "would feel that it was for spite due to his refusal." Baker delicately suggested that continued action in the Startex case "might prove embarassing to the Department." Steelman agreed.[55] In November, another federal mediator visited Tucapau and concluded that "it has long since become a case of attorneys (Union and Management) on one side and N.L.R.B. on the other. All, apparently, have long since consoled themselves to the outcome on such basis."[56] With that, the Department of Labor's Federal Mediation and Conciliation Service unilaterally withdrew.

Under fire about the growing number of unresolved cases from all regions and industries, the NLRB finally determined to end the Startex case in late 1938. In November, NLRB attorney Gerhard P. Van Arkel entered the case with the explicit task of hammering out some kind of settlement. At that time, Walter Montgomery made what he called his final offer: to put fifteen former Startex employees on a preferential hiring list. Because by this time the union had formally filed complaints covering more than a hundred workers, the Tucapau local refused to even consider such a proposal. Under pressure from Van Arkel, the union suggested that Montgomery reinstate fifty workers, to be selected by the union. Montgomery refused. In early 1939, NLRB field examiner Warren Woods personally investigated all 105 cases of alleged discriminatory discharge at Tucapau. He reported that forty-one had merit, two might, forty were weak, and seventeen involved discharges before Montgomery's purchase of the mill. The cases of the seventeen who had been fired by New England Southern were dismissed outright over protests from the union. Working on their own, NLRB staff members reduced the list of complainants to "thirty strong cases." In February they abandoned the idea of pursuing compensatory back pay: "Startex Mills is in such financial condition at the present time that it is unable to pay back pay in any amount worth considering." At this juncture Walter Montgomery offered to "place" twenty of the workers back on jobs at the plant (not necessarily their old jobs) and to put fourteen more on a preferential hiring list. Attorney Gerhard Van Arkel "reluctantly" recommended that the board accept

Montgomery's offer, because it seemed "extremely unlikely that any hearing would result in obtaining any substantial amount of back pay for the employees concerned" and any other course of action involved "the prospect of long-drawn-out litigation."[57]

In trying to grasp how the NLRB interpreted its role of adjudicating labor-management conflicts during the New Deal era, it is instructive to note that at no point during this process were the plaintiffs—the union members of Tucapau—consulted. Nearly a month after Van Arkel had recommended Montgomery's offer be accepted by the board, Van Arkel met with Local 2070's leaders in Washington to explain the board's tentative decision. The shop committee, in Van Arkel's words, "objected bitterly" and claimed that it would settle for nothing less than eighty reinstatements and $30,000 in back pay. Two days later, on 15 March 1939, the NLRB telegrammed Local 2070 with news that the board had unilaterally accepted Montgomery's proposal. The seventy former employees not covered in the settlement immediately appealed, even hiring Olin Johnston to handle their cases. That appeal was never even considered by the NLRB on the advice of its associate general counsel, Thomas I. Emerson, who argued that "it seems particularly important to maintain the integrity of the settlement." Because the settlement was never between the company and the workers but rather between the company and the NLRB, what integrity Emerson intended to preserve is unclear. There were indeed victories in the Startex case: Montgomery had domesticated the union, and the NLRB had kept from tarnishing its already doubtful reputation any further. But no hearing at which the Tucapau workers themselves could formally state their cases was ever held. The settlement was announced in April, and, after more paperwork the Startex case was formally closed by the National Labor Relations Board in Washington on 31 October 1939.[58]

Back in Tucapau, the evictions moved forward once the NLRB had refused to prevent them.[59] Walter Montgomery had the eviction proceedings entered into a magistrate's court at Inman, fourteen miles away, despite the fact that a comparable magistrate's court existed in the village of Tucapau itself. Magistrate R. D. Hicks of Inman "was well known in the community for his bias against the union," whereas Inman itself was known in the wake of the General Strike as a bastion of antiunion sentiment.[60]

The trials began in October 1937. According to the NLRB's Feidelson, "When the first case was tried, the magistrate refused to grant union counsel's request for a jury, did not take any evidence, and signed an order of eviction written out for him by the company attorney." In the second trial, prounion attorney Robert J. Gantt was able to obtain a jury, but Hicks limited the pool to eighteen local men all well known for their antiunion sentiments. To everyone's surprise, even this jury—dominated by downtown merchants, textile mill supervisors, and farmers—ultimately gave a verdict for the defendant. This Hicks immediately set aside. Both cases were appealed to the county courts—one by the union, the other by the company—en route to which the official transcript of the proceedings was prepared in the Startex offices by a company stenographer. An NLRB representative attended eight more similar eviction trials.[61] Local 2070 attempted to mobilize the county against Hicks and obtained nearly a thousand signatures calling for his dismissal. Gov. Olin D. Johnston reentered the case and, after a hearing, suspended Hicks "on the basis of findings that he had falsified the transcript, padded the jury lists, acted arbitrarily and capriciously in refusing to change venue, and conducted himself in a biased, prejudiced, and unjudicial manner."[62]

In the meantime, Walter Montgomery ordered that the evictions in the first two cases—Local 2070 vice president S. P. Caldwell and committeeman P. D. Lavender—be carried out; he completed them in the spring of 1937. The families moved where they could, most finding lodging in the neighboring communities of Wellford and Duncan, but they continued to fight. Even a series of felony charges drummed up against union members failed to shake Local 2070's determination.[63] In large part, the local's resilience was grounded in its exceptional local leadership, for whom the delay and double-dealing surrounding their NLRB case became a cause in and of itself. Yet even their devotion could not provide Tucapau's union loyalists with jobs, food for their tables, or clothes for their children.[64] In February 1939, union officers G. Walter Moore, B. C. Comer, and S. P. Caldwell tersely telegrammed J. Warren Madden that "Startex Case No. X-C-100 should have been tried in 1937. Why? We want this case heard."[65] In response they received the same echoing silence that had greeted CTLRB petitioners five years before.

～

Like the locals at Saxon and Tucapau, Local 1881 at Spartan Mills had emerged from the General Strike unscathed; indeed, local president John Pollard even reported to the CTLRB in December 1934 that relations between the union and company president Walter Montgomery "were most satisfactory."[66] Over the next year and a half, however, those relations deteriorated. On 10 May 1936, Local 1881—still led by John Pollard—struck.

Precisely what prompted the Spartan strike of 1936 was a subject of controversy from the moment the strike began. According to Local 1881, the strike was sparked by spinners protesting the installation of long-draft spinning machinery, which they claimed would exacerbate the stretch-out of their jobs. Pollard also complained of "overwork load in most of the jobs throughout the entire plant," "excessive heat in some of the weaving departments," and "unfair methods used by several second hands in attempting to secure more production from the workers."[67] Yet the Spartanburg press, the business community, and, later, Spartan's management all claimed that Local 1881 had voted to strike in sympathy with the workers of Gaffney Manufacturing Company. The Gaffney mill, located twenty miles east of Spartanburg, was also owned by the Deering-Milliken interests and controlled by Walter Montgomery. It had been on strike for several weeks at the time of the Spartan walkout.[68] The CTLRB's Henry Baker judged the strike to have resulted from a combination of these factors: in his interpretation, the spinning room stretch-out had occurred only when Montgomery installed new machinery so that Spartan Mills could fill orders from strike-bound Gaffney.[69]

In 1934 Walter Montgomery had made a blanket decision to keep the mills under his control closed for the duration of the General Strike. In 1936, however, Montgomery saw the situation as an ideal opportunity to break the union, as he was already trying to do at Gaffney and would soon try at Tucapau. Montgomery reopened the mill the morning after the strike began and was able to recruit a sizable minority of the work force. John Pollard estimated that just over two hundred of the nine hundred employees returned to work in the first two days of the strike, although plant manager Rudolph Johnstone claimed a higher number.[70]

Publicly, Montgomery played the role of wounded benefactor. On the first morning of the strike, he personally addressed the employees gathered around the plant, stating that he was "at a loss to understand" the strike and was willing to "arbitrate any job in the mill."[71] Privately, Montgomery refused to sanction any meetings with Local 1881's shop committee, even after CTLRB representatives offered to broker negotiations. He also refused to allow CTLRB representatives access to the plant for time studies.[72] Stymied, the CTLRB turned to Greenville's F. W. Symmes, president of the Union–Buffalo Mills chain and a director of the American Cotton Manufactures Association. Symmes urged Montgomery to cooperate with the CTLRB, whereupon Montgomery "politely told him to mind his own business."[73] With so many reentering the plant immediately after the strike was called, Montgomery was sure that complete victory over Local 1881 was in sight; he even told one CTLRB agent that he intended to let the strike drift along until he had "cured the workers of their desire to mess with this foolishness."[74]

Led by notoriously antilabor Sheriff Sam M. Henry, city and county police officers swept into the village with speed and numbers unseen in the county since the days of the General Strike at Lyman. In the early hours of 11 May, the police roped off an entire city block surrounding the mill complex and refused to allow anyone passage (later this was extended to cover two square blocks). That evening and Tuesday morning they arrested twelve persons "for 'investigation,'" one because he had been "slow in moving from a roped-off section around the gate." All were detained without charges for varying lengths of time at the city police station before being released. The Spartanburg County clerk of court deputized twenty men to patrol the Spartan neighborhood on the third day of the strike; their security bonds were underwritten by the assistant treasurer and superintendent of the plant.[75]

Montgomery even requested that Gov. Olin Johnston send in the National Guard, a request Johnston refused after Montgomery failed to heed his suggestion that the plant be completely shut down for a twenty-four-hour cooling-off period. Johnston reminded Montgomery that, with his mill situated within city limits, he already had at his disposal both city and county law enforcement agencies, which, he wryly noted, were proving more than adequate for Montgomery's purposes. As the strike entered its second week, sheriff's deputies even began wholesale arrests of anyone entering the city from other known centers of textile unionism. On the night of 17 May, for example, sheriff's deputies arrested eighty-one men found heading into Spartanburg from Inman and Gaffney on suspicion that they were part of an impromptu flying squadron aimed at keeping Spartan Mills closed the following morning.[76]

If Montgomery was confident that the wreckage of Local 1881 was only a matter of time, the union's leaders were equally convinced that time was on their side, especially as the number of workers entering the plant each morning held steady.[77] They were wrong, however. During the first week of June, the strike crumbled as hundreds who had remained out for a month made the decision to return to the mill. In a secret meeting on 8 June between Local 1881's shop committee and two CTLRB agents, the union agreed to call off the strike in order "to save as many employees as possible from losing their jobs" permanently. In the final settlement brokered by the CTLRB, Walter Montgomery agreed to rehire all but thirty-three of his 925 former employees, to help those thirty-three obtain other jobs elsewhere, and to help quash most of Sheriff Sam Henry's conspiracy indictments against various strikers and sympathizers.[78] The strike was over.

Had Montgomery remained true to this settlement, the Spartan strike of 1936 might have disappeared into public memory in the same way that dozens of wildcat strikes in southern textiles during 1935 and 1936 seem to have done. A year after the strike, however, the Spartan local—now, along with the Tucapau local, affiliated with the CIO's Textile Workers Organizing Committee—filed a formal complaint against Spartan Mills with the National Labor Relations Board. According to the union, Spartan Mills had not only failed to reemploy a number of the workers named in the settlement but supervisors had also embarked on a campaign of weeding out other suspected union activists in the wake of the strike. Ultimately, Local 1881 presented the NLRB with fifty-nine names, including members of some of the most prominent and long-term families of Spartan Mills village.[79]

Like the Tucapau and Gaffney cases that accompanied it through the NLRB, the Spartan Mills case ultimately showed, more than anything else, how feeble and unresponsive the NLRB was. At the company's request, NLRB administrators repeatedly postponed any kind of hearing in the case, apparently under the impression that they might in the meantime work out some sort of out-of-court settlement with Montgomery: from 18 November to 22 November, then to 9 December, then to 23 December, and then to 4 January, when the Spartan Mills hearing finally began.[80] For four weeks the NLRB took testimony from both prounion and antiunion witnesses, bringing to the stand some 135 residents of the Spartan Mills community. It was the first time that such a hearing had ever been held in Spartanburg County, and in the balance hung both the NLRB's reputation as a neutral arbiter and the union's continued survival in upcountry South Carolina. As an NLRB official observed, "This is a very, very important case to this community and to the Board."[81]

Yet from the start, the NLRB and its representatives were hostile to Local 1881. Having learned their lesson in trying to defend cases before the CTLRB by themselves, the complainants secured the services of Spartanburg lawyer Robert J. Gantt and two associates. NLRB trial examiner J. M. Brown deeply resented the trio's involvement, privately noting at one point that "had it not been for three adamant, selfish lawyers" the case would already have been settled.[82] On the second day of the hearing, Charles N. Feidelson attempted to negotiate a compromise. When Montgomery turned down the union's proposal, Feidelson "came to the Union the following day and just raised the very devil because we did not make the terms acceptable to Montgomery."[83]

Throughout 1937 and early 1938, NLRB representatives met with Walter Montgomery—although rarely with the union—in an attempt to manufacture a settlement outside of formal NLRB channels. As part of this strategy, the

NLRB delayed issuing its intermediate report in the case until 10 September 1938. The board's trial examiner confirmed significant discrimination, recommending that thirteen of the fifty-nine cases of alleged discrimination be reinstated with back pay and thirty-nine be placed on a preferential hiring list.[84]

From the time that this report was filed until July of 1939 when the case was officially closed, two parties—Walter Montgomery and the staff members of the NLRB—worked to reduce drastically the scope of the decision. Montgomery claimed that such a broad settlement—in conjunction with similar proposed settlements at Gaffney and Tucapau—would financially damage his business beyond repair. In response, the NLRB dropped its demand for the preferential rehiring of the thirty-nine only a week after the filing of the intermediate report.[85] A month later, Feidelson—in conference with the trial examiner—decided that "a formula involving reinstatement of ten and back-pay would suffice" for the rest. As Feidelson saw it, the problem was to concoct a settlement that Montgomery would swallow, not one that would provide a measure of justice to the affected workers.[86]

When Montgomery agreed in late February to reinstate ten workers with back pay, Feidelson recommended that the board authorize this agreement "under the circumstances" and "bearing in mind the interest of the union and the prestige of the Board."[87] On 25 April 1939 the NLRB legitimized that settlement as a formal decision and order without consulting either the union or any of the fifty-nine men and women involved.

The Spartan Mills decision represented a complete defeat for the union. As union official Seth P. Brewer coldly informed one of the NLRB attorneys involved in the final settlement, "If the Board wishes to take arbitrary action in compromising these cases, that is a matter beyond our control."[88] When John W. Pollard—president of Local 1881 and one of the thirty-nine men and women whose names mysteriously disappeared from the final version of the trial examiner's report—protested, Nathan Witt of the board explained to him the rationale behind the board's actions: "As you know, the Board does everything possible in all of its cases to bring them to a conclusion which, in the light of all the circumstances, will best effectuate the policies of the National Labor Relations Act. The Board feels that under the circumstances of this case the settlement was preferable to completion of the case by formal action."[89] In other words, the NLRB's self-conscious attention to its own image and the intransigence of Walter Montgomery had worked in concert to crush the union at Spartan Mills.

In legal terms, the Spartan Mills case represented a great victory for mill owners. It proved definitively that the board was willing to sacrifice virtually anything in order to reach a settlement, a fact that clever manufacturers would exploit for years to come. Although Local 1881 survived at Spartan Mills for many years after the settlement, it never again approached the strength of 1933 through 1936. In human terms, the Spartan settlement—together with concurrent settlements at Gaffney and Tucapau—marked the funeral of any broad-based union movement in upcountry South Carolina.

The practical results of the Spartan Mills settlement were not lost on workers. Writing from a rented farm near Woodruff in July of 1939, former shop committeeman Allen G. Rainwater summed up his feelings about the entire affair. Rainwater began by reviewing the ways in which the NLRB—through its agents—had repeatedly attempted to railroad a settlement through the workers and then blamed the union for being uncooperative; he also blasted Charles Feidelson for overly close personal relations with Walter Montgomery. "We cotton mill people have not got too much sense, but all of us are not crazy," Rainwater declared. "We have got sense enough to know how this case was worked, as dirty as we have been treated and protected in our rights and organizing." Rainwater reviewed the case's history following the hearing: the elimination of the thirty-nine names from the trial examiner's report; the fact that the board allowed Walter Montgomery to choose which ten workers he would rehire; the fact that the board capitulated to Montgomery's claims of financial distress, even while Montgomery "did have enough money to pay two high-powered lawyers" during the hearing and said on the stand "that he paid the sheriff about four or five thousand dollars for mill deputies" during the strike; the hypocrisy of having Montgomery post notices around the mill saying he would not discriminate against the union when he had just disposed of the union's most active supporters; and the subsequent blacklisting of all strike participants who had not been rehired. "The people around Spartan Mills is scared to talk with anyone who is active in the Union," Rainwater reported. "They know that they will be run off in the long run if they are that independent. . . . We sure have had a rotten deal handed us by somebody, God knows who," Rainwater concluded bitterly. "I hope that in any more cases your Board has from this area that you will give them more consideration than you did us. I understand that your Board is set up to protect the rights of workers in their union activities, but under such decision as was handed down in the Spartan Mills case is no more than encouraging the mill owners to discriminate still further." In sum, the Spartan Mills case had taught textile workers "that Montgomery makes his own decision[s], regardless of the Government, because he is more powerful than they in his own home."[90]

The resolutions passed by Local 1881 on 1 April 1939 are perhaps the best epitaph for the Spartan Mills case as well as for the overall experiences of southern textile workers with management and government during the 1930s.[91] Led by John W. Pollard and his shop committee, Local 1881 protested the entire decree "because it represents and accepts the respondent's terms and conditions of settlement throughout, thereby ignoring our efforts at arriving at a settlement through collective bargaining or arbitration, as well as waiving the Intermediate Recommendations of the Trial Examiner. . . . Such a precedent," the committee caustically noted, "smacks of the same type of so-called collective bargaining previously enjoyed by us while employees of the respondent." Montgomery's conduct during the Spartan case had revealed that he was "still too adamant and too powerful to be swerved from its determination to lend nothing but lip service to the theory of collective bargaining." The NLRB's stamp of approval on the final "settlement" not only amounted to an endorsement of Montgomery's tactics but also dramatically set the tone for future NLRB cases in which local and national labor unions would prove the most expendable element of whatever the NLRB understood "collective bargaining" to be. Spartan Mills, the committee further charged, had "usurped from the Board" the authority to set regional and national labor policy "by succeeding in having its initial and only offer of settlement as the final decree in this case. . . . What assurance have we, or the public at large, that this exception shall not become the rule in future cases before the Labor Board?" Finally, the committee complained that at no time had the NLRB explained the practical realities of the case to the workers involved. "During the past months, we have endured much hardship and suffered many hurts, being firm in our conviction that within your sanctuary we would ultimately receive justice," Pollard wrote, "but, frankly, this decree leaves us bewildered." Above all else, the Spartan Mills case proved how easily the NLRB could factor actual workers out of cases set before it. Although the board's wholesale capitulation to Walter Montgomery damaged the credibility of the Roosevelt administration in the eyes of southern textile workers, the board's treatment of the workers themselves had the practical effect of gutting the Wagner Act. As Pollard and the others concluded, "Instead of being a manly redress of our grievances, [the decision] is the crowning humiliation of all. We lay no claim to being interpreters, but this is not assistance—this is not a rectification of injustice—here is only further aggravation."

And with that, southern textile workers' first and last ally—the federal government, whose actions in 1933 had encouraged them to organize in the first place—excused itself from any meaningful involvement in their future

John Pollard, president of the Spartan mills local and chair of the county textile workers' league. (Courtesy of Brooks Pollard)

welfare. That point was not lost on the workers of Spartan Mills. In their final protest, they asked rhetorically "are we to receive from your board only another of the blows which we have been getting all our lives, which sends us still deeper into the night of social and industrial ignominy?"[92] According to the official dossier, the NLRB never responded to this letter. Nor did it ever reply to Allen Rainwater, who, like so many others, disappeared from the record. The board filed these sheets of paper away and closed the case.

6   Southern Textile Unionism and the 1930s: Meaning and Memory

To many outsiders—even historians—the pattern of labor conflict in the industrial South has always presented a puzzle, sweeping dizzily from moments of high drama to decades of apparent quiescence. And as scholars from Jacquelyn Hall to Barbara Griffith have documented, the toll taken on southern workers by their defeats surpasses anything ever experienced by their counterparts elsewhere in the nation. The omnipresent fear reported by union organizers during the CIO's great southern organizing drive of 1946 through 1952 was as incomprehensible to outsiders as it was endemic to the region. In textiles at least, the obvious culprit was the union interlude of 1933 through 1936. That the union movement of the 1930s left profound scars on southern workers is indisputable; precisely why, however, remains a historiographical mystery. The answer lies in the deeper meanings that the union movement acquired as it became part of the overall experience of textile people in the company towns of the American South.

In Spartanburg County, as elsewhere in depression-torn industrial America, the union movement came to embody the best of what "community" could mean in a working-class context.[1] It encompassed a social vision of mutuality, equality, and interdependency that transcended more traditional defining factors such as geography or kinship. In southern textiles, the union movement was able to build upon a preexisting and highly developed sense of mutuality, one based on living together, working together, and, for better or for worse, shared poverty. At its strongest, the union movement was able to insinuate its weft into the very warp of mill-village life. In places like Inman Mills or Lyman, where its dominance was always contested, the union came to define a community set apart and distinct from the mill village as a whole: There were the "union people" and there was everybody else. In places like Tucapau, where the UTWA was stronger, the union ultimately became the arbiter of community, at least in the eyes of the textile workers who joined. Thus, what the UTWA began in southern mills in 1933 had acquired by the mid–1930s localized meaning far beyond anything the national union ever earned.

On the most basic level, the UTWA had to deal with the demographic realities of mill life. Although imposed as a condition of labor from above, the institutional mill village was like a double-edged sword. As much as textile activists decried the paternalism and oppression inherent in the village system, they also realized the important role mill villages played in reinforcing a sense of solidarity among textile workers—the same solidarity that the unions, at their best, were able to exploit. This solidarity existed on two planes: as a bond that united certain residents within the villages and as a line of demarcation that separated residents of a given mill village from all else. While mill villages were, of course, internally divided, villagers consistently distinguished the bounded polis from whatever existed outside. Thus, during the UTWA's 1932 strike at Arcadia, strikers paraded through the nearby campus of the Textile Industrial Institute to protest the use of TII's work-study students—emphatically not part of the Arcadia textile worker community—as strikebreakers.[2]

During the 1930s, local unions frequently demanded that manufacturers recognize this distinction. Resolutions passed by Local 2070 at Startex in late 1936 included not only the usual demands that workers be given the rights "guaranteed under the National Labor Relations Act" but also the demand "that those people who live in the Company houses be given employment before any outsiders are given work."[3] That understanding of the collective was the basis for the moral outrage expressed by union workers at Cowpens Mill and Lyman in the wake of the 1934 General Strike. What galled most was not that they had been fired for union activity or that others had been placed on their jobs; the deepest cut was that the companies in question had hired outsiders—"farm people"—to replace them.

Union officeholding was dominated by men and women who had the longest tenures and highest standings in their respective mill villages. By the 1930s, the nomadic qualities of southern textile workers had become proverbial. As Annie West of Saxon once noted, many "never lived in one village more than two or three months" and "seldom could a family be found that had lived in the same village for a year or more."[4] Yet over time there developed in nearly every southern mill village a "settled cohort" of workers, a group whose geographical tenure gave them the right to both claim and define community in their spheres.

By the 1930s, most southern mill-village residents fell into one of two groups: the settled cohort or the ranks of transients. Which group held the upper hand statistically varied from place to place. Regardless of the ratios, however, it was from among these settled cohorts of workers, not the ranks of the transients, that southern mill workers chose union leaders.[5] Nearly all of the prounion workers discharged in the wake of the 1936 Spartan mills strike had worked for Spartan at least five or ten years. John Pollard, Local 1881's young president, had lived at Spartan since 1919, when his family moved to the village from Converse, nine miles east. Paul Stephens, Local 1881's treasurer, had been born at Saxon and had lived at Spartan since childhood. At Saxon, of the seventeen identifiable union officers active from 1934 to 1936, only two had lived and worked at Saxon for fewer than five years. Seven had lived there between five and ten years, three between ten and twenty, and five between twenty and thirty years. Two had lived there all their lives.[6]

Textile mill villagers had a prior understanding of the collective that transcended mere demographics. It also emerged from and found expression in the voluntary associations that regulated mill-village life, especially the churches and fraternal lodges. The institutional prominence of local union activists reinforced community, both as traditionally defined in the mill village and as defined through the local union. At Tucapau, for instance, all four of Local 2070's officers—Gibson, Caldwell, Comer, and Moore—were also leaders in the Masonic and Odd Fellows lodges. B. C. Comer was a deacon in the Tucapau Baptist church, and G. W. Revels, one of the local's most active rank-and-file members, was a locally prominent Baptist preacher. G. Walter Moore had been a figure in local Democratic Party circles long before he ever joined the union. At Saxon, the first president of Local 1882, Walter G. Gault, was also the superintendent of the Baptist Sunday school. His vice president, Jedediah M. Bevill, was a steward and prominent layman at Saxon Methodist.[7]

Thus, the makeup of local unions, especially their leadership cadres, raised the stakes of labor-management conflict tremendously. Local union officials and rank-and-file activists did not just represent the work force in a textile mill. They represented the settled cohort of workers and residents who traditionally defined "community" in the villages.[8] That these particular men and women would choose to cast their fates with the union had profound consequences. For an owner or superintendent to refuse an audience with, discharge, or evict such people constituted a direct assault on the self-constructed working-class communities that textile workers had labored for decades to build. Union leaders were the very men and women who, through their persistence over time and their institutional ties, held working-class communities together. It was in this social and demographic context that the UTWA operated in Spartanburg County during the mid–1930s.

It is within this context that textile workers' understanding of what the union movement could and should mean must be evaluated. First and foremost, of course, the union represented a battle against intolerable working conditions, particularly the stretch-out.[9] Yet for the vast majority, the movement came to represent much, much more than simple class struggle with a southern accent. It incorporated deep-seated cultural values that existed outside the workplace. Take the idea of making Mother's Day a union holiday, as an Inman Mills worker suggested: "Remember that dear old mother next Sunday. She may be working in one of these sweatshop mills trying to help support her family. Send her a card, or some flowers, or a box of candy. Don't forget mother. Don't fail the U. T. W. of A."[10]

Family concerns underwrote unionism for many. Some workers placed the movement's significance squarely on their hopes and dreams for children and grandchildren. A Pacolet worker urged his neighbors to press on with the movement "that means so much to all textile workers and much more to our children. It is our solemn and sacred duty to strive with all our might to make the textile industry safe for those who follow in our foot-steps. . . . Our only hope and our only protection lies in the UTWA." A Clifton worker asked how anti-union workers would respond in later years when their children asked why they had not worked for change. "Thank God our children at Clifton Mill will never say that about their daddies or mothers," he exclaimed. An Inman worker—realizing that the old chestnut of mill villages being "like a family" often held literal truth in terms of consanguinity—noted that "if all members will work together and organize their families and relatives we will soon have them all." The like-a-family simile could itself be used for the sake of the union, as when this same worker urged his fellows to start "binding ourselves together in one big family to demand our freedom."[11]

Other textile workers wedded the union movement to the preexisting rhythms of daily village life. At Glendale, the local union also served as a booster club for the mill's baseball team. At Clifton No. 1 and elsewhere, the union sponsored ice cream suppers, musical concerts, fish-fries, and cakewalks, just like churches and fraternal lodges. The only difference was that the proceeds of such events, instead of going to Sunday schools or fraternal insurance programs, now went to support striking workers at places like Gaffney. At Inman, Local 1935 chartered a sick benefit club for members and later a women's club "for the purpose of helping the sick and needy," thus structuring the local into the normal mill-village pattern of mutuality in times of need. In case anyone missed the symbolism involved in the creation of this particular women's club—that "union" was becoming synonymous with "community"—the club's by-laws stated that only union members or union sympathizers could become part of its efforts to care for the poor and the ill.[12]

For still others, the union movement came to embody patriotism. If President Roosevelt was both a supporter of unionism in principle and the chief architect of the New Deal, then it was every American worker's patriotic duty to support his or her local union. As an anonymous textile worker from Spartanburg declared, "Now when a man, a capitalist, or an industrial leader turns his back on the Stars and Stripes and on the laborers who have made him what he is, then Africa, the darkest jungles of Africa, is where he belongs. He is unfit to be in a civilized country."[13] Furman Garrett, leader of the locked-out Lyman local and later a UTWA organizer, labeled Gov. Eugene Talmadge's use of concentration camps in Georgia during the General Strike "à la Hitler" and termed police tactics during the 1936 Spartan strike "Fascist." The AFL and CIO were "American Institutions," Garrett believed. "They are defenders of the principles upon which our country rests. We believe in our free institutions, in democracy and in liberty. We want to guard it as a priceless heritage."[14]

The union's role as an avatar of community even extended to issues of public morality. Textile workers were well aware of how the rest of southern society tended to view them: as poor, degraded, immoral, and generally inferior to everyone else in the local white population. That consistent characterization grieved established, law-abiding textile workers, who either denied the charges or blamed them on the transient workers who did not come under the local community's informal patterns of socialization and governance. In Spartanburg, the UTWA functioned as a defense against such stereotyping and against anyone whose actions might bring the community as a whole into further disrepute. The two-month Fairmont strike of late 1935, for instance, was ostensibly over issues of workload and discrimination inside the plant.[15] Its terms of settlement, however, hinted at what really provoked workers. "The management and the entire committee have agreed that the cleaning up of this village as essential," the last paragraph of the settlement read. The company promised to enforce rules against smoking in the mill and against drinking or fighting on the village. It also promised a major overhaul of the village infrastructure, because the dilapidated condition of Fairmont's houses and the fact that they were all painted bright red (the traditional color of African American sharecroppers' shacks) had galled workers for years.[16]

If local unions could arbitrate who did belong in a given community, they could just as well decide who did not, as the Fairmont settlement's reference to house colors implies. Defining community meant defining certain groups or individuals as being out as much as it meant defining others as being in, and so movement culture also acquired a peculiar and self-confining element: race. Racism's dimensions appeared stark in both the rhetoric and the reality of local unions. Although the UTWA had reluctantly agreed to organize black workers during 1933 and 1934, the movement collapsed even faster among African Americans than among whites. Not only did black unionists face the same oppression as did their white counterparts, but they also faced their own small numbers and the implacable hostility of white unionists. White unionists primarily saw "the Negro" as an example of what they believed whites should never be—slaves. "The fight is on and we must be the victors or we shall find ourselves in the midst of another depression that will make slaves of us. Slaves to be bought, sold and traded like the negroes before the Civil War."[17]

On a local level, black workers frequently were caught in the crossfire between unions and management. Seeing how unwelcome they were among the former, by 1936 they mostly sided, at least publicly, with the latter. White unionists blamed black workers for serving as strikebreakers at Saxon in 1935 and at Spartan in 1936, and it was an African American trying to cross an all-white Tucapau picket line who was killed in the only strike-related fatality in Spartanburg County during the 1930s.[18] White textile workers almost never included blacks in their own definitions of community, and so they were also excluded from the union movement, both in principle and in practice.

The unwillingness or inability of southern unionists to accept black workers into their ranks, even at the movement's zenith, reflected the least salutary aspects of southern society. Nevertheless, the union's role in defining community—in taking the best of mill-village mutuality and structuring it into an organization—ultimately became a crusade for the soul of the larger society, including not only black workers but also employers. That effort to enlarge the meaning of struggle, and therefore its goals, never proceeded beyond the linguistic level. The words themselves came haltingly. And yet they give some idea of what the movement's future could have been. "By organization, workers can be human beings instead of just creatures waiting to accept whatever the unmerciful capitalistic barons try to make us accept," a Clifton worker wrote. "If there were no labor organizations there would soon be no humanity." He elaborated on precisely what the union movement had accomplished in terms of local community life: "It has inspired within us a much grater spirit of brotherly love. We no longer look upon our fellow-workers as beings who are separate and far removed from us. Instead, we regard them as human beings who are necessary and important links in the chain of brotherly love. We accept their problems as our problems and together enjoy all that is accomplished. . . . For our fellow-workers are our neighbors regardless of where they may be." Thus, for individuals to oppose the union movement was to refuse "to walk to a greater fullness of life with their fellow-men."[19]

Robert W. Donnahoo, president of the Inman Mills local, once defined the union's goal as "complete economic freedom and social justice." That, as Donnahoo knew, was an aspiration that could potentially redefine community in yet a broader way to include anyone willing to own these goals, whether inside or outside the mill villages. "We hope the general public will take greater interest in our struggles," he noted. In the same way that flying squadrons hoped to extend their understanding of the union and "community" to unorganized mills in 1934, Donnahoo wanted to extend that understanding of community to the "general public."[20]

Of all the ways in which the union movement became interwoven with textile life, however, the two most important spheres in which it tried to alter the very fabric of southern society were religion and electoral politics. In a region and culture steeped in both, that was perhaps inevitable. Yet the union movement's involvement in religion and politics in Spartanburg went beyond simple references to "Jesus, the rebel Carpenter of Nazareth" or to prolabor electioneering. Through the articulation of a consistent prolabor theology on the one hand and direct action on the local political scene on the other, Spartanburg's unionized textile workers fused religion and electoral politics to the labor movement in order to launch a wholesale assault on the very forces that had traditionally been used to keep them in their place.

Southern mill villages were overwhelmingly religious—or at least the settled cohort of workers was. The unity of who defined community in the mill villages, who attended the churches, and who led the local unions automatically gave the union movement a profoundly Christian cast. The county's prounion newspaper, for instance, featured a weekly column on religion and also frequently profiled revivals in and around Spartanburg's working-class neighborhoods.[21] Its editor, Judson Brooks, was also the leading layperson at Saxon Baptist. In such an environment, union supporters naturally reached for religious metaphors when describing their movement and its vision.

To unionists, church and union stood for the same thing: the dignity and redemption of human beings.[22] According to a Clifton worker, Jesus' aim while on earth was "to work for the welfare of man. . . . That is the aim of organized labor today," the worker continued. "Its principle is to aid the toiler, to do good wherever and whenever possible." A speaker at a UTWA rally near Spartan Mills opined, "The union comes next to the Church. . . . My personal opinion is that a real Christian is in favor of an organization which stands for better working conditions." A Glendale worker argued that "organized labor is right and a Christian's duty. A Christian is for better conditions as Christ was and still is." A worker from Clifton No. 1 declared that "organized labor stands for a christian life": "To be a christian you must live a truthful life; you must be a good neighbor; you must try to improve the conditions in this world and make a better place for your children to dwell in. Christ came into this world to improve it and the principles of organized labor will improve it because they are based on Christ's teachings. Christ said, 'I go to prepare a place for you.' Organized labor is striving to prepare a place for the masses of future generations. . . . Let's stand together for the common good of all and great will be our reward," he concluded.[23]

The very act of organization became connected with Christianity. "We find that people were organized as far back as history dates," a Clifton worker noted. "People were organized when Christ was on earth. Christ himself organized his deciples into one unit with one leader and with one aim." A woman from Glendale also made the connection between religion and the union on the basis of calls for unity. "Our people are realizing that in unity there is strength," she wrote. "In creation there was union because God said, 'Let US make man.' In all great churches in the world today, there is strength in the organization of the people. In all the great battles that have been fought, there were united forces working together in order to win the victory. . . . All great men believe in unity."[24]

With these arguments on the table, an individual's refusal to join the union could even be understood as a rejection of the Almighty. "Every honest and intelligent person knows the union is for right, just as they know the church is right, and how can a Christian oppose an organization that stands for right?" asked a Pacolet unionist. "That's what God stands for. He approves nothing else, and if we work to defeat right, it is conclusive proof that there's something the matter with our heart or head." For a Beaumont worker, "The stretch-out system is like the unpardonable sin once you accept it"—that is, refusing to protest the stretch-out amounted to blasphemy. "We only ask for justice. We only want a square deal. We only strive for right," concluded another worker from Pacolet. "Who opposes these? Only ignorant and *unsaved.*"[25]

Perhaps the clearest articulation of how the union movement in Spartanburg intersected with the teachings of Jesus came when, in a highly publicized radio broadcast of August 1936, UTWA organizer Gordon Chastain explained the Lord's Prayer in terms of organized labor. Chastain used "give us this day our daily bread" to attack mill owners who, once having corralled a work force into a village, regularly held them to substandard wages through repeated curtailments. "What day shall we have our daily bread, today as the mill op-

erates, or this month, and next month when it fails to operate shall we fast.
. . . Is it fair that we only have our bread the days we work, when we are not
responsible for our idleness? Shall our children, whom we are responsible
for . . . suffer?" Regarding the forgiveness of trespasses, Chastain noted, "We
have forgiven our trespassers far more than they have forgiven us. We have
been exploited, and our children have been exploited, we have been persecut-
ed because of our efforts to correct this condition, our families, even to the
innocent children, have been made to suffer the pangs of hunger, the degrad-
ing wretchedness of ragged clothes, had the finger of scorn pointed at us as
we trod the highways seeking employment; all because we dared to try and
help ourselves, believing that there is a Supreme Being who will see Justice
done." As for avoiding temptation, Chastain maintained that "God never led
us into temptation. We have been tempted, and have sinned, because of wages
that were entirely inadequate to provide substance for our families." Chastain
cited examples of men and women who had been reduced to theft and pros-
titution in order to feed their families: "Is it fair that we who toil should be
subjected to such an evil, and isn't it right that we should strive to remedy such
conditions?" Regarding God's power and glory, Chastain observed that "the
power and glory is Thine, but cannot shine because of selfishness of man,
because of his greed, and envy, because of jealousness." He concluded that "it
is a mockery to say Amen after repeating the Lord's Prayer, unless we are striving as best we can to make this world better than when we first knew it."[26] Such
were the all-encompassing terms in which textile unionists identified their
movement with what they saw as true Christianity.[27]

Yet the realities of company-town life militated against this interpretation
of Christianity from the beginning. Most religious workers attended village
churches that existed only at the sufferance of the mills. Almost all were on
mill property, and all were financially dependent upon frequent contributions
from the owners, especially for the payment of pastors. The Pentecostal and
Holiness sects that accounted for the rest of any village's churchgoers usually
forbade union membership as a matter of doctrine. The type of religious vision that textile unionists in Spartanburg articulated simply had no place to
go within this system. "We don't make a practice of criticizing the church,"
wrote an anonymous writer from one of the county's mill villages, "but at this
place we have, as leaders in the church, some of the biggest hypocrites that
grace the face of God's green earth."[28]

In mid–1936 a Pacolet Mills unionist had an encounter with a minister that
left him deeply cynical about the institutional church's fidelity. The minister
in question had seemed a "red hot" unionist during Local 1994's heyday, but

his ardor cooled after the local began to decline. He no longer had the courage to criticize the company's policies of stretch-out and layoff, which, the Pacolet unionist noted, amounted to giving such his approval. "My friends, I had rather be an infidel than to approve of such hellish, mean and ungodly methods as that," the unionist declared. "He said his calling would not allow him to be a union man. Now I know whereof I speak, it was the Superintendent's calling that wouldn't allow him to be a union man, and he knows it too."[29] The pastor at Saxon Methodist sided openly with mill owner John A. Law during the 1935–36 strike.[30] With the exception of a very few maverick congregations—such as Saxon Baptist, to which Law had sold a plot of land in a moment of weakness years before—the institutional church remained a conservative social force in the textile South during the 1930s, no matter what workers believed "true Christianity" meant.[31]

If workers' attempts to merge the principles of Christianity and unionism had practical results that were, at best, ambiguous, their experiences with formal politics between 1934 and 1936 were more decisive. Contrary to popular belief—both then and now—textile workers had always been active in southern politics.[32] During the 1920s, Spartanburg's mill villages consistently rang up impressive voting records; a few, like Saxon and Tucapau, were even famous for activism. Yet in the statehouse, mill workers' voices were rarely heard. As in other southern states, South Carolina's political structure provided no electoral unit smaller than county or city government.[33] Whether in isolated rural locations or on the unincorporated edges of cities, villagers found their votes amalgamated to such an extent with the surrounding population that they could not speak politically as textile workers—unless someone with broader support, such as the notorious Cole Blease, chose to court their votes. Figures such as Blease were rare. Spartanburg voters repeatedly sent men to Columbia who had mill-village ties, but only after they had "made good" elsewhere. Their legislative careers, however heartening to those who dreamed of escaping the mill system, did little to ameliorate conditions for those who remained in the factories.[34]

With the election of Spartanburg's Olin D. Johnston to the House of Representatives in 1926, South Carolina politics began to assume a more hopeful dimension. Johnston "quickly emerged as the state's most bellicose advocate of workers' interests," at least in Columbia, and during his eight-year tenure in the house he worked consistently to keep workers' issues in full view.[35] At the same time, voter registration in mill districts continued to rise. UTW leaders urged textile workers to consider a plan of electoral action in the dismal wake of the abortive 1929 strike wave.[36] By 1930, as one historian has noted, "One out of every four Spartanburg residents lived in a mill village and as many as forty percent of the county's eligible voters were tied to the textile industry. As a result, the candidate that grabbed the mill vote stood on the verge of victory." Local politicians took notice. Spartanburg County's 1932 campaign resembled nothing so much as a "traveling road show," with candidates for every office vying for mill-village votes with promises of antistretch-out legislation, workman's compensation, and a legally mandated eight-hour day.[37] Although textile workers cast their ballots accordingly, they gained nothing tangible over the next two years.

In 1934 the Democratic Party's primary occurred on the very eve of the General Strike. Registration at all the textile boxes (mill village ballot boxes) in Spartanburg County was high: 938 at the three Cliftons, 507 at Drayton, 554 at Pacolet Mills, 904 at Lyman, 609 at Tucapau, and 686 at Saxon.[38] Taking their cue from the New Deal victories of 1932, at least three avowedly prolabor candidates ran for the state's house of representatives, and others contended for lesser posts. Yet the UTWA apparently did not enter this election as a distinct force, and textile votes were scattered among the various candidates. The only recognizable barometer of worker support came in the gubernatorial race, where lawyer and former textile worker Olin D. Johnston swept every mill box except one.[39]

While Johnston went on to win the governor's chair in the November elections, most of the county's other prolabor candidates suffered defeat. Only H. C. Godfrey, local minister, textile worker, and erstwhile UTWA activist, managed to win a spot on the county's statehouse delegation. True to his campaign promises, Godfrey spent virtually all of the 1935 legislative session as a one-man campaign for an antistretch-out bill, to no avail. Of some twenty-nine labor initiatives proposed during the term, "all, including measures to fix minimum wage and hour levels, ban antiunion discrimination, prevent evictions during strikes, and establish a separate state department of labor, save one . . . either drowned in committee or sunk on the Senate floor."[40]

Workers hoped that the next elections would provide a very different story. By early 1936, textile unionists in Spartanburg County had come to understand that any real, lasting, structural changes would have to come through the arena of electoral politics. The UTWA entered the campaign of 1936 at the grass-roots level, beginning with precinct meetings to elect the county's Democratic executive committee.[41] In June, labor elements across the state—headed by the UTWA in Spartanburg County—successfully convinced Governor Johnston to appoint John W. Nates, UTWA organizer and Spartanburg resident, as the first head of South Carolina's new Department of Labor. As Jud-

son Brooks observed, "The laboring people are becoming more and more ed-
ucated to the fact that they can get what they want by concerted action."[42]
Throughout the spring, political activity among textile workers in the county ran high, as union members urged each other, in the words of an Inman
Mills worker, to "get busy" and "put men in office who are as fair to us as they
are to the moneyed interests."[43]

Such men were hard to find, especially among South Carolina's seasoned
politicians. The obvious answer lay in the UTWA's providing not only the
votes but also the candidates. Textile worker hopes of effecting real political
change mounted over the late spring and summer as unionist after unionist
announced his candidacy. J. P. "Uncle Jimmie" Gibbs, who claimed to have
first joined a textile union in 1906 and was a popular speaker at UTWA rallies,
entered the race for county coroner. Lawyer John C. Williams, who began
working in the mills as a spinner at the age of eleven and later worked his way
through college and law school to become Olin Johnston's law partner, offered
himself for solicitor of the state's Seventh Judicial Circuit. William Fred Ponder, the only prolabor candidate to win election to the state's house two years
earlier, ran for the state senate. He reminded voters how he had gone into the
mills as a child after his father died and how, working part time, he had worked
his way through both Chesnee High School (as valedictorian) and Wofford
College. Paul Stephens, treasurer of Local 1881 at Spartan Mills; Furman Garrett, secretary of Local 2191 at Lyman; Robert W. Donnahoo, UTWA organizer and former president of Local 1935 at Inman Mills; Enoch M. Sisk, a member of the Saxon Mills shop committee; and G. W. Revels, Baptist minister and
outspoken rank-and-file member of Local 2070 at Tucapau, all entered the race
for the South Carolina House of Representatives.[44]

All of these men had been politically active before 1936, but for all except
Ponder and Williams these were their first experiences as candidates. Their
platforms were designed not only to attract UTWA members but also to appeal
to a broad spectrum of New Deal supporters. Robert Donnahoo, for instance,
announced a wide-ranging progressive platform that favored shorter legislative sessions (to encourage "rigid economy of government"), free textbooks
for secondary school students, rural electrification and sewerage (especially
for mill villages), state ratification of the proposed child labor amendment to
the U.S. Constitution, a state social security program, and improvements in
the state workman's compensation law. Furman Garrett ran "with full knowledge of the plight of many of the citizens of this industrial as well as agricultural county." Garrett aimed his campaign directly and exclusively at textile
workers, calling for equal representation for labor on social security boards and

commissions, shorter working hours to create more jobs for the unemployed, a higher minimum wage, a state law protecting labor's right to organize, free hospitalization for the poor, old-age pensions for workers, "preservation of civil liberties" in South Carolina, and a general cooperation with Governor Johnston in his "progressive program for progressive labor legislation." Like Donnahoo, Garrett also supported free textbooks for grammar-school students, amendments to South Carolina's workman's compensation law, and the state's ratification of the proposed child labor amendment to the Constitution.[45]

These candidates and their platforms electrified the wavering ranks of prounion textile workers.[46] "The biggest thing on our minds these days is the coming election," wrote a Beaumont worker in late July. "And with that on our minds we urge all working people to get together and elect to the various offices some men whose hearts are with us." A Pacolet worker noted that Spartanburg textile workers—some fifteen thousand strong—had more than enough power to swing all county elections. Referring to antiunion incumbent sheriff Sam M. Henry, "Just to oust him would be a tremendous victory for the laboring class in this county. . . . His crushing political defeat will bring joy and gladness to the hearts of men he has wronged and mistreated and to the fair and honest union people of our county."[47]

Unfortunately, electoral timing doomed these political aspirations. By late 1934 the UTWA had succeeded in galvanizing the vast majority of southern textile workers, but at the time of the fall primaries the union movement's function was still primarily one of protest. Union supporters believed that continual witness against the crimes of the mill owners, coupled with unwavering faith in President Roosevelt and his New Deal, would be enough to transform the southern textile landscape. By 1936 the surviving ranks of prounion workers in South Carolina knew all too well that effective and permanent change could come only through formal politics. The cost of having gained that experiential knowledge, however, was higher than anyone had expected. The defeats of late 1934, 1935, and early 1936 had taken their toll. The union movement was in disarray across the state; in many mill villages, a blanket of fear, shaken off during the union's heyday, had returned. To put it more succinctly, in 1934 the union movement in the textile South had the numbers but not the vision; in 1936 the union movement had the vision but no longer possessed the numbers.

In the election, voters from outside the mill villages failed to support most of the UTWA's favored candidates, and even mill-village support for avowedly prolabor candidates was uneven. At the Tucapau box, for instance, about half the voting totals almost precisely duplicated the divide between union and non-union. In the race for circuit solicitor, John C. Williams defeated Samuel R. Watt by a vote of 519-246; for Congress, prolabor Joseph R. Bryson of Greenville won with 509 votes; for state senate, William Fred Ponder won with 479 votes; and for county sheriff, union-endorsed Jack Kendrick defeated the notorious Sam Henry by a vote of 499-248. In more complicated state house races, however, Tucapauans preferred candidates from their own section of the county, regardless of how they stood on labor issues. Four of the eight men Tucapauans wished to represent Spartanburg in the state legislature were indeed UTWA activists: Tucapauan G. W. Revels (496 votes), Saxonite E. M. Sisk (424 votes), prolabor Spartanburg lawyer John C. Lanham (501 votes), and Lyman unionist Furman Garrett (the top vote-getter at Tucapau, with 506 votes). The other four men Tucapauans endorsed by similar margins, however, were local candidates who had weak or nonexistent labor platforms: Tracy J. Gaines (485 votes), G. M. Hill (481 votes), W. R. Kerr (493 votes), and Burley A. Holland (388 votes). These men's Tucapau victories came at the expense of UTWA organizer Robert W. Donnahoo, who only received 168 votes, and Spartan Mills activist Paul Stephens, who only received 129.[48]

Thus, even in Spartanburg County's most unionized precinct, the politics of neighborhood ultimately triumphed over the politics of class. On 2 September 1936 virtually the entire slate of prounion candidates went down to defeat at the county level. Even Sheriff Henry was narrowly reelected to office. Defeat in the 1936 elections completely demoralized what was left of the labor movement in Spartanburg County. "I had been informed by seemingly reliable men that there were close to twenty thousand . . . union people in our county, and if that was true, there was certainly a lot of 'scab' votes cast, and our safe and sane candidates went down to overwhelming defeat," wrote a "shocked" and deeply wounded Pacolet unionist in the aftermath of the election. "There is something radically wrong somewhere," he mourned. "Anyway, we must get busy, or our cause will tumble in the South. May God help us all. . . . Wake up, people, wake up."[49]

Most workers and union activists, however, were too stunned to respond. The number of reports from local union correspondents in the Una *News-Review* plummeted immediately after the election, never to recover. Manufacturers saw the election as a sure sign that the union's power in Spartanburg had been permanently broken. "Since the manufacturers carried the election, they are beginning to fire the labor leaders," observed Judson Brooks. "They think they will scatter the flock by destroying the leaders."[50] They thought correctly, and by Christmas of 1936 the union movement in Spartanburg was moribund.[51]

It is within this overall context that the manufacturers' assault on textile unionism after 1934 must be understood. Unionism meant much more than simple labor-management relations inside a mill; it could encompass virtually every aspect of human existence. In many southern mill villages, the union became the chief mechanism through which community was expressed. It fed the hungry and visited the sick. It provided recreation. It reinforced family ties. It reinvigorated the political process. It guarded community virtue. Through it, workers could try to reduce their workloads in the plant and follow Jesus at the same time.

But like the more informal mill-village mutualities that had preceded it, this powerful sense of community rested on a shaky foundation. Regardless of what kinds of communities textile workers were able to create in the artificial worlds of mill villages, the villages themselves were ultimately the property of management. The only effective counterbalance to wholesale interference in village affairs was the company's desire to keep a stable work force in residence. A union automatically rendered such a work force unstable, at least in the eyes of mill owners and managers, who acted accordingly.

A few manufacturers realized the source of the UTWA's local power and even attempted to co-opt the themes of community and mutuality through the formation of company unions. At Lyman, for instance, this organization's purpose was "to promote good feeling, harmony and full cooperation between the employes and the management" and also "to deal with the management on questions relating to wages, working conditions, general improvement of the plant and village, cost reductions, quality of production, education, recreation, religious exercise, and sanitation—in short, to make Lyman a better place in which to live and work." These were precisely the same goals as articulated by local UTWA activists. The UTWA and Pacific Mills disagreed, however, on what type of relationship between workers and management would produce such a rosy future. For the UTWA—and for the worker-defined communities that provided the backbone of its support in the mill villages—this vision would become reality only when management gave full recognition to the communities the workers had constructed for themselves, including the union. For Pacific Mills, that recognition was entirely dependent on the workers' obedience, which, as the by-laws of the Lyman company union specified, included not joining any outside labor-related organization. Acquiescence to paternalism thus became the keystone of management's social vision. As the

Lyman by-laws concluded, "Every member shall perform his or her duties for Pacific Mills in such a way that this Association and the management will have the esteem and confidence of such members to this end that the residents of the town of Lyman will be happy and contented and may uphold the reputation that as a mill town Lyman has no superior in the South."[52]

Few companies tried to combat the UTWA on such a sophisticated level. All of them, however, exercised ultimate authority through their control of housing. That housing was at the root of manufacturers' power cannot be overemphasized: Through the administration of company towns, textile managers were able at will to define the human components of mill-village life. Manufacturers had always used selective eviction in order to alter community demographics. During times of labor unrest, evictions often became a company's key tactic in breaking a union. For a union, no matter how amicable negotiations with a company might have been, underlying everything was the threat of a strike. For a company that had its own village, underlying everything else was the threat of eviction. Evictions cut to the heart of what community could and did mean in the mill villages of Spartanburg County. Even more than the questions of who held the keys to the mill gates or the National Guard armories, the fact that textile corporations could physically remove offending individuals and families from their homes struck at the foundations of worker-constructed communities.

The Startex evictions were a case in point. During the 1936 shutdown, Walter Montgomery eventually issued eviction notices to some thirty-two families. The list included all four officers of Local 2070 (Cloyd Gibson, S. P. Caldwell, B. C. Comer, and G. Walter Moore) and the most active rank-and-file members. With only a few exceptions, the evictees as a group were men and women of standing within the workers' community at Tucapau. Even NLRB investigators were struck by the reverence with which Tucapau residents regarded elderly rank-and-filers P. D. and Janie Lavender. From the beginning, Walter Montgomery viewed eviction cases as a last-ditch effort to eviscerate both the union and the union-centered community at Tucapau. His most revealing tactic along these lines was, of course, the decision to enter the cases in the Inman magistrate's court of R. D. Hicks rather than at the local magistrate's court of William C. O'Shields.

When the original Tucapau mill and village were constructed in 1894, the incorporators had been confounded by one farming family who refused to sell their land in the heart of the proposed complex. The O'Shields clan thus later came to play a large and independent role in community life. William C. O'Shields took advantage of the newly urbanized environment to erect a general store, movie theater, and other conveniences for village residents. According to the NLRB, mill management was continually irked by the competition O'Shields's grocery gave to the company store. When Tucapau Mills barred Local 2070 from using its community building as a union hall, O'Shields allowed the local to meet on his premises. Although O'Shields was not himself prounion, he was friendly with many of Local 2070's leaders and an integral part of the textile worker community at Tucapau. That was why Walter Montgomery refused to enter the Startex eviction cases in the Tucapau magistrate's court.[53] Magistrate Hicks, however, was the epitome of what Inman's Chamber of Commerce would have termed a "leading man." In addition to serving as magistrate, he was the proprietor of the Inman telephone exchange and operated one of the finest Elberta peach farms in South Carolina.[54] Hicks's antiunion bias and outrageous conduct in the eviction trials have already been noted. From the workers' point of view, it was more than a blatant case of antiunion discrimination to try the eviction cases before Hicks instead of O'Shields. It was a direct, and ultimately successful, attack on their community.

That attack was dependent on the company-town set-up. In a lengthy letter to Secretary of Labor Frances Perkins in the fall of 1937, G. Walter Moore attempted to explain both the arrangement and the ways in which evictions cut at the heart of the union movement as well as workers' conceptions of what community meant more generally.[55] "You are possibly aware of the fact that the cotton mill corporations own the houses in which the operatives live and always when there is an employment contract made, there is a rent contract made incident to the employment of the workers," Moore began. "It goes further . . . the corporation gives the power to employ special officers to police these cotton mill villages; and they usually control the schools and often the churches in the community." Reviewing the history of the Startex case before the NLRB, Moore declared, "Unless you are here, you cannot conceive of the petty oppression, coercive discrimination worked upon the union employees through the agency of the corporation, under these labor conditions." Under state law, Moore reminded Perkins, "Occupancy [of a mill house] is but an incident of employment." Upon discharge from the company, for whatever reason, mill employees and their families were required by law to vacate their houses at the mill's pleasure. According to Moore, Walter Montgomery was using this law "as an agency against the active union workers." Yet "the Labor Relations Board has taken the position that they have nothing to do with the rental contracts and have steadily refused to lend their power and aid to hold the workers in their homes."

As every southern textile worker understood, such a stand by the NLRB utterly negated any rights textile workers might have been promised regarding the organization of local unions, or indeed any self-activity whatsoever. In refusing to accept jurisdiction in the Startex eviction cases, the NLRB gave its consent to the entire system of mill-village paternalism and oppression. The mill's use of state law to force evictions, as well as the filing of "petty charges" against active unionists, were all part of the company's larger plot to "create the impression that they [the union workers] are communist and anarchists and not desirable citizens in the community." It was a closed system, Moore wrote: "They are able to frame these charges, because . . . the authority of appointing their own peace officers is granted to them under the State Law. . . . Not only that, but the mill corporations make and promulgate the rules that govern the conduct of the operators in their own homes. . . . All this power and control of the home and the conduct of the operator [is] used to oppress and blacken the reputation of the good men who are union men" and, ultimately, "to destroy not only the union, but the union people themselves." While the NLRB dawdled on the Startex case, Moore claimed that "the workers' homes are being broken up and the union people scattered to the four winds." Insofar as preserving the union was concerned, a favorable decision would be meaningless if the company were allowed in the meantime to drive away all known union activists. Moore appealed to Perkins that "some policy may be mapped out and some real relief granted to us from a condition where the corporation invades the peace and tranquility of our homes," where an industrial corporation had the legal right to vivisect working-class communities at will. "A labor contract involves much more than wages and working conditions in the mills," Moore concluded. If neither the Department of Labor nor the National Labor Relations Board was willing to recognize that fact, then the Wagner Act was a dead letter in the textile South.

Such was indeed the case. In the company-town world of the textile South, any labor conflict was bound to take in not only issues of wages, hours, and working conditions inside the mill but also virtually every other aspect of textile life, because every aspect was in some way either really or potentially under the control of the corporation. It is impossible to understand the "episodic" or "apocalyptic" nature of labor protest in the industrial South without understanding one central fact: Nothing could go onto the bargaining table in a company town—especially during the explosive time of a strike—without everything going onto that bargaining table.

Thus, to call into question the mill's absolute right to increase work assignments in the plant was also, necessarily, to question much more—the mill's right to fire workers deemed guilty of moral transgressions, or its right to require that workers trade at the company store, or its right to "suggest" which way workers vote in a particular election. The moment workers challenged a company over any major issue, every facet of their lives was thrown into play, for better or for worse. As Jacquelyn Hall et al. have noted, "Meshing the ethos of the mill village with the vocabulary of protest that emerged as the national climate of opinion shifted to the left, southern workers spoke out against injustices taken for granted in less troubled times. In doing so, they pushed at the boundaries of political debate."[56] In such a context, defeat obviously meant much more than just losing a strike.

This was the dynamic that eluded the normal rhythms of contractual labor-management relations practiced elsewhere in industrial America. It likewise eluded the protective regulations of the National Labor Relations Board, which in practice not only validated a narrower conception of labor-management relations but also coerced both workers and managers into accepting that definition. In this sense, the jurisdictional views of the NLRB played directly into the hands of southern manufacturers, who knew that even if they were forced to concede a measure of workplace control to the NLRB they had myriad other formal and informal methods of regulation at their disposal. Southern workers' disappointment in the NLRB stemmed precisely from this disjuncture. Nowhere was that, or the ways in which the union could become synonymous with community in the fullest sense, more clear than in the hidden transcript of the Saxon strike of 1935–36.

In familiar historical contexts, the Saxon strike of 1935 seems incomprehensible. Local 1882 had emerged from the General Strike of 1934 virtually unscathed, but the local's leaders must have known the dangers of striking at a time when their parent union was widely perceived as a powerless wreck. Closer to home, they saw the rapidly declining power of textile unionism in all but a handful of upper South Carolina's myriad textile plants. Ostensibly, Local 1882 struck out of frustration. Although John A. Law was courteous and always met with the local's negotiating committee upon their request, he categorically refused to entertain grievances. (It was not collective bargaining, declared a UTWA organizer—it was "collective arguing.") The strike, at least from official accounts, was a clear-cut case of wages and working conditions. Yet these grievances were nothing new to either workers or management at Saxon Mills; they were the daily conditions of labor and had been for some time. Moreover, as local union leaders such as Annie West must have known, they were the types of grievances that neither striking workers nor government boards were likely to remedy. Although stretch-out was an endemic problem, in and of itself it would not appear cause for weary South Carolina unionists to strike again so soon after September 1934. Why were Saxon workers willing to lay so much on the line in such a lengthy strike?

The key lies in evidence not found in the cases of the National Labor Relations Board, in the files of the Federal Mediation and Conciliation Service, or in local newspapers. For all its customized benefits, life at Saxon was often excruciating for workers. Energized by his exacting ideals of textile paternalism, John A. Law tried to micromanage the community whose infrastructure he owned. Saxon's residential neighborhoods had a salutary reputation, for instance, but only because "we had to do that. That was part of living there. . . . You had to keep the place clean, keep the weeds cut. . . . You had to keep it clean and neat, inside and out." Anyone caught tampering with any of Law's carefully sited shade trees and shrubs was subject to dismissal.[57]

Thus, the Saxon strike was about much more than the stretch-out. The men and women of Saxon wanted water fountains in the mill. They wanted plant guards removed from two gates so that their children could continue traditional patterns of visiting. They wanted to know who controlled the village streets, were they county roads or company property like everything else, and in any event what law enforcement agency had the right to patrol them. They wanted to wrest control of the Saxon school district—which included the neighboring communities of Una and Powell Knitting—from the direct personal control of John A. Law and his staff. Most of all, they wanted the removal of Marjorie Potwin.[58]

In his attempt to regulate the rhythms of life and labor at Saxon, Law had a partner: Marjorie Potwin, a Columbia University graduate student whom he had met in New York, hired as a welfare worker for his village, and eventually embraced as lover. Saxon village policy was carried out, and increasingly promulgated, by Potwin at Law's behest. Her very presence occupied the epicenter of the Saxon strike—unspoken in all but a few official records.[59]

Potwin's pioneering sociological study of the Saxon village has earned her an enduring place in southern textile historiography. Her conduct while an employee of the company—a position that gave her access to the information upon which her study was based—has garnered less attention. Textile workers at Saxon despised her. Ruby Lee, a second hand's daughter, was denied a mill job after she refused to tell Potwin who her father-in-law planned to vote for in an upcoming school board election.[60] In her capacity as company nurse, Potwin canvassed Saxon on a white horse given her by Law—"and the ones that was out sick, . . . she would ride that horse to the back door, rear that horse's feet in the door part, and demand them get back up there immediately, or lose their job and get off this mill village."[61] As former Saxon residents related half a century later, Law and Potwin flaunted their affair.[62] Such flagrant adultery on the part of a worker would almost certainly have resulted in dismissal and eviction—and at Potwin's hands.

Potwin did have a magnanimous side, as represented in the school commencements and Christmas celebrations she organized every year, but what gestures she made were entirely a function of her drive for control and her desire to protect her employer's reputation.[63] Even Evelyn Neal—from a prominent supervisory family—found Potwin "domineering. She was the boss of everything—she took over. And if she told you to do anything, no matter who you were, you better do it—because she'd go right straight to Mr. Law, and you'd either get fired or you'd do it. And everybody knew that."[64] As Beatrice Norton concluded, "She was over the school, she was over the mill, she was over the help in the mill. She was the boss."[65]

Conversely, UTWA Local 1882 drew its strength from what even an anti-union worker admitted were "some of the families that had been on the mill village as long as it had been there."[66] Hal Corn, whose family and in-laws had been at Saxon for decades and who became a leading figure in Local 1882, "hated Miss Potwin with a passion. And she hated him." By the 1930s, Corn—whose father had been a supervisor at the mill—no longer worked for Saxon; he was "independent, he worked for himself" and lived just off the Saxon village. "But he fought her—see, she controlled the school, and he tried his best to keep her off of the trustees."[67]

Each of the key union families—Bevill, Satterfield, Sisk, Gault, Corn, Lovelace, and Brooks—combined long tenure in the village with long-standing grievances against either Potwin or the mill company more generally. Despite reams of NLRB documentation to the contrary, Saxon workers remain united about what really prompted and fueled the strike of 1935–36: the arbitrary and abusive misuse of power. Certainly, the stretch-out and union recognition were issues at Saxon, but it was Marjorie Potwin who provided the moral impetus for striking. The questions were complex. Was Saxon the personal property and baliwick of John A. Law, as he argued? Or, was it a community of some twelve hundred men, women, and children, with four churches, a school, several grocery stores, a baseball team, and one of the most renowned community bands in the region? Which was the true Saxon Mills?

Although there are hints of these dynamics in the archival evidence—the request for open gates at the plant was presented in writing and there are two vague references to Potwin—none of these issues was covered in the official record that, for the federal government at least, summed up the Saxon case.

Local union leaders may have tailored their demands to fit the most profitable NLRB mold, but the NLRB's regulatory mechanisms themselves only admitted a small segment of worker grievances, not including such thorny problems as water fountains and adultery. Official documents state that in early 1936 both Law and the local suddenly became more disposed to negotiate. What they fail to mention is that only the removal of Potwin from the Saxon scene—considered by the unionists a major victory, if not a publicly acknowledged one—had convinced the workers to return to the bargaining table.

That workers at Saxon cared more about the removal of Marjorie Potwin than about improving wages does not necessarily mean that they were backward, or pre-modern, or otherwise deluded and therefore dismissible. What it does mean is that Saxon workers conceived of the conflict holistically. The question was not so much about the size of paychecks as it was the very nature of the industrial community in which Saxonites lived. In this sense, Local 1882's conception of industrial conflict was broader than the records suggest. Had they allowed the chips on the bargaining table to include only wages and the stretch-out, they would have been drastically limiting not only the parameters of contractual labor-management relations but also their potential control over the working-class community they had worked so hard to build.

Oral testimony from workers at Saxon and elsewhere—including Spartan and Tucapau—suggests that open industrial conflict was considered a viable option only when it raised the chance of altering the basic rhythms of industrial life. Otherwise, why bother? The so-called episodic nature of southern labor activism was in reality a rational response to regional conditions. Only when workers perceived a window of opportunity sufficiently large to transform their entire world did they risk the pain of overt struggle. New Deal legislation did indeed have a profound impact on southern organizing, but not the one most historians have cited. As NLRB records from the 1930s make abundantly clear, when workers discovered that neither the Wagner Act nor sympathetic politicians were willing or able to open the parameters of struggle wide enough to make such struggle worth the fight, "quiescence" returned.

Lost in this easy recitation is the extraordinary realpolitik and pervasive pathos that lay concealed beneath the ebbing of textile worker activism. The scars left by "1934"—by the General Strike and its complex aftermath—proved so deep and enduring precisely because so much more than a textile workers' union had been at stake. While workers at a handful of southern mills fought on into the 1940s and beyond, most went back to their old lives, shutting doors in their minds and in their souls as they cauterized the wounds left from the hopes and dreams of 1934 through 1936. It was this turning away, this painful process of dissociation, which outside observers later subsumed under the descriptive word *quiescence*. The "quiescence" of southern workers in the wake of the 1930s was neither irrational nor inexplicable. It was a social product manufactured experientially through a collective experience of defeat. Nowhere was the arduous path back to quiescence more clearly marked out than in the life of Annie Laura West, former secretary of UTWA Local 1882 at Saxon Mills and for a time one of the most prominent union activists in Spartanburg County.

Annie West was finally fired by Saxon Mills in late 1936 as part of the manufacturers' post-election purge. Impoverished and defeated, she moved to Una, the working-class suburb that gave refuge to other outcast union veterans. What was left of the community of suffering and vision, struggle and hope, came to her aid. Scattered friends slipped her money when they could, while local families who remembered what she had done and what they had all once stood for sent her sewing when their own meager incomes allowed it. More than anything else, she waited. In 1939 West's spirits revived briefly when a reconstituted UTWA made a belated attempt to reorganize the South (chapter 8). Afterward, she attempted to secure work as an organizer or office worker with the UTWA, but to no avail. She even attended the UTWA's 1939 and 1941 conventions as a delegate-at-large at her own expense.[68]

In mid–1941, the Spartanburg Central Labor Union finally concluded that the textile workers' struggle was over, expelling all inactive locals (including Local 1882) and all the unemployed delegates that still attended local CLU meetings, including Annie West, then the Central Labor Union's own vice president. A year later, West contacted her old hero Francis Gorman. "I would almost give ten years of my life to be able to help other people, and feel that I was helping build the union that was all it can be for the people," she wrote, but "I hope that neither you nor anyone else will ever be treated as I have been."[69]

As Annie West's hopes of becoming a union organizer faded and her economic situation became increasingly desperate, she again turned to the textile mills. "Each time I asked for work in the mill, I was politely told that no help was needed," she later wrote. "For months, I had only the money I could make sewing for the people around here, which amounted to less than $3.00 per week, sometimes not that much."[70] In the fall of 1940, she secured work at the Dixie Shirt Factory, a new firm set up and controlled by the Montgomery-Milliken interests, but was fired after only a short time in the plant because she could not keep up with ever-rising production quotas.[71] In mid–1942, West was able to get a second textile job, this time through the offices of an old schoolmate now working as a supervisor at the Mayfair Cotton Mills of Arcadia. Friends and even her brother Barney (a member of the Railway Carmen's union at Spartanburg) advised her to "not let anyone know [she] had ever belonged to a union." West tried to take her brother's advice, but by her own admission she was still a fervent believer in the union cause: "I can no more ignore what is happening and not help in the fight for the survival of unionism than I can live without breathing," she wrote. In December she was fired for trying to organize a local union at Arcadia.[72]

West nearly despaired of any future employment prospects in South Carolina after her dismissal from Arcadia, but in the superheated economic climate of World War II she was finally able to obtain employment in April 1943 at a local defense plant. Cautious and worn down by past struggles, she nevertheless entered the lists one last time. Still working as a battery-filler, West telegrammed the Federal Mediation and Conciliation Service in August with details of the stretch-out at the Warrior Duck Mill. Federal mediator Fred Beck did journey to Spartanburg and took up the issue of the battery hands' workload with the plant superintendent. But as Beck candidly noted, there was little he could do. "I explained to Miss West that since this mill was unorganized and no recognized committee set up it was difficult to determine whether an excessive work load exists, since to present to Mr. Irwin the battery filler's side of the complaint would necessarily mean the calling of battery fillers to testify to their work load." Beck left West with the unhelpful advice that she organize the plant first and then, if necessary, get back in touch with Washington.[73] Shortly after her involvement with Federal Mediation—and her attendance at the South Carolina Federation of Labor's annual convention in 1943—West lost her job again. She never returned to public work.

Throughout her years in exile from the UTWA, Annie West struggled to retain the faith in the union movement that had motivated her during the 1930s. "I might starve to death but I would not change my mind about Unionism," she wrote to Francis Gorman in 1940. "You know me and you know, I love the movement and it means more than life," she wrote again in 1941. In 1942 she added, "You know I've always felt about the Labor movement, it always comes first, and I did not put self first." Yet the vicissitudes that tore the remnants of the movement after 1936 ultimately disillusioned even Annie West. She saw her expulsion from the Central Labor Union in 1941 as having been politically motivated; certain leaders in the building trades unions, she charged, had been made uneasy by her one-woman union label campaign against local department stores. She later mourned that the revived UTWA and its Southern Cotton Textile Federation had become a "racket" set up by her former union colleagues. When she tried to bring the UTWA back to first principles by calling for a new southern organizing campaign, other UTWA activists deserted her. "My spirit has been crushed," she told Francis Gorman in mid–1942. In 1944 she vowed never to trust anyone in the union movement again. Yet even in her darkest moments West was forced to admit that "I'm as much a true blue union member as I was in the General Strike and the '36 convention, etc., and shall die that way."[74]

In the spring of 1944, *ten years* after joining the union, Annie West sent her last letter to Francis Gorman. "I'm not as young as I used to be," she noted and obliquely gave notice that she would soon be leaving behind the last of her union aspirations for a career as a "settled housewife."[75] In 1945 West married a carpenter from north of Spartanburg and moved to the country not far from Lyman, where they raised their only child, a son. In 1969 the family moved back to Una, just across the railroad tracks from Saxon. Every day until her death in 1986, Annie Bryant could gaze out her front window and see the twin smokestacks of Saxon Mills rising over the neighborhood. What she thought at such moments is unknown, because, like most of the veterans of the southern union movement of the 1930s, she kept her silence. After so many years of struggle, Annie Laura West Bryant had finally become quiescent. With thousands of other southern textile workers, she became, in her words, one of the "forgotten ones." Even among her most intimate friends and relations, including her son, she never again spoke of the "Ideal" that she and others had fought so hard and so long to realize.[76]

7   The Politics of Survival

For most American workers, the late 1930s were years of epochal change. Beginning with spectacular sit-down strikes in the northern mass-production industries and the creation of the Congress of Industrial Organizations (CIO), organized labor stormed the bastions of industry that had so effectively resisted unionization. These were watershed years, when the United Automobile Workers of America captured Flint and the United Mine Workers finally won decisive battles in Appalachia. Yet in the South, this high-water mark had come much earlier and been much less successful. The year 1937 was a moment of euphoria nationally, of grand beginnings and of the ratification of many hopes. In the textile South, those hopes had already been dashed. The year meant nothing in Greenville. Sit-downs in Flint were meaningless in Honea Path. By the time America went to war, the southern labor movement occupied a fundamentally different structural position than its northern counterpart. In the North, unions had achieved major breakthroughs in all major mass-production industries.[1] But in the two key southern industries—textiles and wood products—no such breakthroughs had occurred. During the late 1930s and 1940s, most American workers believed, and with just cause, that they were marching toward a new social order. Southern workers found themselves in the last downward spirals of an odyssey leading from the very same hopes to the destruction of their unions and the extinction of the social vision those unions had represented. To understand what this critical disjunction meant in human terms is to begin to comprehend the heritage of fear and resignation that became the most paralyzing aspect of the southern industrial experience in the twentieth century.

In Spartanburg County, the first and most obvious casualty of these dynamics was the CIO itself. An organizing powerhouse in the North, the CIO fared miserably in the South, especially in textiles.[2] Initially formed as an industrial organizing committee within the American Federation of Labor, the CIO broke with the more conservative, craft-oriented AFL in 1936. The United Textile Workers of America—pathetic and bankrupt in the wake of the General Strike and its aftermath—voluntarily disbanded, sending its leaders and locals into the newly formed Textile Workers Organizing Committee (TWOC). That committee, like its better-known counterpart in the steel industry, was supposed to sweep textile workers nationwide into the CIO. Organizing would be its first priority; union-building on the local level would come later. When the CIO first came to Spartanburg in the spring of 1937, it found the remnants of the labor movement ready and willing to cooperate for what both the CIO and local activists viewed as "reorganization."[3] Within three years, however, the vast majority of these workers, having clung to union dreams for so long, deserted the CIO. Neither the CIO's Textile Workers Organizing Committee nor the AFL's United Textile Workers of America (UTWA)—resuscitated by disgruntled textile unionists in 1938—provided the vehicle that southern textile workers felt they needed to realize the social vision their union aspirations represented—the vehicle they required to rally wavering colleagues and recapture the momentum of 1933 and 1934.

In April 1937 TWOC's Greenville office convinced the leaders of the Tucapau local—who had time on their hands as their discrimination cases languished—to take charge of the Spartanburg area. The so-called Tucapau Four—Cloyd Gibson, S. P. Caldwell, B. C. Comer, and G. Walter Moore—were tested and dedicated organizers directly from a local mill. Gibson and Comer were known as compelling orators, and Moore's administrative expertise had been solely responsible for preventing the Tucapau cases from evaporating in Washington. Along with John Pollard and others, the four crisscrossed South Carolina zealously during 1937 and 1938. These men were pragmatists. Gibson, for example, knew—as earlier disciples of Roosevelt's New Deal had not—that the Wagner Act itself was no substitute for unionism and that only solid locals would be able to manipulate New Deal machinery effectively. "The workers realize that without a strong militant organization they will be beaten down again as they have been in the past," he wrote in July 1937. "The Wagner Act will not benefit them unless they have a strong union to act as a 'positive force' to help enforce the law."[4]

Prospects seemed bright.[5] S. P. Caldwell reported in August that "workers are signing blue cards as fast as we can get to them, regardless of the opposition from the manufacturers."[6] Yet TWOC ultimately withered, in Spartanburg as elsewhere in the South, for three interlocking reasons: It failed to find any official means of addressing the stretch-out, it failed to secure contracts at organized mills, and it failed to resolve the scores of pending southern textile cases before the National Labor Relations Board, as promised.[7] Over time, southern textile workers became convinced that TWOC was at best inept. At worst, they suspected that the new union did not really have their interests at heart.[8]

In the matter of organizing, the Textile Workers Organizing Committee found itself between management opposition and the union's need to differentiate itself from the old UTWA.[9] TWOC would not request an NLRB election until it was absolutely sure of its majority in a mill, nor would it charter a local until such an election had been won. In that way it hoped to avoid the debacle of 1934, when the General Strike had revealed how thin the UTWA's support actually was in many mills.[10] The new union also adopted a "no-strike-if-at-all-possible" policy.[11] To workers watching the last shreds of their movement slip away, these tactics seemed less those of prudence than those of hesitancy and delay. At the same time, there was the problem of renewed management opposition. Although in 1933 and 1934 the UTWA had been able to organize with comparatively minor interference from owners and managers, by 1937 and 1938 TWOC faced a united front of mill officials armed with experiential knowledge of where such organizing, if left unchecked, could lead.[12]

Nowhere were TWOC's inadequacies more evident than at Beaumont. The Beaumont union—formerly the UTWA's Local 1705—was the oldest surviving textile local in Spartanburg County and one of the oldest in South Carolina. It had struggled from 1935 through 1937 with only a handful of active members, but after an intensive campaign of reorganization the Textile Workers Organizing Committee took the plant by a vote of 291-208 on 18 February 1938. As a federal mediator later noted, "This is the first case (in the immediate section) that has been taken up for contractual relationship [under TWOC], and as such is the test case."[13] TWOC's success in obtaining contractual relations at Beaumont would affect not only the future of the Beaumont local but also the CIO's future in South Carolina more generally.

Company president Dudley L. Jennings knew that and fought the very idea of a contract from the beginning. On 5 July 1938 TWOC filed unfair labor practices charges against Jennings, and six days later Beaumont and other area mills announced a general 15 percent wage reduction, nearly provoking a strike.[14] TWOC negotiator Seth P. Brewer used the threatened walkout to push for contractual provisions—such as a closed shop—far beyond anything a southern industrial union had ever achieved. The result was deadlock. As mediator D. Yates Heafner noted, "That the manufacturers as well as the organization have the full backing of their . . . constituents in this case is little doubted."[15]

With pressure mounting, TWOC called a protest strike on 29 September 1938. Only a minority of Beaumont workers responded, but they were enough to keep the plant down for more than a month. Jennings steadfastly refused to make any hard promises as long as workers remained off their jobs. The best TWOC could obtain—with help from both federal mediators and the South Carolina Department of Labor—was a "peculiar" verbal agreement embodying "a basic understanding . . . on practically all points of the contract."[16]

The plan was for union and management to reduce these understandings to writing as soon as the mill resumed operations; instead, according to TWOC, the company continued to stall while it weeded the most troublesome unionists from its work force. Negotiations collapsed in a stormy meeting on 4 January 1939. In early April, the Textile Workers Organizing Committee formally withdrew, to the disgust of Beaumont workers who blamed the debacle more on the union than on Dudley Jennings. Even the NLRB agreed. "The strike of September, 1938, should never have been called," regional director Charles N. Feidelson fumed. "Sole responsibility for the failure of the TWOC to secure a contract rests on the personal ineptitude of the TWOC leadership in the Spartanburg area." NLRB attorney Thomas Emerson agreed that "the failure to secure a contract was due to the bungling and poor management of the T.W.O.C.'s representatives and not to the Company's alleged failure to bargain."[17]

The NLRB sealed the CIO's death warrant at Beaumont in December 1939 when it dismissed all of TWOC's allegations of discriminatory discharge.[18] Beaumont's dwindling union cadre, estranged from the CIO, flirted briefly with independent unionism before returning to the AFL in early 1941.[19] They never got their contract, and the local disbanded shortly thereafter.[20] According to the NLRB's Feidelson, the entire affair indicated how "miserably" "the old-line unions have . . . botched their organizing jobs in South Carolina."[21]

To textile workers in the mills, all of this only exacerbated their sense of criminal incompetence in the handling of the lingering Tucapau case. Tucapau unionists had responded enthusiastically to the CIO from the moment of its inception.[22] Within a year, however, they had concluded that TWOC itself was part of the problem. In August 1938, G. Walter Moore complained to TWOC regional director R. R. Lawrence that his constituents had little more idea of the disposition of their NLRB case than they had possessed a year before. "I believe there is a reason for this but we do not believe the representatives of the T.W.O.C. has human principle enough . . . to tell the truth about it. We do not want the sympathy of the T.W.O.C.," he declared. "We want a square deal." The delays and bargaining had convinced Tucapau unionists that "the T.W.O.C. as a whole is a racket. . . . Mr. Lawrence, we are making a death plea to you for help in securing a hearing on this case. We joined the T.W.O.C. with the assurance that we would get such help and if there is nothing you can do be man enough to say so."[23]

Given TWOC's apparent inactivity on the Tucapau case and its policy in chartering locals solely on the basis of NLRB elections, Moore wondered whether it even considered Tucapau part of its union. By December, Tucapauans had also heard rumors that TWOC officials had asked the NLRB to hear two younger cases before Tucapau's. "If the T.W.O.C. done this," Moore stormed, "I feel that it was the most underhanded dirty piece of work that has ever been handed the union people at Tucapau."[24]

After TWOC refused to file additional discrimination charges authorized by the local, Moore even appealed to CIO head John L. Lewis. "I noticed that Mr. R. R. Lawrence . . . made the statement in the C.I.O. convention at Pittsburgh that the southern workers wanted organization," Moore wrote. "I will agree with Mr. Lawrence on this question but how is Mr. Lawrence or his staff going to organize the southern worker when they will give one worker a blue card and the other a stab in the back?" In general, Moore and his associates decried TWOC's centralization, which they claimed deprived rank-and-file southern workers of any voice in an organization ostensibly administered for their benefit. "I realize the T.W.O.C. cannot put all of their time to the discrimination cases," he wearily concluded, "but they will never organize the textile workers in this section of the south with this underhand[ed] work going on."[25] The final disposition of the case destroyed the CIO at Tucapau.[26]

As a result of the Textile Workers Organizing Committee's poor southern performance, dozens of surviving textile locals—including all but one in Spartanburg County—bolted the CIO in 1939 and 1940. They realigned with the AFL's reconstituted UTWA and its new southern arm, the Southern Cotton Textile Federation (SCTF).[27] The SCTF represented a fundamental critique of how earlier union movements—both TWOC and the old UTWA—had handled southern textile workers and their union vision.[28] In December 1938, when Francis Gorman left the CIO, he specifically promised that southern textile workers would "run their own affairs" in the revived UTWA.[29]

When the SCTF was formally organized in Atlanta on 28 January 1939, its leadership was dominated by Spartanburg County's most experienced unionists: John Pollard from Spartan Mills, Furman Garrett from Lyman, Robert Donnahoo from Inman Mills, Annie Laura West from Saxon, and organizer

Gordon Chastain.[30] The federation's literature—probably written by Pollard—echoed the theme of self-rule. Attacking the "shackles of dictatorship" placed on southern textile workers by the "TWOC Monstrosity," the SCTF promised in one pamphlet to offer "at last . . . a Union where democracy will really be practiced and not simply a word spoken as a slogan." Denouncing the "secret chamber meetings" that they alleged had characterized TWOC, Pollard and his colleagues pledged to "Build a Union of Southern Textile Workers—For Southern Textile Workers—That will be run exclusively by Southern Textile Workers in each mill and community."[31]

But the SCTF flowered early and briefly at the UTWA's reinaugural convention of 8–10 May 1939. On paper at least, the new UTWA was the first American textile union to have significant southern representation. At the convention, fifty-five of the eighty-three participating locals and sixty-three of the 126 delegates were southern; southerners dominated five of the nine permanent committees and constituted half of those elected to office. Southern delegates controlled much of the convention and in fact "gave the south quite a play up." Yet paper credentials crippled the new movement from the beginning. The existence of many southern locals was tenuous at best. At least four Spartanburg delegates represented locals that were effectively defunct, one of them perhaps even imaginary. As for those present, a CIO mole reported, "I don't think there was six good locals in the south."[32] Simultaneously facing a weak membership base, the "UTWA" stigma, and the new union's almost total lack of funds and organizers, the SCTF withered almost instantly. By 1940 it was a dead letter, and in 1942 its existence was formally terminated.

In returning to the UTWA-AFL, textile workers attempted to recapture some of the sense of mission and local initiative that they felt had decayed under TWOC leadership. Yet neither a renewed sense of mission nor local initiative could compensate for the combination of dynamics that steadily ate away at unionism in the textile South. Hostile management, an erratic national economy, and the bureaucratic nightmare of NLRB proceedings were factors over which no union—AFL or CIO—had any real control. The NLRB, conceived as a means of worker empowerment, had become by late 1938 a mechanism of containment as a result of the declining electoral clout of the New Deal. With economic indicators again falling, New Dealers in Washington—including NLRB administrators—saw room for domestic maneuvering reduced to zero. The resulting political retreat had devastating consequences for workers everywhere. Spartanburg's activists, sensing that what was left of their movement was dangerously becalmed, placed the blame on the most visible target: the CIO's tendency toward autocracy and centralization. "They have set themselves up as little Hitlers," Tucapau's G. Walter Moore charged of TWOC's leaders.[33]

But the problems of the Textile Workers Organizing Committee, and southern workers' dissatisfaction with it, were ultimately as irrelevant as they were real. Beneath the surface both were overshadowed by the stark reality that the southern labor movement had less and less real substance. The AFL-CIO schism in textiles only weakened southern unionism further (map 3).

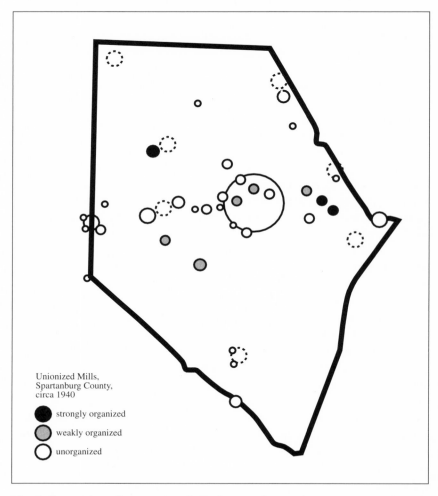

Unionized Mills,
Spartanburg County,
circa 1940

● strongly organized

◐ weakly organized

○ unorganized

Map 3. Spartanburg County, circa 1940, showing degree of unionization at all mills and villages. (Courtesy of L. A. Waldrep)

Such was the situation as the nation entered World War II. As it did elsewhere in the United States, war brought new prosperity to economically stricken manufacturing communities in the textile South. The sudden shift to maximum production also created new strains on workers and thus new possibilities for worker protest. Across the country, unions seized upon wartime protections to consolidate their positions in key plants and industries. In the South, however, the CIO's drives of the late 1930s had ended dismally, depriving southern unions of the necessary beachheads. Elsewhere, World War II presented industrial unions with an unprecedented opportunity for entrenchment and expansion, but only in cities and industries where unions had already managed a negotiable presence. Neither the CIO's TWUA nor the AFL's revived UTWA were in such a position.

Spartanburg's textile manufacturers greeted the war with the same hosannahs voiced by their associates elsewhere, renovating their mills and hiring thousands of new workers. Experienced workers laid off due to the vicissitudes of the 1930s were, of course, the first to be reabsorbed into the work force, but wartime personnel demands were much greater than this ready pool could supply. Despite the depression, automobiles became an increasing part of the rural South during the 1930s; with the economic jolt of war, commuting to and from factory work suddenly became a real option for rural people. Only a few Spartanburg mills added company housing to their villages.[34] Most chose to recruit once again from the countryside.

The explosion of new workers, few of whom had prior experience in textiles and none of whom lived in mill villages, permanently altered the relationship between mill corporations and mill-village residents. Mill workers now came from all over the county and occupied a much wider spectrum on the socioeconomic scale than before. These facts, coupled with the very real rise in wartime wages, dispelled much of mill work's long-standing pariah status. Mill owners no longer considered their company-owned villages the sole, or even primary, source of new employees, and many began to dispose of residential holdings during or immediately after the war. New workers, neither living in the villages nor having experienced the struggles of the 1930s, found expressions of mill-village culture—including what was left of the union movement—both alien and irrelevant. Perhaps an array of stable and entrenched local unions in Spartanburg could have found ways to incorporate this wave of new employees, as happened elsewhere in industrial America. In Spartanburg County, however, only six local unions had survived. Four of these—at Startex, Beaumont, Spartan, and Fairmont—were too weak and demoralized to take any advantage of the situation; their memberships, already low, were swamped. Only the locals at Inman Mills and Clifton met the war with any vigor.

One aspect of wartime production seemed obvious to seasoned workers: The stretch-out continued. Despite the fact that both the AFL and the CIO had signed no-strike pledges for the duration of the war, textile workers in Spartanburg—along with workers across the country—repeatedly took matters into their own hands when neither their unions nor the War Labor Board gave satisfaction. The six organized mill complexes of Spartanburg County saw at least twenty-three work stoppages between 1940 and 1945: eight at Startex, seven at the Cliftons, three at Inman Mills, two at Beaumont, two at Spartan, and one at Fairmont.[35] Workers at unorganized plants also walked out on occasion. Brief strikes hit Whitney, Drayton, Lyman, and even Arcadia.[36]

Union leaders hoped that the renewed sense of militancy would translate into new local unions.[37] In fact, the major effect of wartime strikes was to corrode union strength in Spartanburg's organized plants rather than to assist the organization of new ones. The sheer act of striking—in violation not only of wartime no-strike pledges but also of specific contractual grievance procedures—undermined local unions' legitimacy and robbed them of whatever moral high ground they had gained through the patriotic posturing of AFL and CIO leaders. In the plants, the specific pattern of wartime strikes—nearly all of which were provoked by, and even confined to, specific groups of workers—divided even unionized workers. When one group, such as doffers, walked off the job and caused an entire plant to close, both union and non-union workers were forced to pay the penalty in terms of time, money, and morale. The results were deep and bitter divisions in union ranks, causing many workers to abandon textile unionism and draining the dedication of those who remained.

Nowhere were these dynamics clearer, and the harvest more bitter, than at Inman Mills. In 1937 what was left of UTWA Local 1935 rallied behind the Textile Workers Organizing Committee. A year later, the CIO won an election there by a vote of 295-194. For two years TWOC Local 255 remained active without a contract. In August 1939, plagued by both its inability to accomplish anything locally and the prospect that Local 255 would also return to the AFL, the CIO abandoned the plant. The revived UTWA won the plant in December 1940 by a surprising vote of 502-181, resurrecting old Local 1935 and delivering a contract in March 1941. With a contract in place and a record 73 percent level of support inside the plant, textile unionism seemed to have come to Inman Mills to stay.[38]

Structurally, however, Local 1935 was considerably weaker than anyone suspected. Union support was uneven from department to department, and the conflicts, disappointments, and frustrations of the previous eight years had taken root in complementary ways. With every new crisis, organizing drive, or NLRB election, antiunion workers in the plant became even more hostile to the very idea of textile unionism. Cynicism multiplied among Inman Mills's active unionists, who had already endured two institutional shifts and what they perceived as shoddy treatment from both sets of union officials. Like the leadership cadres of so many other southern locals that reaffiliated with the UTWA between 1938 and 1942, their allegiance to any force or institution outside their own local union hall was questionable. Finally, the vast majority of the workers at Inman Mills were exhausted. Textile unionism, to them, was becoming more a burden than a boon. With every new twist of events that affected the union movement at Inman Mills after 1941, more and more rank-and-file members deserted.

It took eight more years to destroy the Inman Mills local. The process began with a seemingly innocuous workload case, the kind that always set the tone for labor-management relations in southern textiles. Simmering resentment among spinning doffers caused three wildcat strikes in mid–1943.[39] Once the doffers' controversy was settled, battery-fillers began demanding a reduction in their revised workloads. On 2 February 1944, the spinning overseer ordered them to accept new job assignments, at least provisionally. They refused. Two days later, the exasperated plant manager told the entire work force that anyone unwilling to work on assigned jobs would have to leave the premises immediately. Not only did the battery-fillers walk out as a body, but approximately a third of the entire work force also followed.[40]

The strike—which lasted seven weeks—shattered the union movement at Inman Mills. Prounion workers who stayed in the plant felt that they were obeying contractual obligations as well as the general no-strike pledge signed by the AFL for the duration of the war. Those who struck felt they had reached the absolute limits of endurance in what they termed an ongoing stretch-out. Local 1935's leaders were torn. Although they publicly tried to distance themselves from the strike, their sympathy toward the strikers and the anemic quality of their pleas for contractual obedience were obvious. Some officers struck; others stayed on their jobs. During the strike's first week, the actual number working fluctuated daily as individuals drifted back and forth across the lines of debate. Ultimately, some 324 workers—about 40 percent of the plant's production work force—chose to support the strike.[41]

At first, management viewed the strike as yet another of the petty work stoppages that had plagued the plant; they promised full reinstatement without penalty to anyone who would return to work within a week. Few did. After the toll of operating on such a curtailed basis became evident, Inman Mills formally handed the case to the War Labor Board. On 24 March 1944, the Fourth Regional War Labor Board ordered strikers back into the plant under threat of arrest. In the stinging decision that followed, the board declared that it "has too much of importance to do without taking on issues which can and ought to be settled under the grievance procedure of the contract. Neither the Company nor the Union ought to be permitted, just because they prefer it, to cast aside their contract obligations." The War Labor Board ordered both sides to submit the issues precipitating the strike to immediate arbitration, but it also ruled that the 324 remaining strikers had indeed forfeited seniority and benefits and would have to reapply for work through the company's employment office. "The mere recital of the facts of the case is sufficient to show that these workers have no one except themselves to blame for their present predicament," the board concluded. "They have deliberately taken their jobs and their seniority away from themselves."[42]

The situation was much more complicated from the strikers' point of view. In their opinion, the company had by 1944 spent more than a decade stretching out its workers. Joining the AFL had not helped. Joining the CIO had not helped. Appeals to government boards had not helped. Obtaining contractual relations had not helped. To them, the company's order of 4 February was notice of a final showdown between the union movement and Inman Mills, a gauntlet that already-battered unionists could not ignore. The stretch-out at Inman was once again a matter of principle, as before at so many other southern mills. The contract's existence was immaterial, because, strikers argued, the company violated it in either spirit or letter daily. Annie Laura West of Saxon, who knew as much about the formal mechanics of labor-management relations as anyone in South Carolina, captured the moral issues at play in the strike when she noted that "some of my own cousins are 'scabbing' up there and I don't think I'll be claiming them as relatives any more."[43] War Labor Board or no War Labor Board, these were the broad strokes in which Inman strikers painted their struggle in the spring of 1944.

Whichever side actually held the moral high ground in the 1944 strike, the conflict ruptured Local 1935's relationship with the UTWA. After being expelled from the union in September 1944, J. C. Shelton—who had led the Inman local since the mid–1930s—considered steering an independent course, perhaps in association with dissatisfied union workers at Spartan and Startex.[44] Later he decided to try swinging the local once again into the TWUA-CIO, although that was easier said than done. As a TWUA organizer noted, "The workers of the Inman Mills over a long period of time have met with one defeat after another in trying to build an organization." In a mid–1945 election the CIO triumphed by a vote of 340-167, but its strength in the plant remained minimal.[45] In 1947 the TWUA noted that unionists were still being plagued by "opposition within their own ranks" and that despite some concrete improvements in working conditions "they had been unable to build a good substantial dues paying membership."[46]

The UTWA continued to meddle, capitalizing on each and every misstep the TWUA made—and encouraged by Local 731's officers, who remained distrustful of CIO leadership.[47] During the 1947 contract negotiations, a TWUA representative was forced to admit to management that Local 731's membership hung at only 37 percent and to union officials that past history utterly precluded the possibility of a strike. The result was one of the weakest union contracts ever signed in a region known for weak contracts.[48] When it expired in 1948, the UTWA petitioned for a new election. The TWUA immediately sent a team of organizers to rebuild the local, but by then Local 731's officers were ready to desert the TWUA for a second time. Perhaps they hoped to regroup as an independent body, but whatever their plans, they sadly underestimated the numbers of exhausted and embittered workers who were ready to abandon textile unionism completely. In the election of 28 April 1949, the vote was 227 for the TWUA-CIO, 57 for the UTWA-AFL, and 417 for no union at all.[49]

And that was the end of the union movement at Inman Mills. For a few, the vision that had so inspired in earlier years was difficult to abandon. In late 1950, when the TWUA attempted to retrieve Local 731's charter and books, treasurer J. B. Clayton refused to release them. Clayton, as well as J. C. Shelton and other union stalwarts, repeatedly expressed hope for the mill's eventual reorganization; Local 731's officers even suggested that they be allowed to continue paying their union dues in secret. Although state director Charles Auslander was willing to countenance such an arrangement, TWUA treasurer William Pollock balked at the idea of maintaining a local "where we have no members." On 19 January 1951 the TWUA formally revoked Local 731's charter. For the remaining prounion workers at Inman Mills, it was just another betrayal. In a final show of defiance, the former officers of Local 731—including J. C. Shelton, who had witnessed the local's birth in 1933—raided the local's bank account for $250 on the day before Auslander arrived to close it out.[50]

By the late 1940s, the structural estrangement of the southern and northern labor movements was complete. In the wake of the organization of northern industry, both the AFL and the CIO turned increasingly to matters of administration, a process that blurred the distinctions between them and led to their merger in 1954. Furthermore, America's postwar cultural environment—

with anticommunism its centerpiece—proved a cruel turnabout for American unions, legitimizing vicious antiunion sentiment at precisely the moment wartime protections were lifted. Politically, this antiunion sentiment found its fullest expression in the Taft-Hartley Act of 1947, which substantially revised and curtailed union powers previously established under the Wagner Act.[51] Elsewhere, established unions fought desperately to retain their wartime gains. Southern unions found themselves in a particularly vulnerable position, because in most cases they still represented only a fraction of the regional work force.

The AFL virtually abandoned the industrial South. In 1946 the CIO announced one last ambitious attempt to bring southern workers under the union banner: its great Southern Organizing Drive.[52] Although not officially terminated until 1954, "Operation Dixie" was a public failure as early as 1947, when its collapse in textiles was apparent. In Spartanburg—where the CIO drive set up its state headquarters—the TWUA never managed more than a toehold at any plant, losing two early NLRB elections (Arcadia and Fairforest Finishing) and never even making it to elections in four other major campaigns (Lyman, Saxon, Arkwright, and Cowpens Mill).[53]

In the lone textile plant the TWUA did win, the union was literally driven from the mill after a protracted power struggle. The TWUA's Glendale campaign began in December 1946. It had better prospects than earlier efforts. Salaried TWUA representatives worked hand-in-hand with volunteer organizers from neighboring Clifton, where the TWUA still bargained from a position of considerable strength. On 28 February 1947 the TWUA won Glendale by a vote of 388-271, but absentee owner J. L. Stiefel and Sons fought the union aggressively both in the mill and at the bargaining table. In mid–1947 the TWUA's lead negotiator termed the situation "futile." The TWUA filed NLRB charges against the company in early 1948, but the union's certification lapsed while those charges were pending (under new NLRB provisions courtesy of the Taft-Hartley Act). With several union committee members already discharged and the rest exhausted and afraid, the TWUA knew it could never win another election. It withdrew, leaving antiunion scars for years to come.[54]

As a worker and volunteer organizer from neighboring Greenville summarized, Operation Dixie's collapse convinced textile workers across the South "that the whole CIO campaign is a flop, and many of them express their regret that they had ever confided in the CIO."[55] In the spring of 1949, Inman Mills president James A. Chapman sent an account of Local 731's demise, without comment, to Stanley Converse, president of the Clifton Manufacturing Company, one of the last South Carolina mills under TWUA contract. We've done our jobs, Chapman seemed to be saying for himself and other area executives; now it's time for you to do yours.[56]

By mid–1949, Spartanburg County's union movement seemed destined for extinction. Three-quarters of the county's textile workers labored in nonunion plants; the Beaumont and Inman locals had been eviscerated; and the remaining UTWA locals—at Spartan, Startex, and Fairmont—were moribund, decimated by wartime strikes and effectively domesticated by management.[57] TWUA Local 325 at the three Clifton plants had become the last obstacle to a union-free textile industry in Spartanburg County, and it was on Local 325 that the ultimate fate of the Spartanburg union movement came to rest.

8   Last Stand: The Clifton Strike of 1949–50

The six-months' strike at the three mills of the Clifton Manufacturing Company in 1949 and 1950 has no place in the existing historiography of the American South. After all, it occurred in the feckless wake of the most ambitious southern organizing drive in history; in an isolated setting; at the mills of a small, family-owned company—not Burlington, not Cannon; and against the wishes of the parent union involved. Yet the Clifton strike was more than just a random showdown between workers and managers in a South Carolina backwater. Both its local origins and its localized execution bespoke older understandings of unionism and community, understandings that to managers and union officials alike seemed out of place in the postwar era of orderly contractualized labor-management relations.

These understandings were directly descended from the ideals of the 1930s. The scenes enacted at the Cliftons during 1949 and 1950 constituted the concluding act to a drama that had begun sixteen years before. At its best, the textile workers' movement of the 1930s had structured the union into a critical nexus, where it functioned simultaneously to define, maintain, and defend the communities textile workers had labored so hard to build. Elsewhere in Spartanburg County, the movement had been either destroyed or domesticated. By the late 1940s, TWUA Local 325 at the Cliftons was the sole survivor. Nowhere else in Spartanburg County had this peculiar understanding of what unionism could mean been allowed to mature for so long or to such depths.

The early history of unionism at the Clifton plants was not particularly different from that of other southern mills, with the exception of its endurance. UTWA locals 1834 and 1735 at Clifton No. 1 and No. 2 survived the vicissitudes of the mid–1930s largely intact. In 1938, following two threatened strikes over working conditions and a wage reduction, the Textile Workers Organizing Committee won elections at both plants by votes of 237-154 and

201-57.[1] Labor relations appeared placid during 1939, but once it became clear that no contract was forthcoming, prounion workers embarked upon a coordinated program of direct action, culminating in a strike at No. 2 in April 1940.[2] Federal mediators prevented further deterioration only by convincing the company to put a few compromises into writing—a grudging step toward contractual relations.[3] More unfruitful negotiations led to a spinners' strike at No. 1 in April 1941 and a threatened general strike in May.[4] With the union's staying power so evident, the company finally consented to serious negotiations that ended on 10 December 1941 with a contract covering both plants.[5] In mid-1942, Local 325 used a wildcat strike by disgruntled doffers at No. 3 (the so-called Converse mill) to lever itself into a position of power there as well. After escalating the stoppage into a full-scale strike of all three mills, the company consented to an immediate NLRB election, which the TWUA won handily, 355-50. Plant No. 3 came under contract two days later on 9 July 1942.[6]

With company and union both accustomed to such antagonism, contractual relations proved difficult. At least eight wildcat work stoppages disrupted production at the three plants between 1942 and 1944.[7] Both sides repeatedly had to resort to either federal mediation or arbitration in order to settle ongoing workload conflicts.[8] In late 1942, Local 325 secretary Earl Smith reported that "our situation at Clifton continues to go from bad to worse."[9] Smith believed that the company was trying to wear down the union by refusing to settle any grievances at the local level. Management seemed to be making a concerted effort to circumvent contractual channels. Although soon-to-be company president Stanley Converse made "all kinds of promises," his supervisors were "not making any effort to abide by the provisions of the agreement." It was Smith's conclusion that "probably they want us to strike so they can accuse us of violating the agreement, then they will call on the war labor board" and thereby use the culturally sanctioned powers of the government to eviscerate the union.[10]

Within a year, however, the atmosphere at the Cliftons had improved dramatically. By early 1944 it appeared that the company had finally decided to work with the union on the union's terms. Although the reasons for that change of heart remain unclear, managers could not have ignored Local 325's resilience. Textile unionism at the Cliftons had exceptional leadership, both in quality and quantity. Not only did the local have strong men such as H. M. Branch, Earl Smith, W. E. Lands, and Luke Tindall at its helm during the 1930s and 1940s, but it also had a surprisingly large and active pool of shop stewards and committeemen on which to draw.[11] At Inman, a handful of strong leaders had been coupled with hundreds whose loyalties were doubtful, and apathy reigned at Spartan and Tucapau by the mid-1940s. But the Clifton union still functioned on every conceivable level, so much so that even a temporarily empty rung at the bottom of the leadership ladder—such as a shop steward's post in No. 3's cloth room in late 1944—was cause for notice and concern.[12] Local 325's broad-based leadership pool enabled the union to survive at the Cliftons long after it had crumbled at other mills; a TWUA staff member once judged it "the best Local Union in South Carolina."[13] Once Stanley Converse decided to cooperate, labor-management relations assumed an orderly appearance. By 1945 contractual mechanics had become routine at the three plants of the Clifton Manufacturing Company.

By mid-1949, however, the TWUA found itself fighting the most desperate rearguard battle of its existence, both at the Cliftons and across the South. Explanations for this turnabout have never been hard to find. It was the Taft-Hartley Act, or it was the removal of sheltering wartime governmental controls. It was the unpredictable rhythms of textile economics in the postwar decade, or it was the paralysis of the National Labor Relations Board. It was the general political climate of a nation turning away from Rooseveltian ideals, or it was the deserved fate of ignorant, backward southern workers who did not know what unionism meant. In upcountry South Carolina, the battlefield was already bloody. Promising union drives at plants like Lyman, Glendale, and Buffalo had ended in disaster. Strikes and intraunion squabbling steadily tore away at the TWUA's membership in Rock Hill. In notoriously antiunion Greenville, the management of Woodside Mills spent the late 1940s in a continuous effort to promote an all-out union-busting strike against the TWUA. They finally succeeded in mid-1950, erasing the union's only Greenville toehold. And in Cherokee County next door to the Cliftons, the Hamrick and Milliken interests succeeded in crushing the TWUA at Gaffney and Blacksburg during 1946 and 1947 in what arguably remain two of the most vicious labor strikes in southern history.

In this devolving endgame, the TWUA scrambled to salvage whatever it could, while mill owners and managers closed in for what they hoped would be the final kill. In Spartanburg County, the last target was Local 325. Since assuming the presidency of the Clifton company in mid-1945, Stanley Converse had grudgingly played along with the union. He never made contractual relations easy, but neither was he willing to resort to the extreme techniques that so characterized antiunion offensives elsewhere in the South. As both regional and national political climates chilled, however, Converse found him-

Panoramic view of Clifton, 1949, featuring the No. 1 complex. At bottom right is "the flat," where much of the excitement of the 1949–50 strike took place. The No. 1 company store is the balconied building at the picture's center; houses on Main Street and Middle Street are to the left. Mill No. 2 and part of the No. 2 village are visible at upper right. (Courtesy of Converse College)

self under pressure from all sides—especially from South Carolina's other textile manufacturers—to exterminate the TWUA's Clifton stronghold.[14]

Inside the plants, the relatively amicable working relationship between union and company began to deteriorate in late 1947. To the union, it seemed that the company—after several years of working in good faith—had reverted to its former policies: refusing to settle grievances, willfully violating the contract, and, of course, the stretch-out. In this increasingly charged atmosphere, practically anything could have set off a strike at the Cliftons in 1949: job classification problems at No. 1 or ongoing conflict between battery-fillers and an overseer at No. 2.[15] Like grievances were replicated at varying levels of intensity across all departments in all three Clifton mills. That was why what began as a wildcat strike by a dozen loom-fixers at No. 3 quickly escalated into a full-scale war between TWUA Local 325 and the Clifton Manufacturing Company.

The complicated ballet that precipitated the official strike vote on 8 December 1949 had deep roots.[16] Throughout the early spring of 1948, loom-fixers at No. 3 had been talking to their supervisors about "putting on warp boys or cutting down the size of their sections." (Loom-fixers at the Converse mill were required to fix on between 90 and 104 looms and were also responsible for tying on and taking off warps, whereas loom-fixers at No. 1 and No. 2 had the assistance of an extra worker, a "warp boy.") On 28 May 1948, George Adair—former president of Local 325 and shop steward for weaving at No. 3—called his fellow loom-fixers together just as the first shift was giving way to second. When plant manager H. B. Davis went to the weave room tower to investigate, Adair demanded immediate workload adjustments. Davis reminded the twenty-one loom-fixers present of the contractual provisions for filing a grievance, warning Adair in particular that, as shop steward, it was his responsibility to make sure the union adhered to the contract. Adair retorted that "when they put in a grievance the company would put them off or refuse to meet with them" and that grievance procedures took too long anyway. Davis tried to argue Adair back into the contract, but unionist Troy Sisk interrupted "to make their position plain": "They wanted warp boys put on all sections or the jobs cut down to equal a warp boy." After more wrangling, Adair finally agreed to file a formal grievance, and Davis promised to bring the matter up with his superiors over the weekend.[17]

Once again, it seemed that the mechanics of contractual relations had effectively broken down, leaving no other option but direct action. From the company's standpoint, spokespeople for Local 325 were blatantly violating the provisions of the contract. In the union's opinion, the company had been violating the contract in spirit, and occasionally in letter, for some time, thus rendering it null and void insofar as their actions inside the mill were concerned. At heart was an issue of dignity, whether supervisors of the Clifton Manufacturing Company were willing to give workers the minimum respect to which they felt they were entitled—and which those workers had hoped a structured labor-management contract would provide. If contractual provisions failed to ensure workers that respect, then everyone returned to square one.

Week after week of conferences proved unavailing.[18] On 30 June 1948 the loom-fixers agreed among themselves not to tie on any more warps until the company quit stalling; a wildcat strike was averted only after an emergency shop committee meeting and a verbal promise of immediate adjustments from general manager T. I. Stafford.[19] Company officials continued to meet with the No. 3 shop committee, but even after the company admitted that the addition of warp boys might improve work in the weave room, neither side could agree on precisely how the workloads should be reconfigured. On 24 February 1949 both sides handed over the controversy to an arbitrator, who sustained the union's position on 17 May 1949. He ordered the company to add warp boys on all sections.[20]

That should have ended the matter, but as weeks passed and the company did nothing, tempers again began to rise. On 18 July 1949 the company finally added warp boys in the second weave room, raising the loom-fixers to 108 or 116 looms each from 91 to 97 and eliminating one loom-fixing job. On 15 August the company restarted the smaller forty-inch looms that had been standing idle in the first weave room. It also added warp boys, eliminated another loom-fixing position on each shift, and raised loom assignments from ninety-three to 139 and 140. The loom-fixers immediately claimed that the new assignments made their jobs even more onerous than they had been. Conferences between managers and the incensed loom-fixers came and went during August, September, and October. In the meantime, the loom-fixers worked at their new assignments, protesting continually.[21]

At 7 A.M. on 31 October 1949, the beleaguered loom-fixers at No. 3 began a guerilla campaign against the Clifton Manufacturing Company. As the first-shift fixers entered the mill, Robert Emory of the first weave room and Troy Sisk of the second told their supervisors that they were unilaterally returning to their old job assignments. Apparently under orders from Stafford or Converse (who seem to have been expecting something), weaving overseer P. H. Dickson informed all twenty-seven loom-fixers on all three shifts that their new assignments remained unchanged. Under orders from George Adair, the two first-shift loom-fixers who had been reduced to spare hands returned to their old fixing jobs. Dickson retaliated by sending them home for insubordination, whereupon all but one of the first-shift loom-fixers retreated to the No. 3 tower. They stayed there until 3 P.M. and then went home as a group.[22]

For the next week the loom-fixers at No. 3 played a cat-and-mouse game with management in what amounted to a sit-down strike. At the beginning of each shift, they would enter the plant, assume the starting positions on their old jobs, and turn their pick clocks. A spokesman—usually Troy Sisk or George Adair—would tell the supervisors that they "were still waiting for a Conference," and then the entire group would walk out. Sometimes they would go to the tower, sometimes (if the tower was too cold) to the men's dressing room. Sometimes they would disappear entirely. Sometimes they could be found elsewhere in the mill. At 10 A.M. on Thursday, P. H. Dickson caught Robert Emory in earnest conversation with two weavers, and half an hour later loom-fixer Frank James was sighted on the spare floor, talking to another weaver. Second-shift loom-fixers fanned out and were spotted by supervisors in both the spinning and slashing departments. Everyone watched everyone else. Only one loom-fixer out of twenty-seven remained working. A third-shift nonunion loom-fixer privately told his supervisor that "he would like to work and was willing to work, but that he was afraid to because somebody might knock him in the head." Another nonunion fixer even asked for a few days off on account of his bad heart, complaining that he could not stand the ever-rising pressure inside the mill. By 10:30 P.M. Wednesday night, 759 flags were up (looms not running due to mechanical malfunctions) and seven warps were off at No. 3.[23]

The loom-fixers hoped that the growing number of stopped-off looms would pressure the company into an immediate conference and, hopefully, some immediate action. By 10:30 A.M. on Monday, 7 November, more than a thousand looms were idle at No. 3. At 8:45 A.M. the next morning, supervisors officially discontinued weaving, and two hours later they began to shut down machinery in the slashing and carding departments. At 11 A.M. the entire work force of No. 3 was sent home.[24]

That day—8 November 1949—the strike also spread to plants Nos. 1 and 2. On the night before, loom-fixers at these mills had voted to back up their comrades in what even some unionists were calling a sit-down strike.[25] Within a few days, Stanley Converse closed both No. 1 and No. 2 as well. The TWUA and company officials convened three meetings in an attempt to settle the crisis and negotiate a new contract. "All they have offered is a renewal of the Old Agreement," a TWUA staffer complained.[26] Calling the existing contract "perhaps the worst around," TWUA state director Charles Auslander declared that "the company has given evidence that they intend to, if possible, break the union."[27] The old contract expired at midnight on 8 December, and the following day the members of Local 325 voted overwhelmingly to strike the plants.[28]

This was not a strike that the TWUA expected or even wanted.[29] Once it was in progress, however, everyone understood how much rode upon it. On the scene, E. L. Smith begged the international union for funds "in order to save one of the few and oldest Locals in the State. We know that it will be a severe blow to the Organizing efforts in South Carolina if for the sake of a few thousand dollars this Local is allowed to fold up."[30] The strike's first month passed peaceably. Everyone marked time while Stanley Converse tried to operate No. 1 using only his supervisors. Strikers picketed the plants, held rallies, and received food, fuel, and medicine courtesy of the union commissaries established at each mill, and TWUA officials made a few desultory calls on management.[31]

A month later, however, both the stakes of the battle and the rules of the game changed dramatically. After more than a week of rumors, Stanley Converse announced on 10 January that he planned to reopen the mills "as soon as possible" and "for the mutual benefit of all persons involved." Contract negotiations would resume only after workers had returned to their jobs and following an ill-defined "period of observation." A second memo notified workers that the mills would officially reopen on Tuesday, 24 January, at 8 A.M.[32]

On the day that Stanley Converse announced his intention to reopen the mills, the question at Clifton ceased to be one of industrial collective bargaining, of workloads and contracts. It was reduced overnight to a much simpler proposition: Were the Cliftons a cohesive working-class community, united behind the institutional superstructure of TWUA Local 325, or were they not? Competing answers to that question were reflected in both the large number of strikers who remained out and the subsequent experiences of the small number who went back in. The strike became an elemental moral contest, sweeping along in its path every other facet of human life in the Cliftons, from sex to race to religion. It affected workers' conceptions of themselves and each other at the deepest levels. The issue had come down to this: What did community really mean? As long as the appearance of labor relations remained calm, the prevailing understanding of community as union could be maintained without overt conflict. In this context, the strike was transformed into an ongoing test of the utility, the durability, and, ultimately, the cost of what we may call "community unionism."[33]

Of workers at all of Spartanburg County's mills, the men and women at Clifton were uniquely armed for the struggle they faced in the early months of 1950. Union membership was higher than at any of the TWUA's other organized South Carolina plants, and so, arguably, was the level of institutional identification between Local 325 and the broader worker-constructed collective. Local 325's leadership had handled the various crises and issues of the 1940s deftly and avoided the schismatic politics that hamstrung unionists at Inman Mills. The Cliftons had mostly avoided the wartime influx of commuting workers. The company's three sprawling villages held a more sufficient labor reservoir, and Stanley Converse's ongoing policy of preferential hiring—first from the villages, then from the immediate neighborhood, and only then from elsewhere—cushioned Local 325 from the textile work force's 1940s demographic makeover. Not only were understandings of "community" and "union" inherited from the 1930s still in place, but the bounds of the collective of workers and their families who shared these understandings—structured into TWUA Local 325—also remained largely intact.

As at Saxon in 1935 and 1936, every resource went into the struggle. All the social conventions that enabled Cliftonians to get along on a daily basis—the cosmetics of mill-village life—were cast aside. Name-calling was the most evident symptom of this social state.[34] The patter was designed to keep striker morale up and strikebreaker morale down, especially on picket lines, but there were darker sides to the verbal abuse that rang back and forth across the Cliftons every day of the strike's second phase. Race and sex—the two issues that so complexly underlay southern social mores—surfaced immediately.[35] Strikers played the race card shamelessly, labeling one strikebreaker who was bringing black workers through the gates a "nigger-loving skunk" and telling another that he was "more black than a negro" and "ought to have to go to church with them and live with them."[36] Likewise, sex—crass, violent, and illicit—suddenly became a public matter. Boyce Blackwood claimed that a striker "pulled his trouser legs up to his knees and yelled 'you goddamn street walker'" at his wife Pearl.[37] Striker Ola Bagwell publicly warned one strikebreaker that "he had better stay down here and watch his wife, she might slip off and go to the fair again," while picket captain Carrie Justice urged that strikebreaker Leona Tisdale "put a sack over your face, pull your dress up to your knees and shake that thing for old rooster."[38]

It all added up not only to an expression of long-held resentments against certain workers by certain others but also to a general sentiment (on the union side) that strikebreaking workers were no longer due the conventional respect of day-to-day social relations. It was this understanding, this intention to give disrespect to those who crossed picket lines, that caused certain male pickets to urinate at precisely the spot under the No. 2 bridge where strikebreaking women weavers in No. 2's upper weave room could see them.[39] As one picket captain asked, "I'd be ashamed if I was a scab. Why don't you stay out with us good respectable people?"[40]

In short, strikebreakers forfeited their right to a place in the social order of the Cliftons, a place that had always afforded certain degrees of mutuality and tolerance, even protection. As shop steward Furman Mabry later recalled, "Now if you'd ever done anything that people didn't know about, when you crossed that picket line, it all come out right there—you knowed what people had done and what they hadn't done." Mabry knew of one man, hired from outside the village to serve as a watchman during the strike, who had secretly "run a car off at Lawson's Fork" in order to collect the insurance. "That come out when he crossed that picket line."[41] A man at No. 2 who had been receiving long-distance medical care for sterility discovered that suddenly everyone in the village, in addition to the postal clerks responsible for mailing his samples, knew about his condition.[42] As a picket captain yelled over a loudspeaker to a female strikebreaker, "You had a baby before you married, didn't you? . . . It was a yellow girl. Everybody knows it. If your brother was living you wouldn't be down here. He would beat you to death."[43]

Anywhere they went, strikebreakers could expect abuse. It is impossible to overstate how coordinated, intensive, and continual the verbal attacks were. On 17 February, for instance, strikebreaker Viola Mason tried to cross the No. 1 village to see her friend Mary Carr. On her way down the street, two young girls saw her and shouted, "Look at the scab going to see another scab. Why don't you hold your head back, it might rain and drown you." While she stood on Carr's porch, a passerby cursed her, as did one of the original two girls on her way home. Carr was not in. As Mason turned to leave, neighbor Caldwell White called her "B. O. Mason" and added, "They don't want you over there— you stink too bad." Minutes later she was verbally harassed by several members of the ardently prounion Kirby family. Four days later, Mason ventured out to get some milk from a neighbor. On the way down the street, Mrs. Luther Tindall called Mason a scab from her porch; on the way back, Edna Bible called her "B. O. Mason"; and just as she stepped into her own yard, Caldwell White again began to harangue her.[44]

Beyond the realm of the verbal, the favorite weapon of the Clifton strikers was the automobile. By 1949, private cars had only just begun to come into common ownership in southern mill villages, but they, too, provided an arena for extending Local 325's efforts at enforcing community solidarity. In an explicit modern version of the traditional southern charivari, striking workers patrolled village streets—especially at odd hours of the night—honking their horns, sometimes alone, sometimes in parade formation.[45]

Most obviously, such conduct amounted to a highly visible but basically harmless act of protest against villagers who were crossing picket lines. In practical terms, strikers hoped that a constant nighttime ruckus would keep fearful strikebreakers awake and sap their ability to work. At bottom, however, these were acts of ownership by Clifton workers who sought to delineate and patrol the precise geographic bounds of the community they claimed to represent. The charivaris not only covered village streets on which strikebreakers lived but also symbolically covered territory such as the schoolhouse, the churches, and the residences of the Cliftons' few professional men and women, as well as the rural neighborhoods that had strikebreaking reputations.[46]

Union pickets at the No. 1 flat, early 1950, as taken from the No. 1 watchtower by a company supervisor. (Courtesy of Michael Hembree)

If control of village streets was such a prize, then denying strikebreakers access to those same streets held a power of its own. Strikers frequently stepped out in front of strikebreakers as they drove, forcing them to stop. Sometimes they tried to coax them from their cars.[47] Strikebreakers—especially supervisors—learned to check their driveways every morning for nails and tacks. It mattered little to some strikers that many of these men were not covered by the contract and therefore had to work or face immediate discharge. It had ceased to be a union-versus-management conflict. It was a community-versus-company conflict, and anyone who crossed the lines from within the community, regardless of their job in the mill, was deemed guilty of having violated the principles that the strikers were using the union to defend. Thus, in the month of January alone, supervisory families such as the Pliny Shropshiers, Ben Dearyburys, and George McCarleys—all resident in the community for decades—found their driveways vandalized.[48]

Whether verbal taunts or automotive assaults were involved, the compressed social geography of the villages came constantly into play. Much of the company housing at Clifton was duplex. Some homes were occupied by single large families, but most held two families at once. Trouble came when strikers and strikebreakers found themselves co-resident. Indeed, the thin walls dividing them could become just another weapon in the strikers' arsenal. According to staunch company supporter J. E. Barber, the striking Otis Seals family made life "miserable" for strikebreakers living near them, and the strikebreaking Fred White family found itself targeted by "a continuous disturbance" consisting of "loud talking, laughing, beating on [the] connecting door with their fists," and even firecrackers at the hands of their prounion neighbors.[49]

Porches were crucial. Traditionally, socialization in mill communities was sustained on the wide company-house porches, one of the few amenities of mill-village life. In what could approach ritual, workers and their families would sit on their porches in the late afternoons and evenings, calling to and visiting with one another. In the strike situation, porches became fortresses from which pro- and antiunion workers launched private offensives.[50] Intraporch shouting matches became common as the strike wore on. One evening in February, as strikebreakers Jesse Tinsley and Annie Lou Mullinax talked from their respective porches, striker Geraldine Sullivan came out onto a third porch and began railing against the two in a verbal fight that ultimately involved two other families on two other porches. Later, Mullinax complained that Sullivan "starts a fuss with her or any member of her family every time they stick their heads out of the house. . . . And George Sanders wife [on a sixth porch] sits around and eggs it on."[51]

One gauge of how deeply the strike tore into the Cliftons was the role played by children. To some, children's conduct became the strike's most controversial aspect. To others, it was a natural by-product of an action predicated on total polarization of the community. In a conflict in which one of the union's most widely distributed leaflets proclaimed "Striking Is a Family Affair," it stood to reason that children would enter the struggle as much as anyone else.[52] The ten-year-old son of one striker was accused of putting up signs in the garage the two families shared that were aimed at his strikebreaking neighbor. Another strikebreaker reported that two of his neighbors' sons, always marble afficionados, had started using slingshots to pepper his house during the night. Some strikebreakers had to arrange private transportation to take their children to and from school after some strikers' children graduated from taunts to physical attacks. And one strikebreaker even reported being called an "old yellow scab" by a three-year-old boy at the company store to the approving laughs of the child's parents and siblings.[53]

The physical toll this abuse took on strikebreakers was enormous. At the end of January, Rollie D. Shropshier, Sr., of No. 1—for decades one of Stanley Converse's most trusted supervisors—finally collapsed. "This is to let you know why I failed to stay at work when I went back in," an agonized Shropshier wrote to Converse, "as I told you on the day I first come out that I was not phisically able to be worried with a mob like that."[54] In part, that is what the strikers were trying to accomplish. Every single strikebreaker deterred from entering the plants represented an immense symbolic victory for the strikers. Even if they kept working, physically wrecked strikebreakers were, at bottom, not very effective strikebreakers. That was the brutal logic behind the nighttime disturbances, whether in duplex housing, at the plant gates, or on the streets. "I bet you every night seems like a million years," a picket captain smugly noted. "They go home, can't sleep and eat. We know why. They pass that picket line."[55]

The strike divided families, shattered friendships, and revealed previously hidden fault lines deep in Clifton's social terrain. Mary Carr, for instance, was from one of Clifton's oldest families and worked for the company as its payroll manager. She personified Clifton's elite in what she had always thought of as the best ways, and she was totally unprepared for the barrage of hatred that came her way. Strikers tacked her driveway and called her a "White Devil" and a "low-life heifer." Nothing that anyone had ever said to her in the previously ordered rhythms of mill-village life had given her any reason to suspect she would become such a target. In early February, however, a chance encounter with two strikers solved the mystery. Carr was passing down the street when striker Evelyn Hylemon called to Bertie "Pete" Holcombe, "There she is, Pete, tell 'er what she said, tell 'er where she can hear you." Holcombe replied with stunning brevity: "She knows what she said—she called us White Trash."[56] In the textile South, there was no more demeaning epithet. In short, the Clifton strike revealed social divisions within the Cliftons' community structures that in less anguished times remained wholly or partially submerged. Bertie Holcombe was part of the portion of the local population that defined itself through TWUA Local 325, and Mary Carr was not.

Three other groups who did not belong to Local 325 also found their social positions within village life clarified: blacks, outsiders, and supervisors. Blacks, the majority of whom labored outside the plant in jobs excluded by the contract, faced the dismal choice of either continuing to work or being fired. "Community," as defined by the majority of Clifton's white unionists, did not include blacks, and so it followed logically that the labor contract (itself a partial ratification of that understanding of community) would not cover black jobs. As Anderson Gray, a carpenter's helper, later recalled, "I couldn't join [the union]—I worked on the outside. . . . When the mill struck, that didn't include my job, so I had to work on." Most blacks chose to keep working.[57] In early March, supervisor C. W. Wooten barely forestalled a mass revolt by black workers at No. 2, who were beginning to fear for their physical safety. Unidentified strikers even told a black cook from the village's most respected African American family that "they would drag her out" if she continued to babysit for a strikebreaker's children.[58]

Although not directly involved in the strike, nonresidents who had Clifton business were also subject to striker discipline. At various points strikers threatened to boycott a local insurance salesman (unless his wife ceased working), a local auto shop (unless its proprietor refused to handle strikebreaker's cars), and even one of the mill's machinery suppliers.[59] Because all of Clifton's supervisors lived in the villages as a matter of company policy, and many, perhaps most, had worked their ways up from production jobs and had friends and relatives on the picket lines, their positions were volatile.[60] At least four low-level supervisors stayed out in deference to Local 325; others who worked harbored well-known prounion sentiments. All faced abuse at the hands of strikers.[61]

Blacks, outsiders, and supervisors were at least partially structured out of the understanding of the collective that Local 325 had come to represent, and so unionists at least partially expected their conduct. Not so for production workers, who implicated themselves in the strike by choice.[62] As during the strikes of the 1930s, replacement workers hired from outside the village faced the worst ire. A picket captain invited strikers to come and "watch these country hoogers coming in over us. They are the backbone of the world but they will cross the picket lines."[63] In the case of scabs from neighboring Cowpens, the events of the mid–1930s resonated even more strongly. Memories ran long in textile communities. When Cowpens workers began to appear on the scene, the wrath of the union community came down squarely upon them. These were the very ones who had taken jobs away from Cowpens Mill unionists during the strikes of 1934, and no one at the Cliftons had forgotten. "Cowpens scabs. Double-crossing scabs. You know what they done at Cowpens," one union picket called. "They scabbed on them there and come down here and scabbed" as well.[64]

With Local 325's deep psychological roots in the local population, it stood to reason that the Clifton strike would disrupt the institutional life of all other community organizations. Hardest hit, of course, were the churches. Strikebreakers were harassed to and from church, and their homes were vandalized while they were away; strikers even urged supervisors to withdraw from church life entirely because their presence was "tearing it up."[65] Part of the problem was that many working supervisors were, as self-styled community leaders, also church activists. As shop steward Furman Mabry once hollered over the public address system, "If people wanted to see a bunch of scabs, just go to church tonight." The conflation of strikebreaking, supervising, and church-going, like everything else in the strike, could become intensely personal. One morning picket captain Ola Bagwell confronted Mary Barber—a prominent Methodist and member of a long-standing supervisory family—as she headed for the mill. Bagwell asked why Barber "didn't get out and do her mission work Sunday afternoon" and then answered the question: "I know the reason, you were afraid to, you old freckle face hussey, you ain't nothing, you old low down rat, thief, cheat, robber, good for nothing."[66]

Sunday morning services began to resemble armed camps, especially at No. 2, where the leadership of Second Baptist Church was almost equally divided between union leaders and supervisors. Weaving overseer George McCarley later recalled the result from his perspective: "Some of the deacons that was in the church . . . belonged to the union, and when you went in the gate down there . . . you was anything that they wanted you to be: a rascal, or a S.O.B., or anything else. On Sunday morning . . . the preacher would ask, 'Brother So-and-so, will you lead us in prayer?' Well, that fellow, he might have called me a S.O.B. on Friday afternoon." McCarley stayed away from church for more than a decade thereafter.[67]

In this climate, pro- and antiunion observers alike were amazed by how little physical violence actually occurred. Unionists and strikebreakers swore out dozen of warrants against each other for threats and verbal assaults, but physical assaults were few.[68] Most that did occur seem to have stemmed from personal grievances as much as strike activity and took place outside the mill villages.[69] Few were reported to the police, even fewer went to trial, and only a handful resulted in convictions. Perhaps the most provocative incident occurred at Cherokee County's Daniel Morgan mill village, where a female striker reportedly attacked a member of the highway patrol with an axe after he had ordered a group of women to cease putting up signs warning against scab-bing at the Cliftons.[70] With these exceptions, however, all the damage inflicted during the Clifton strike was either economic or psychological. And that, especially the latter, was enough.

As the strike wore on, the company and the union played a game of chess across the villages, the company selectively trying to recruit new strikebreak-ers from the more doubtful ranks of strikers, the union trying to enforce its picket lines in the same manner. For the union, that meant constant surveil-lance as well as circumspection. Too little attention could allow a wavering striker to desert unnoticed, and too much pressure could drive one into the company's arms. When it seemed that a striker was considering bolting, he or she invariably received serious personal attention from the union. Union-ists watched both supervisors and their houses to see who was visiting or be-ing visited. On an evening in late January, for instance, spinner Mary Wyatt went to her overseer's home to tell him that she would be in the following Monday; before she had gotten back down the hill, she was accosted by strik-ing neighbors Toy and Hazel Whitt and Willis and Maud Ogle, who pleaded with her for almost twenty minutes to change her mind.[71] After it became common knowledge that Maurice White of Gaffney had decided to commute to a strikebreaker's job, more than fifty Clifton unionists made the thirty-mile round trip to dissuade him.[72] Friends, relatives, neighbors, and strangers were all involved in these private attempts to hold the picket line. After weaver F. D. Horn made the decision to return to work, his brother-in-law Arnold Dickson visited him in a vain attempt to keep him out. When Horn reiterated his in-tention, Dickson "told him that if he (Horn) waked up and found his tires cut, cow dead, or his window lights knocked out don't blame me."[73]

The responses gathered by company officials as they canvassed the villages provide perhaps the most revealing testimony of what the strike meant to individual rank-and-file Clifton workers. Although the company did recruit a few new strikebreakers this way, for the most part the workers they inter-viewed knew what crossing the picket line meant and were unwilling to take that step. It was all very complex. Mrs. Denver Clark of No. 1, for instance, told T. I. Stafford that "there was too much disturbance 'down there'—she could hear them at No. 2 from her house." Mrs. Clark told Stafford that her family "wouldn't mind" returning once the strike was settled, but that "they couldn't take all the yelling and the things they said—she didn't like having so many people 'feel bad at her.'" Her sister-in-law, a third-shift spinner, also told Stafford that she would return "as soon as they get it settled. . . . I miss the

money but would rather have a union," Mrs. John Clark said simply, then added what "having the union" meant to her in practical terms: "I would rather
have the friends."[74]

Down at No. 2, overseers hand-delivered recruitment notices in late February and early March to several dozen workers. Only one definitely agreed to
return to the mill; the rest held their ground, for various reasons and with
widely varying levels of commitment. Corene Whitt told her supervisor "that
she was ready to return to work but that . . . she was afraid that they may do
something to her or her home." Nannie Worthy "said that she wanted to go
back to work but that she guessed not under the conditions." Union committeeman Scoval Baker replied that although he did not approve of much striker conduct "he had two girls and he did not want anyone calling them names
on account of him returning to work." Lois Vaughn said "she was ready and
wanted to come back to work but that she could not cross the picket line for
someone might tell her of some meanness she had done in the past." Ella Gray,
however, said "she had too many friends on [the] outside to go back to work"
and that "she wanted to be where she could hold her head up and speak to
everybody" when the strike was over. Pauline Lee's mother declared that "she
had rather her girls would walk the streets and beg than to go back to work and
cross the picket line." Horace Coleman said "he sure would like to see things
settled but that he wanted to see the working man get everything that he could
because when he became old he had no one to care for him." Arlie Stapleton
accused the bearers of the notice of "running around with papers" trying to
"knock [the union] out of a contract." Jess Thornton said "he could not 'scab'
on the Lord and he sure would not 'scab' on his fellow-man." And Nellie Frady
concluded that "she was not ready until a contract was signed as this was the
only thing left for the working class of people." Some men and women had
gone so far with Local 325 that they found turning back inconceivable.[75]

Loyalty and betrayal, conviction and coercion, shattered friendships and
broken confidences, social vision and class division exposed for all to see, community solidarity of a sort and for a price, hearkening back to seven decades
of mill-village life and nearly two decades of unionism at the Cliftons—all
these amounted to the private transcript of the TWUA's Clifton strike of 1949
and 1950. In a very real sense, they represent in their totality what the strike
meant to the men and women of Clifton. Yet it is important to remember that
while these dramas were playing out at the local level, other proceedings—the
official record of the strike as preserved in news media accounts and company and union records—were moving forward as well.

In late December, Charles Auslander described his frustration in trying to negotiate a settlement: "Mr. Converse . . . is possibly one of the worst people I have ever had to do business with. You can't get a definite answer or anything out of him. His actions are kiddish and ridiculous. While I realize that this strike is a hardship to the people and a financial burden to the International union . . . , Converse has given us nothing at all to give to the people. If anything, he has tried to subtract from our present agreement."[76] Company officials continued to hold out hope that the strike was gradually weakening. Never did the trickle of strikers back into the mills achieve greater volume, but neither did it subside entirely, and it, combined with strikebreakers recruited from elsewhere, posed a serious threat to the strike's indefinite continuation. In late March—when the company had about three hundred "productive workers" reporting each day—the TWUA finally filed failure-to-bargain charges against the company with the NLRB. That brought Converse back to the negotiating table.[77] On 25 April 1950 both sides finally signed a new contract.

The settlement itself was, to TWUA officials at least, a severe compromise, but as Charles Auslander noted, "We were able to save our union." Clifton unionists certainly celebrated the event.[78] Throughout the summer and early fall of 1950, the TWUA was occupied with administrative battles in trying to get all of its members back into the plants. In a stunning arbitration victory the union managed to reinstate all but four of nearly one thousand strikers.[79] By Christmas of 1950, all facets of the Clifton strike had been resolved—at least on the official level.

In the hearts and minds of the participants, however, the deep breaches of community occasioned by the strike would take more than arbitration to heal. During the strike, the polarization of the Cliftons had been nearly total.[80] "Most of the people felt so strong one way or the other," paymaster Betty Hughes Carr recalled. "You were either for it or you were against it," her sister-in-law Mary Carr added. To the Carrs, the actions of the prounion majority amounted to an inconceivable rent in the fabric of the community they had known all their lives. The same was true from the union perspective: That some would even think of crossing picket lines established by neighbors was a source of outrage. Looking back after nearly half a century, unionist Ruth Barber summed up the sensation in one sharp word: "Bitterness. You felt like where you were standing up for something to better things, and you felt like, well, they were going against that."[81]

Thus, to striker Delbert Willis, the crux of the matter was that those who crossed the picket lines "wouldn't cooperate with us."[82] With stakes as high as they obviously were, the matter of not cooperating represented a serious break in community relations that no signing of a mere labor agreement could ever heal. "Let's get a good contract and get back in that mill[,] then we will all be friends together," a picket captain urged his friends and neighbors during the strike. "As it is somebody has already lost their friends," he added. Another picket presciently noted, "Everybody on the outside will remember them, working against the people like they do."[83]

The union's victory celebrations ebbed, leaving on both sides of the union divide a profound and painful ambivalence still evident half a century later. "I don't think most of them's ever got over it," said former striker Elbert Stapleton. "It was a sore spot, to a certain extent, for a long, long time," unionist Georgia Seals admitted. "It still is, a little."[84] Most chose silence as the most effective medicine—but not everyone. As Pauline Bible noted, "Every now and then, you know, it will come up, 'Well, you *did* go in and work against us,' you know, or something like that. We don't have no words over it, but still, you know, every once and awhile it will come up."[85]

The problem was how to reconstruct community in the aftermath. To live as openly divided as Clifton residents had during the strike proved untenable, especially because both unionists and strikebreakers knew, as a condition of ending the strike, that they would all soon be living and working side by side as before. Both sides attempted to pick up the pieces. In essence, they tried to restore to the Cliftons the understanding of community that had existed before 1933, an understanding rooted in kinship and neighborhood and stripped of the ideological ramifications that community as unionism had brought. Never again would the union command the communal authority of the 1930s and 1940s. As the strike revealed, the cost was just too high. Even as the most diehard unionists came to grips with such post-strike realities, changes in the Clifton mills' work force and villages steadily undermined the near total identification of village–work force–union that had undergird the Clifton strike. Following the regional trend, Clifton Manufacturing began to sell its company housing in 1952. As older workers retired and younger ones began to choose more lucrative employment elsewhere, the number of mill-village residents actually working in the mills declined steadily. In their places, of course, were commuters who had little or no stake in Clifton village life. Within only a few years of the strike, Local 325 had become just a labor union, its role confined to contractual mechanics inside the mill, its membership stagnant and its morale anemic.[86]

Ibera Holt, a former Clifton worker, was postmaster at Converse at the time of the strike. She remembered her days in the mill during the 1930s and sided quietly with the union. "We don't forget that it happened—we know that it happened—but we don't let it interfere with our feelings," she later explained. "We just accept it and try as best we can. But you can't forget something that's happened, once it's happened. It's like driving a nail in a board. You can pull that nail out, but that hole is going to be there. And that's the way it is with forgetting things. You can remove the bitterness, but you can't remove the fact that it happened."[87] In the wake of so many disappointments, the industrial South became a land of holes, a thin horizon of silences and shattered dreams.

In all the years that the Clifton mills sustained human life on the banks of the Pacolet, there were two events that inhabitants agreed defined their lives together in moments of collective anguish. The first was the great flood of 1903 in which sixty or more Clifton residents perished. The second was the strike of 1949 and 1950. Each marked the generation it touched, leaving an indelible imprint on village memory "because it damaged things and tore up things, the flood did—and the strike tore up some things too."[1]

What obtained in Clifton in 1949 and 1950—and in hundreds of other communities during the heady years from 1933 through 1937—was the articulation, in battle, of a social vision rooted in a particular culture. This culture was predicated upon a mutuality rooted, in turn, in poverty and in a specific socioeconomic milieu: the southern textile mill village. It was at best an ambivalent medium. Mill-village culture operated in tandem with (and ultimately at the sufferance of) the mill system itself. The space for protest or debate was always limited. Even in its best moments, village life informed workers' experiences in such ways that certain goals and tactics were rendered inconceivable or at least undesirable. And yet it was precisely this culture that supported mill workers' aspirations. The transcendent value of mill-village culture lay in the extent to which it reflected the best in human endeavor. In places like Clifton and Saxon and Tucapau, the mutuality of relationships provided the only workable defense. In this, Spartanburg's workers—and the southern textile world they inhabited—were not so far removed from their counterparts elsewhere. Thus, the story of Spartanburg's textile workers lies at the heart of the Western industrial experience.

It is appropriate at this juncture to specify precisely what Spartanburg's textile workers did and did not attempt. At no point in their struggles did they ever try to break out of the mill-village system. They attacked its most glaring inequities, but escape from the mills was not their goal. Rather, they sought to take the best of what they knew and enlarge upon that knowledge, with the union's help, so as to transform their lives and worlds. Their struggle was for the soul of the mill village. That they attempted to further this struggle through an alliance with organized labor is not, under the circumstances of the 1930s and 1940s, surprising. More significant is that on so many occasions they merged private struggles with public acts in order to catapult their hopes into general view. Prompted by a social and political environment only a bit more encouraging than that to which they were accustomed and by their own increasingly desperate straits, they gave themselves permission to engage in what they knew was serious work.

In short, the mutualities of the mill village provided a basis for community unionism, a unionism grounded in the particular, not only in the particulars of factory life but also informed at every level by a localized understanding of what constituted the collective. The working men and women of Spartanburg County knew what they wanted not because their union leaders or their employers or anyone else told them so. Rather, they possessed experiential knowledge—at first courtesy of their shared lives and later by virtue of their shared struggle—that their goals were necessary for the preservation of basic dignity. The strikebound Cliftons were not so much unionized communities as they were industrialized communities acting as a unit under what happened to be a union flag.

Union officials rarely understood how, for most southern workers, most of the time, allegiance to the union—any union—was a pragmatic decision, a tactical step. Even in communities like the Cliftons where a local union became an entrenched part of neighborhood life, what developed in the textile South was not a "union culture" (as historians have observed in any number of northern and midwestern industrial cities). It was, rather, a realignment—a refining—of preexisting cultural elements under union auspices. Seen from afar, the sudden advances and retreats southern workers made during the 1930s do indeed seem quixotic, even (at their worst) self-defeating. The internal record of the Clifton strike lays nothing more bare than the underlying complexities of public protest. Is this class consciousness? Is it autonomy? Is it, in its evocation of rights and privileges within the prevailing system, mere articulation of negotiated loyalties, the necessary give-and-take of paternalism?

None of these ways of viewing struggle are very helpful in understanding what happened at the Cliftons in 1949 and 1950. The fact that human lives are immersed and encoded within systems—social, cultural, and economic—beyond their immediate control seems beyond dispute. Nor does our understanding that within these systems men and women struggle to carve out their own lives, spheres in which autonomy—to at least some degree—may prevail. We may call this condition of daily existence "contingency," in which the possibilities for direct assault on the inequities of life fluctuate unevenly from moment to moment and place to place. What still seemed possible at the Cliftons in 1949 was only a faint and lingering dream downriver at Pacolet Mills. The strike itself, both in its origins and its execution, repeatedly bewildered union officials, for whom the mechanics of wage raises, work assignments, and arbitration had all but eclipsed real knowledge of industrial life.

In this light, the myriad conflicts of the 1930s—not just in Spartanburg County—take on new significance. Beneath the sanctioning power of Roosevelt's New Deal, American workers suddenly perceived opportunities to address their living and working conditions at breadths and depths previously inconceivable. In city after city, town after town, and industry after industry they attempted new alliances with employers, neighbors, unions, and federal and state governments. They experimented with new tactics: the sit-down, the slowdown, strikes, boycotts, and appeals to federal agencies. The modern script of orderly, contractual relations between workers and their employers was not yet written, or at least not yet accepted by workers. They tried anything and everything. The significance of their actions was local but not provincial. What does it mean, in historical terms, to exchange long-standing fear for the kind of hope that generates action? The "labor movement" in Spartanburg County was really a series of insurgencies fueled by similar circumstances but always particular in both context and execution. In 1934, past losses had increased the barrier of fear at Woodruff far beyond anything workers at Clifton could imagine. What looked like the proverbial window of opportunity at Spartan seemed shut on workers at Pelham and Chesnee. The leadership that distinguished the Tucapau local had no counterpart at Arkwright or Jackson Mill. Any understanding of how hope and fear make their appearances in public life must rest on the particularities of struggle: *one* mill village, *one* strike, *one* striker.

The Saxon conflict of 1935 and 1936 is a case in point. Just as the strike constituted the high-water mark of external protest in the Saxon community, so did it also represent the highest moment of community mobilization. According to Beatrice Norton, then an enthusiastic striker:

> We had a good time! . . . We enjoyed it. *Every family* was joined together as a unit, a group, as one. And we really enjoyed each other. We learned a lot about our neighbor. We learned about their problems—if there was one sick in the family we knew about it, went to see them, we took things to

them that we had to provide for them. We sat up with them, we'd wait on them, and things of that sort. . . . It brought people together as never before. . . . After that strike, I knew everyone's first name, all their children's names—if they had a cat or dog I could tell you their names! That's how close it took us.[2]

So close, in fact, that even expulsion from the village could not entirely efface ties forged during the strike. The Saxon village was surrounded by the independent, railroad-dominated neighborhoods of Hayne, Una, and Spartanburg's West End, and it was there that many Saxon activists later found refuge. Together, and assisted by the defiant leadership of the Saxon Baptist Church, they maintained a tenuous fellowship for decades thereafter.

But that was as far as community unionism could take Saxon workers in the wake of the collapse of the broader union movement of the 1930s. The Saxon strike ended with John A. Law's promise to remove Marjorie Potwin from the mill's payroll. She withdrew to the mountains of western North Carolina, where she remained as Law's mistress and eventual second wife. Potwin's departure may have felt like a victory to workers, but accomplishing that immediate objective robbed Local 1882 of the moral purpose that had animated it. Interest in the local flagged even before Law set out on his private campaign to root its most ardent supporters from both mill and village. In the union's place came pain and loss. "Oh, it tore up the community, there's no doubt about it. It tore up families, and friends, and everything," a strike veteran recalled. Spiritual communion in the predominately prounion Baptist congregation never recovered, and up the street the riven Methodist church "never was the same." The movement even left visible scars. John A. Law had once built a community bandstand for the renowned Saxon band, but after the union began to use this favorite space for rallies, Law had the facility dismantled.[3]

Nor did the fates of those most closely identified with the Saxon movement encourage future public expression. Annie Laura West's plight has already been noted. Others paid similar prices or even higher ones. A Saxon resident for more than two decades, Jedediah Bevill was one of the most beloved members of the working-class community. "He took a big part in the Methodist church. He was superintendent of the Sunday school, and he was a big believer in the union." Exile—if only to Whitlock Street a half-mile away—broke his spirit. "It just killed him. In fact, I always felt like that might have been partly the cause of his death. He grieved so over the conditions that the community and all was in." Less than a year later, "he died, he died in the State Hospital: he had a nervous breakdown." Saxon never returned to being the community that textile workers had once known—or thought they knew. Even for those who kept alive the union dream, cautious ambivalence—at best—replaced hope. "It was a *good* place to live, way back. It was. And I don't know whether you could say Miss Potwin ruined it, or whether you could say the union ruined it, or what ruined it. I guess what was going to be was going to be."[4]

Ambivalence, like silence, is a form of retreat, a protective stance against both public assault and private grief. What insulates against fear also, unfortunately, insulates against hope as well. The risks of public life remain what they always have been—great. In the wake of the Saxon strike, some blamed the union, some the company; some made their peace by moving away, either at the company's behest or on their own; and a few held out private hopes that the union would return, someday. Virtually all chose silence.[5]

In the prevailing social and political climate, hope was a luxury few could afford, which makes the stories of those who kept the hopes of the 1930s alive all the more remarkable. Beatrice Norton was a young homemaker at the time of the Saxon strike. She was the child of mill workers and married to a mill worker. Her mother, Daisy McGaha, had migrated alone to the Greenville mills from the North Carolina mountains. McGaha and her second husband, Hamp Hamby, never found the satisfaction they sought within the mill system, but they knew little else and so they persevered, from mill to mill. Along the way, they and their daughter accumulated firsthand knowledge of what oppression meant in human terms. At a Greenville mill, her stepfather—in the mill at age seven—was caught by his boss skinny-dipping in the mill pond when he should have been working. "So he took him upstairs and wanted [the boy's] father to whip him. And his father said 'I'll quit before I will. You've done beat the devil out of him, I'm not going to hit him any more. . . . You can fire away if you want to, but I'm not going to whip my child any more. You've done beat him enough.' So they told him . . . he'd have to move." At Spartan Mills, Norton's future father-in-law lost two fingers in a card-room accident: "They carried him to the hospital, but they didn't wait: and there wasn't no telephones, and he had to walk all the way back . . . with his hand a-throbbing and aching. And they wanted him to come back in the next morning to work in that condition, and he just told them no, and they said he had to get off the mill village, he couldn't stay there any longer." As Beatrice Norton concluded, "If you'd ever worked in one of these mills, then you'd know what we called slaughterhouses. It wasn't for cattle to be slaughtered—it was for humans. They were brought up ignorant, they grew up without school, they were told what to do: when to go to bed, when to get up, and when to get to that mill! They woke 'em up at five o'clock every morning with the whistle."

By the 1930s, the Norton family had become a fixture at Saxon village, and Beatrice herself had settled down. The stories she heard on both sides of her family were not after all very different from those told by thousands of other textile workers. Nor was the enthusiasm with which the Nortons supported the union movement of the 1930s unusual. What made Beatrice Norton different were the lessons she took from the movement, the Saxon strike, and its resolution. To Norton, the expulsion of Marjorie Potwin amounted to a real victory, whatever UTWA Local 1882's fate. First of all, there was the exultant feeling of being able to stand up against the sources of oppression:

> It felt like—we'll, I've heard of people being on the chain gang and carrying those chains around their legs, and trying to walk and work. Well, it couldn't have been more binding than if we'd have had it around our necks, and wasn't allowed to speak and wasn't allowed to do nothing only except just exactly what they told us to do. No more, no less. Exactly. When the strike came, we were free of that chain, that binding chain. And so it was a freedom to us. It was a joy to us. And it simply was the happiest times of our lives.

She remembered that joy. "I learned to love, I learned to understand, and I learned I was a human, not an animal. Not one with a chain around my neck to be led around and told when to do this and what to do and how to do it and when to stop. They couldn't do me thataway no more. It gave me backbone and the courage to stand up and say 'Look, I'm human. I can do so much. I'm willing to do to my ability. But don't push me.'" She remembered what it was like to love and speak in the midst of struggle. The strike "was a defining moment. It was a have-to, to just survive. To survive, to have dignity, to have food on our tables, to have even the *privilege* of going in and asking to be let off of the job because you're sick. All that was accomplished through that little eight-month strike." And so she remembered what it was like for a community to be united. Afterward, Norton returned to her private life as wife and mother. To all appearances she was no different from any of her Saxon neighbors. Inside, however, was a different story, and when Norton heard of the Brown Lung Association's fight against byssinosis in the 1970s, she knew in her heart that it was time to turn back forty years of silence. "I felt like that this was another bridge I had to cross to get help to those people in that mill—still in that mill, needing help. After all those years, I felt like I had to help."[6]

"It brought people together as never before," Beatrice Norton concluded of the Saxon strike. "It was good to bring people together. Now people—

I believe they need another [strike], because *now* people are scared. They're scared to death. They don't know who lives next door. And they act as if they care less." As Norton understood, fear and hope—these two most basic human emotions—are each the other's reverse. In one's absence the other obtains. Both are, at base, organically related components of politics itself. As the American writer Wendell Berry has noted, "It seems plain that the voice of our despair defines our hope exactly; it seems, indeed, that we cannot know of hope without knowledge of despair, just as we know joy precisely to the extent that we know sorrow."[7] One of the more jarring disjunctures in American intellectual and political life is the gulf, evident throughout the twentieth century, between the America portrayed by the nation's poets and novelists and the America alluded to, both directly and indirectly, in established political discourse.[8]

So often, the fragile public phases of the politics of hope are nothing more than the results of the forced confrontation between heart and mind in agony. The received culture of which Americans, like Spartanburg's textile workers, are all partakers militates against an open understanding of the dialectical relationship between hope and fear. What Spartanburg workers accomplished, they did under a specific set of conditions (the New Deal and the stretch-out) and using a specific vehicle (the union) toward specific ends (transforming mill life). That challenge came neither easily nor naturally but was prompted by the encounter between their desperation and their vision, the possibilities of which they saw within the interior life of their culture. Only in extremis does it seem possible to lift ourselves out of the more subterranean channels of human endeavor.

Where fear prevails, it effectively prevents the kind of social awareness that allows individuals to give hope both voice and life. In practical terms, the results of fear usually prove more tangible than those of hope. For most people, most of the time, fear functions—socially—as silence and paralysis. According to the distance between observer and the observed, that paralysis may be characterized as "quiescence" or "acquiescence," "apathy," "disempowerment," or "lack of consciousness." At extreme distances it may even be mistaken for contentment.

Fear predominates in societies to precisely the extent that previous defeats have left aching social and psychological voids. For most of the textile South, the General Strike of 1934 provided that moment. For a substantial minority of communities, defeat took longer but was ultimately more total. As Phoebe Cato remembered of the Saxon strike's cold aftermath, "I know there was an unrest, an uneasy feeling about it, and as a child it made me feel afraid—*which we had never been before.*"[9] Cato's view was a child's, not yet fully introduced to the vagaries of industrial life. Certainly, fear was present in Saxon and Una long before 1936—fear of unemployment, of eviction, and of accidental maiming or death. Yet she was correct in sensing a heightened tension. That was something new, whether it happened suddenly and in the immediate wake of September 1934 or gradually over the course of a decade or more.

A few of Spartanburg's local union leaders managed to escape the subsequent carnage, but the vast majority of men, women, and children touched by the movement did not. The resulting conspiracy of silence—so poignantly documented by Jacquelyn Hall and others—betrays not only anguish but also the extent to which southern workers felt robbed of all future ability to address social and power relationships basic to the functioning of their lives, both individually and collectively. The space in which they had permitted themselves to engage in such work had been demolished. Beatrice Norton was one of the few extraordinary veterans of the 1930s able to deal constructively with the experience of defeat. The rest, weary and wounded, remade their private lives in much the same molds as before the insurgency.

What was missing in them—and present in Norton—was a constructive acknowledgment of pain, an understanding, essentially moral, capable of reconciling the certain or even deadly risks of a given course of action with the absolute necessity of undertaking it. In modern circles, "spiritual" is a suspect word evoking a swift and usually negative identification with one or another religious tradition. Yet as an alternative descriptor of worldview, the word is appropriate in considering the economy of the human heart. Southern workers had a spiritual understanding of their struggle that transcended both rationality and any quick ideological fix. That much is clear, both from their testimony and in light of the enormous risks they took. They undertook public struggle because it was the right thing to do, because their previous lives—together, in the mill villages—armed them ethically to resist the evils of the stretch-out.[10]

They acted out of desperation. The stretch-out was destroying their lives. In historical terms, this is the problem of pain. Southern workers who engaged in strikes during the 1930s did so in a culture overwhelmingly grounded in a particular theological tradition: Protestant Christianity. That they so often sought to paint the union struggle in biblical terms or attempted a theological wedding between strike and church was no accident. Their religion and their unions were public manifestations of the same underlying ethical assumptions. For all its inhibiting effects, the prevailing modes of Protestant Christianity provided some southern workers with a particular way of dealing with pain—an understanding of the necessity of individual and even collective suffering in the accomplishment of any greater good, what many would have termed "the cross." In this redemptive context, suffering—either in the mill or on the picket line—lost the power of shame. At no point did they ennoble the physical depredations they endured. Rather, they ennobled the spiritual manifestations of endurance itself, the qualities of mutuality and solidarity. It was precisely this sensibility that provoked another textile worker, years later, to risk organizing his mill with the justification that "somebody's got to suffer. Those people down in Gastonia who started it all [in 1929], they had to suffer for me."[11]

That struggle involves suffering is axiomatic. How an individual or group chooses to view the attendant pain, both in the moment of protest and in the aftermath, defines a movement. Through most of the twentieth century, American workers and organized labor consistently accepted mainstream ideological categories of achievement, of "winning" and "losing."[12] What that has most often left them with, of course, is losing. These narrow categories represent a belief system that perverts the complex meanings of suffering and struggle, conflating and reducing all such experience to a flat, immobilizing sense of loss. For the majority of southern workers who did not possess the ethical underpinnings of Beatrice Norton, the 1930s became the bitter story of defeat, plain and simple.

The prevalence of this sense of loss—of defeat or betrayal—lies at the heart of the American working-class experience in the twentieth century. Was there ever any alternative? The African American struggles of the 1950s and 1960s suggest so. The participants in what became known as the American civil rights movement located their ethical foundations not in the broader culture (servant, after all, to those responsible for their oppression) but rather in the power of their experientially grounded convictions as to what a just American society might look like. In this they were not so very different from the textile workers of the 1930s. What civil rights activists had—and what the vast majority of southern textile workers did not—was an understanding and acceptance of suffering within the context of the moral necessity of action.

As the flying squadron and sit-down became the memorable organizing tools for labor in the 1930s, so did tactical nonviolence became the cornerstone of the civil rights movement in the early 1960s. Martin Luther King, Jr., later averred that nonviolence "was grasped by the Negro masses because it embodied the dignity of struggle, of moral conviction and self-sacrifice."[13] Although King exaggerated the extent to which American blacks embraced Ghandian resistance, his observation of what nonresistance embodied on the street was astute. Dignity of struggle, moral conviction, and self-sacrifice—again, it was a moral understanding that reconciled the certain and even deadly risks of protest with the absolute necessity of undertaking it. It was precisely the physical evidence of this understanding that electrified other blacks as well as white America at large. As King put it, "Negroes, by the hundreds and by the thousands, marching toward him, knowing they are going to jail, wanting to go to jail, willing to accept the confinement, willing to risk the beatings and the uncertain justice of the southern courts."[14]

Like participants in the other great social movements in American history—the American Revolution or the Populist insurgency, for example—civil rights activists achieved not only a rare sense of self-possession and mission but also the development of vehicles, both tactical and institutional, with which to achieve their goals. This state of being is perhaps best described in the phrase "engaged living" (or, in what poor terminology the host culture affords, "empowerment"). In simplest terms, engaged living is fear transcended, the product of an underlying belief system that enables men and women to take public steps. In practice, fear becomes subject to hope and loses its capacity to immobilize. What was grasped by the civil rights movement as a whole, collectively, has only been reached episodically, even individually, within the American labor movement.[15] Outside of Flint, the Appalachian coalfields, and a very few other places, no mobilized culture of aspiration has arisen in working-class America since the 1930s. In the vacuum necessarily resides an immobilized culture of defeat.

In such a context, even working-class "victories" remain persuasive only so long as their practical benefits—the fruits of "victory" according to prevailing wisdom—remain conspicuously present. In the 1990s, the cloak of silence was no less muffling at Arcadia, where the union never regained power after the UTWA's disastrous strike of 1932, than at the Cliftons, where the union enjoyed thirty years of contractual relations and expired (with the mills' closing) through no fault of its own. Elsewhere, union power still exists in the formal world of collective bargaining, but silence continues to encroach upon institutions increasingly removed from the reality of pain. Without a culture of aspiration able to deal with human suffering in constructive ways, the politics of hope and fear remain reduced to the cold mathematics of profit and loss, forever seeking ratification in a world devoid of redemption.

Epilogue

For workers who had so ardently sought to impose a more equitable level of community upon lives in which so much was controlled by others, the destruction of the union movement of the 1930s and 1940s brought a return to quiescence. Organizers from the TWUA and its successors visited Spartanburg and other South Carolina textile centers periodically, but never again would unionism gain a foothold here. The costs of this form of public life, from Arcadia down through Clifton, had proven too high. The risks were too great. The real power to alter South Carolina's social and political infrastructures was too concentrated and seemingly forever beyond reach.

A handful of veteran local activists retained enough influence among the powerful to escape Spartanburg entirely. Robert Donnahoo of Inman Mills, Paul Stephens of Spartan, G. Walter Moore of Tucapau, and others obtained employment from federal and state labor departments. As conciliators and inspectors, they later dealt with the same mills they had once fought to organize. John Pollard, Furman Garrett, and the "Tucapau Four" all worked as union organizers, at least for a time. Yet all reached a point where peace was required. For most, such peace had to be made in Spartanburg County. This was a peace predicated on silence. John Pollard, the photogenic UTWA spokesman from Spartan Mills, became a postal clerk and never spoke of the union to his children or co-workers. Annie West, heroine of the Saxon strike, became the wife of a local carpenter. Furman Garrett died an alcoholic in Greer. B. C. Comer, S. P. Caldwell, Cloyd Gibson, and Walter Moore all later managed small businesses within sight of Startex's smokestacks. Charlie McAbee, Spartanburg's man on the UTWA's national executive board during the General Strike, was quietly rehired by Inman Mills and subsequently promoted into supervision. He remained in Inman for the rest of his very long life, and he, too, kept his silence. Others disappeared—men like George Garland, who led the union fight at Cowpens Mill, and J. O. Blum of Drayton, the county's flying squadron co-ordinator in 1934. None of the mills involved in the events of the 1930s were ever again organized by any union of any kind. In 1983 UTWA Local 1881 at Spartan Mills, still a slight force in the plant, was finally decertified by a narrow majority in an NLRB election. In 1984 the weak Startex local disbanded rather than challenge the company in pending contract negotiations. In many ways, Local 2070 had been the first among Spartanburg County's textile unions during the heyday of the 1930s. Appropriately, it was also the last.

Back on the Pacolet River, where the industrial revolution in Spartanburg County began, the textile world ground to an end. The Glendale mill closed in 1961.[1] In 1965, Virginia-based Dan River Mills purchased the aging Clifton plants in a move designed to increase Dan River's market share in basic textiles. On 7 January 1969 Dan River announced the closing of mill No. 1, followed by mill No. 2 exactly nine months later.[2] The shutdown was painfully slow. "The people who brought in the cotton and opened it up went first, and then into the card room," followed by spinning and weaving. "They'd stop off a set of looms, and then that would get that person out of a job," and so on down the line.[3] A few workers were transferred to the Converse mill, which even at this late date Dan River pledged to operate. Others, distrusting their new employer more by the month, fled to plants elsewhere in the county. On 15 December 1971 Dan River announced the shuttering of No. 3 as well. The last bolts of cloth left Converse six weeks later. The textile era on the upper Pacolet was over.[4]

The Clifton company had sold its residential holdings to its employees during the 1950s at bargain prices. Unlike their counterparts in villages elsewhere, most of Clifton's residents kept their homes. Even as the older generation of workers began to die out, the three Clifton villages retained much of their old atmosphere and cohesiveness. Dan River's early promises had buoyed community spirits: "Everybody thought, you know, when Dan River was taking over, we was sitting on top of the world."[5] In part because hopes were so high, Dan River's decision to abandon the Cliftons stunned all.[6] Years later, former workers still struggled for words to describe the experience. "You heard tell of breaking up a chicken's nest, an old setting hen? That's about how it was." "It was just like a death." "It broke your heart." "It was like you'd lost a brother." As Vessie Bagwell of No. 2 concluded, "To the majority of the people it was like me. . . . .I felt like my world had come to an end."[7]

In a sense, it had. Fortunately for hundreds of former Clifton workers, Spartanburg County's industrial renaissance during the 1960s and early 1970s provided employment opportunities at precisely the moment Clifton workers desperately needed them: Arrow Automotive and Koehler in Spartanburg, Hoechst's massive synthetic fiber plant, and Collins and Aikman in nearby Cowpens.[8] For those in their fifties and sixties, prospects were bleak. Some suffered.[9] But for younger workers, reemployment was generally swift. Indeed, the new jobs in the new plants—generally with better pay and benefits than Clifton had ever offered—proved, in the long run, "a blessing in disguise."[10]

Economically, at least. Work elsewhere also shattered the unity of life and labor that had bound residents together and informed protest across the textile South. The point was not lost on Clifton residents, who went into a state of mourning that lingered decades later. "It just broke everything apart," Ibera Holt recalled.[11] From the Spartanburg suburb of Ben Avon, Abbie Lee Croxdale explained, "The worst thing about it was—these people, you grew up with them. You'd known them all your life, and they knew you all your life. . . . They were just like your family. You take your family—when they're growing up, they're growing up right there together, but after they get grown, one goes here, one goes yonder. Well, that's the way the village was. It's just like a family being separated, and them going every way and everywhere."[12]

The death of the Cliftons did indeed represent a social and industrial coming of age for Spartanburg County. The Pacolet flows quietly now, unimpeded. But if in its passing the age gave up the bewildering varieties of intimidation and social control that had defined life within it, it also relinquished the

Shuttered mill and dam, Clifton No. 1, 1999. (Courtesy of Mark Olencki)

peculiar culture of mutuality and reciprocity that those structures had engendered.[13] When Spartanburg County's textile workers cast their lot with the union in the 1930s, they did so because they saw through the anguish of their existence to a world whose vague contours resembled the social relations they had managed to create among themselves. Their culture armed them with experiential knowledge that the world did not have to remain as they knew, that better was possible, and that their children need not inherit wind. The end of their world marked the end of those dreams. We still search for others.

Notes

INTRODUCTION

1. Rich, introduction to *The Best American Poetry 1996*, 23.
2. The silences in the wake of the General Strike have been noted by numerous historians, most poignantly in Hall et al., *Like a Family*, and George Stoney and Judith Helfand's documentary film *The Uprising of '34* (1995).

CHAPTER I: SHARED LIVES

1. The literature on the southern textile industry's development and on the peculiar culture it engendered is voluminous. Period accounts of mills, workers, and communities include Thompson, *From the Cotton Field to the Cotton Mill;* Kohn, *The Cotton Mills of South Carolina;* Mitchell, *The Rise of Cotton Mills in the South;* Potwin, *Cotton Mill People of the Piedmont;* MacDonald, *Southern Mill Hills;* Rhyne, *Some Southern Cotton Mill Workers and Their Villages;* and Pope, *Millhands and Preachers.* Modern appraisals must begin with Hall et al., pathbreaking *Like a Family*, although the definitive account of textile industrialization from a structural perspective will likely remain Carlton, *Mill and Town in South Carolina.* Prompted by *Like a Family* and related efforts, other scholarship on southern textiles has included DeNatale, "Bynum"; Tullos, *Habits of Industry;* and Flamming, *Creating the Modern South.* For intraregional, transindustry comparisons, see also Cobb, *Industrialization and Southern Society;* Eller, *Miners, Millhands, and Mountaineers;* Kelley, *Hammer and Hoe;* and Shifflett, *Coal Towns.*
2. In a feature article on the state's textile mills in early 1880, the Charleston *News and Courier* devoted considerable space to "those little miniature manufactories which are so thickly crowded in between Greenville and Spartanburg, and which appear to thrive and grow rich in a region which seems utterly desolate and cut off from the world." Although the *News and Courier* undoubtedly exaggerated these mills' profitability—the local press frequently referred to their financial difficulties and erratic production schedules—it did provide an adequate overview of the operations themselves. Typical was the Cedar Hill factory (modern Apalache) with

eight hundred spindles, sixteen looms, and thirty employees. Glendale, the largest mill, boasted 5,000 spindles, 120 looms, and 120 employees. Each mill formed the nucleus of a factory settlement, but except for Glendale these were minuscule. Fingerville in 1882 contained only the wood-frame mill, a cotton gin, a grist mill, a blacksmith shop, a store, and "eleven Cabins for Operatives." *News and Courier* article reprinted in *Carolina Spartan,* 18 Feb 1880, and *Spartanburg Herald,* 18 Feb 1880; Fingerville description from *Carolina Spartan,* 31 May 1882. For the early southern textile industry more generally, see Lander, *The Textile Industry in Ante-Bellum South Carolina;* Griffin and Standard, "The Cotton Textile Industry in Ante-Bellum North Carolina"; and Beatty, "Textile Labor in the North Carolina Piedmont."

3. What became the Clifton Manufacturing Company on 19 January began as a purely South Carolinian phenomenon. All of the company's incorporators were either businessmen from Spartanburg or resident managers at Glendale. The capitalization, which reached a locally unprecedented $500,000 in its initial phase, was solicited via open subscription. Although it drew from sources as far away as Baltimore and the textile Northeast, most of it came from South Carolina, predominately from upcountry businessmen and Charleston investors. *Carolina Spartan,* 7, 21 Jan. , 4 Feb. , 3 March 1880, 19 Jan., 23 March, 27 July 1881; Hembree and Moore, *A Place Called Clifton,* 17, 22–23.

4. *Carolina Spartan,* 27 July, 24 Aug. 1881, 18 Jan., 29 March 1882. The isolated and phenomenal natures of early mill-and-village complexes were emphasized by Englishman T. M. Young during his tour of American textile operations in 1901. Young's description of Cooleemee, N.C., could have applied with equal force to the early Cliftons: "A place with no history at all, and not to be found upon a map that I have seen, but said to be somewhere about thirty miles along a single track of railway which connects Winston-Salem with Charlotte." T. M. Young in *The American Cotton Industry: A Study of Work and Workers,* as quoted in Wingerd, "Rethinking Paternalism," 5.

5. *Carolina Spartan,* 27 Sept. 1882.

6. *Carolina Spartan,* 28 June 1882.

7. *Carolina Spartan,* 12 March 1884.

8. Barry's account of his southern organizing tour was originally printed in the *Philadelphia Press,* then in the Charleston *News and Courier,* and finally in Spartanburg, where the *Carolina Spartan* invited local manufacturers to refute the charges. D. E. Converse claimed that only a few ten-year-olds worked at Clifton (certainly no five- or six-year-olds as Barry had charged), and that although "we never want them before they are twelve years of age," greedy parents were often guilty of forcing younger children on supervisors. Converse excused low wages by citing the South's lower cost and standard of living and defended the company store as a necessary, noncoercive institution. While admitting to the twelve-hour day, Converse maintained that children worked less than the full regimen: "Their work is

light, and admits of moving around and taking much exercise. During the day they have several recesses, ten to twenty minutes, when the boys go out on the sand and play and the little girls romp in the halls. The fact is the children beg to be permitted to work in the factory." *Carolina Spartan,* 18 Jan. 1888.

9. *Carolina Spartan,* 9 Jan. 1889.

10. The organization of Spartan Mills in 1888 and 1889 heralded these new economic arrangements. Spartan (Spartanburg city's first major industrial complex) was first incorporated in 1888, with local leadership under the popular installment plan. Within a year, however, the company's president—local businessman J. H. Montgomery—had abandoned the installment plan in order to recruit "outside capitalists." What happened next took nearly everyone by surprise: "Just before the masons began to lay the foundation, President Montgomery received a dispatch from his mill engineer, Captain Greene, to meet him at once in New York. . . . When he got there, Captain Greene, who is a stockholder in and treasurer of the Whitefield mills, laid before him the plan of moving said mills to Spartanburg. They talked the matter over and were pleased with the project. The President of the Whitefield mill, Mr. Milligan [Milliken], knew nothing of this matter. Captain Greene had an interview with him and he was favorably impressed with the idea of bringing the spindles to the cotton fields. He called the directors together and a trade was soon effected." Spartan Mills opened with the sacked Whitefield mill's machinery in 1890. Henceforth the announcement that "a Boston Company" had invested heavily in or purchased land for a Spartanburg mill would be greeted without comment. *Carolina Spartan,* 14 March, 4 April, 9 May, 18 July, 5 Dec. 1888, 27 Feb., 15 May 1889 (quotation); Thompson, "A Managerial History of a Cotton Textile Firm," 38–55.

11. This is a central argument in Hall et al., *Like a Family*.

12. The more itinerant the worker, the more frequently he or she seems to have shared this view. One of the few Spartanburg workers I interviewed who took this position was Arkwright's Clayton Faulkner, who worked in eleven different mills in two states between 1927 and 1938 and labeled the accompanying villages "all about the same." Interview with Clayton Faulkner.

13. The odyssey of the Textile Industrial Institute was virtually unique in the textile South. The school—later Spartanburg Methodist Junior College—was founded with the intent of providing high school and college-level instruction to textile workers and their children. For a full but highly partisan account of the school's history by its founder, see Camak, *Human Gold from Southern Mill Hills*.

14. These examples are drawn from unrecorded conversations with dozens of retired textile workers in the Spartanburg area.

15. For a detailed (although biased) examination of how life and structure related in Spartanburg's Saxon community, see Potwin, *Cotton Mill People of the Piedmont,* chapters 4–6.

16. Interview with Aaron McConnell and Etrulia McConnell. When, as a child, Aaron "Jack" Thornton visited relatives in the country, his grandmother would

often point out an African American tenant farmer's shack. "She would let me know"—surely with irony—that "that was a Clifton house." Interview with Aaron Thornton.

17. In Spartanburg city, some supervisors, professionals, and clerical workers were able to choose residence outside the village. Throughout this period, mill workers of all types did emanate from town or from the adjacent countryside, but their numbers were always few in comparison with those of village residents. Some mills even required village residency as a condition of employment. Because of the clear demarcation between company-owned property and other space, "on" and "off" became the accepted terms for describing one's physical relation to any given village.

18. Labor contracts were a brief feature in southern mill life. When Robert Atkins agreed to work for the Clifton Manufacturing Company in early 1882, he contracted "to move my family to Clifton, S.C., and occupy one of their tenements at that place, and for the entire year of 1882 furnish my faithful services when wanted, and also that of my children as operatives in their Factory, and do hereby bargain to so continue in their employ until all advances made to me by them are paid in full. I also agree to submit to and support all Rules and Regulations existing in the Factory and on the place customary in such cases." (Hembree and Moore, *A Place Called Clifton*, 27.) Even after the passing of such contracts, however, the key points on which Atkins conceded remained central elements in the company-worker relationship in southern textiles.

19. Interview with Georgia Seals and Ibera Holt. Mill people were notoriously itinerant, and many mountain recruits lasted for only short periods in the unfamiliar industrial setting. "A lot of 'em didn't like the mill . . . and they would leave. That's why they kept bringing people in, see." Interview with Furman Mabry and Louise (Vaughn) Mabry. Recruiting in the Tennessee and southwestern Virginia mountains is discussed in the interviews with Pettit Calvert, Venie Calvert, John Roland Brown, Helen (Cash) Brown, Aaron McConnell, and Etrulia McConnell.

20. Interview with Aaron Thornton.

21. Interview with John Roland Brown and Helen (Cash) Brown.

22. Interview with Vernon Foster.

23. Interviews with Aaron McConnell, Etrulia McConnell, Zelia Ann (Chapman) Mabry, Pettit Calvert, and Venie Calvert.

24. When asked whether she was a proficient worker, Pauline Bible of Clifton replied dryly, "Apparently. Pretty good, I reckon. Or they'd have let me go if I hadn't of been, because they did let some of 'em go when they couldn't keep up jobs." Interview with Pauline Bible.

25. Interviews with A. Beatrice Norton and Ruby Bevill. As Hall et al. have noted, "Even the most routine jobs required initiative, creativity, and dexterity, traits that were transmitted from worker to work and added some dignity to mere toil." *Like a Family*, 45.

26. Louise Mabry, in interview with Furman Mabry and Louise (Vaughn) Mabry; interview with Zelia Ann (Chapman) Mabry.

27. Hall et al., *Like a Family*, 105–9.

28. Interviews with Marie (Vaughan) Coggins, Hoyt Jones, and Marie Jones. As Coggins implies, many mill families came to have a single village that served as a base for excursions elsewhere. Whitney garnered such a reputation in this regard that the story of a family on the highway, their wagon laden with household goods, "heading back to Whitney!" entered Spartanburg folklore. D. E. Camak, writing from his perspective as a reformer, observed of his Spartanburg youth that "it was seldom possible to go up a street without seeing loads of household stuff on the move. . . . It was a restless human sea, never still, always seeking its level and never finding it; thousands constantly going where thousands had just been, all of them hunting the rainbow pot of 'something better farther on.'" *Human Gold from Southern Mill Hills*, 25.

29. From Saxon: "If they didn't do what mill officials required of them, if they didn't just obey orders down to the very teeth, they let 'em go—had to move out. If they found any fault at all with the family—it didn't have to be the worker—if one of the families, say for instance, one got arrested for something, or one sassed the bossman for something, it would be connected to the work. They'd let the whole family go." From Clifton: "Every town had a bootlegger. . . . If somebody got out on a Saturday night or a Sunday, got drunk and shut out, Monday morning was moving day. If you ever caused confusion in the community, it was moving day." Interviews with A. Beatrice Norton and George McCarley.

30. Figures for Saxon Mills in August 1926 revealed that of 168 families in the village, fifty-one had been there less than five years, sixty-five between five and fourteen years, forty-one between fifteen and twenty-four years, and eleven since the mill began operations in 1900. Potwin, *Cotton Mill People of the Piedmont*, 73.

31. Interviews with Homer Lee Harrison and Elbert Stapleton. Mary Wingerd made the same point: "Workers put great store in the close personal relationships that developed within the village confines, declaring that 'most everybody stayed put' and 'hardly nobody ever left.' However, the community they remember is the story of those who stayed. The core families, those who lived within the village itself, and who by virtue of their persistence defined the meaning of community, tended to remain in place throughout their working lives, creating stable and interlocking relationships that persisted over generations. But it is important to specify that for those who floated in and out of the mill or who resided outside the boundaries of the village—possibly at times a third of the work force—the bonds of solidarity were more tenuous and depended on how well individuals conformed to group norms. In short, employment in the mill did not mean automatic membership in the community, nor was social control the province of management alone." Wingerd, "Rethinking Paternalism," 12–13. For the effect the settled cohort of workers had on shaping the dynamics of protest during the 1930s, see chapter 5.

32. Interviews with Georgia Seals and Ibera Holt; interviews with Elbert Stapleton and Homer Lee Harrison.

33. Interview with Vessie M. Bagwell.

34. Both size and amenities were issues in supervisory housing, which tended to be larger and fancier. As a Cliftonite put it, "It was something else if you had hot water—you had to be a bossman if you had hot water and a bathtub." Interview with Furman Mabry and Louise (Vaughn) Mabry.

35. Interview with J. Luther Campbell.

36. Interview with Paul Dearybury and Virl Dearybury.

37. The Saxon situation was more representative: "The second hands [assistant foremen] . . . had worked up from fixing looms and proved their ability and had been promoted. But the overseers were not. They brought them in from other places." Interview with Fred Jewell.

38. As Hall et al. have observed in their larger consideration of supervision and authority in textile communities, "The contradictions of authority bore most heavily on overseers and second hands, who were most deeply enmeshed in the social life of the close-knit communities where the mills were located" (*Like a Family*, 96). Mary Wingerd elaborates: "They attended the same churches and schools, and even managers' children usually worked at least for a time in the mill. . . . By articulating a community identity that included managers, workers were able to hold them somewhat accountable to its norms. As long as managers tied their own identities to the constructed conceptions of family and community, they were doubly bound" ("Rethinking Paternalism," 18).

39. Interview with Jasper DeYoung and Mae DeYoung. Joe Love, who also remembered the 500 side as being "kind of rough," tried to explain the complex social geography at Tucapau, which in addition to Hickory Street included three other well-defined neighborhoods: the central village, "New Town" (on the north side), and "Red Egypt" (across the bridge on the south side). "There was this section over here, they had their own little thing, and this section over here had theirs. . . . They didn't mix and mingle," he recalled. Interview with Joe Love.

40. Interview with A. Beatrice Norton. More circumspectly, a Saxon supervisor agreed: "These little houses were built for the one employee, really, and they kind of hand-picked what they wanted to go in those houses, too. They didn't just let everybody move in them. They were few, and they were nice." Interview with Fred Jewell.

41. Interviews with Aaron Thornton, Aaron McConnell, Etrulia McConnell, Furman Mabry, and Louise (Vaughn) Mabry.

42. Interview with Georgia Seals and Ibera Holt.

43. *Carolina Spartan,* 12 March 1884.

44. Interview with F. Vard Whitt. Some mill executives touted "welfare work," ranging from YMCAs to night schools to extension clubs, but in only a few cases did such programs make a lasting impression. When the Pacolet Manufacturing

Company completely reconstructed its village in the 1920s, it embarked on an elaborate program of company-sponsored activities, ranging from a Mandolin Club to courses in "practical motherhood" to a local chapter of the Red Cross. Much of this highly touted work, however, was scrapped during the early days of the Great Depression. By the 1920s, Spartan Mills also sponsored an array of amenities: a community building, a gymasium, four baseball diamonds, a hospital, a community band, fraternal lodges, a Boy Scout troop, clubs, and "activities of all kinds." Wesley House, a Spartan Mills institution for decades, was financed by the Methodist church and modeled on Chicago's Hull House. Operated by itinerant Methodist deaconesses, it included a free library and kindergarten. By the 1930s, however, Spartan Mills was clearly exceptional. As a Spartan employee admitted, elsewhere "you could count the community buildings or YMCAs on one hand." Dozier, *Pictured Story;* interviews with Elbert J. Pye, Paul O. Taylor (quotation), Vernon Foster, and Ernest C. Hawkins.

45. Hall et al. recognize the importance of visiting in the pre-mill rural context but limit its village importance to the socialization of women. *Like a Family,* 20, 170–71.

46. Interview with Georgia Seals and Ibera Holt. Most mill villages were, after all, walking communities. As Joe Love recalled of 1920s' Tucapau, "I'd go a whole year and not see twenty-five cars." Interview with Joe Love.

47. Interview with Herman Bagwell.

48. Interviews with Pauline Bible, John Roland Brown, Helen (Cash) Brown, Zelia Ann (Chapman) Mabry, Pettit Calvert, and Venie Calvert.

49. Interview with A. Beatrice Norton.

50. "After supper every night, all the women folks, they would gather up on somebody's front porch. Might not be the same one every day; two or three houses, and all the kids would be there, you know, playing together." Interview with Joe Love. At Clifton No. 2, the favorite spot for the men was a grove of shade trees by the upper company store. "Our enjoyment, when I was growing up as a kid. . . . They built a bench in between some big old trees; it would seat about fifteen or twenty people. And after supper, people would go out there, and the men would smoke, and the kids, and you could hear some awful good tales out there. That was one of the enjoyments. And you would have people from different places, and they would tell about their life when they were young, and all this. It was an education." Interview with Aaron Thornton; also interviews with Pettit Calvert, Venie Calvert, Howard Croxdale, Abbie Lee Croxdale, and Marie (Vaughan) Coggins.

51. Interview with A. Beatrice Norton, emphasis added.

52. The various Clifton lodges are described in Moore and Hembree, *A Place Called Clifton,* 158–63.

53. Fraternalism waned during the second quarter of the twentieth century. Insurance-based secret societies lost their appeal as commercial life insurance be-

came widespread, and younger generations of mill-village men chose baseball over Masonic ritual. Even in its heyday, fraternalism remained almost exclusively the province of white men, especially supervisors. As an expression of community solidarity, fraternalism could only stretch so far, however. Appropriately, the legacy of mill-village fraternalism was a tendency for Masonic lodges to become social clubs for supervisors. As late as 1952, Paul Dearybury discovered upon being promoted at Clifton No. 3 that "every overseer, I think in every mill on the river, was a Mason except me." Necessarily, oral evidence on fraternalism's importance is sketchy and comes primarily from the children and grandchildren of participants. Interviews with Delbert Willis, Nell Willis, Howard Croxdale, Abbie Lee Croxdale, Elbert Stapleton, Aaron Thornton, Paul Dearybury, and Virl Dearybury; Hembree and Moore, *A Place Called Clifton,* 158–63.

54. Perry, *Textile League Baseball,* 6–11. Hall et al. note the existence of textile league baseball but emphasize the corporate perspective (organized mill sports as a means of social control). *Like a Family,* 136–37.

55. Jackson played for Brandon Mill of Greenville and Victor Mill of Greer from 1905 to 1908 before moving on to the Philadelphia Athletics. After his expulsion from professional baseball, he ended his sports career back in South Carolina, coaching (and occasionally playing) at Winnsboro Mills, Woodside of Greenville, and elsewhere. Perry, *Textile League Baseball,* 28–33, 111–15.

56. Interviews with Pauline Bible, Howard Croxdale, Abbie Lee Croxdale, and Herman Bagwell. Although baseball was of paramount importance, some mills did occasionally field teams in other sports, including men's and women's basketball at Spartan, Converse, and elsewhere.

57. Perry, *Textile League Baseball,* 47–48.

58. Ibid., 86.

59. Interview with M. A. Worley.

60. "Of course ball players, they got special privileges on the job," noted Jasper DeYoung of Tucapau. At Lyman, mill superintendent W. L. Howard was also the team manager and "crazy about baseball," according to one of his players. "Back then, you know, every mill that was any size, they had scouts, and they'd send them all around South Carolina. . . . And a good ball player, well, didn't have to worry about working. They'd put you on a so-called job, but that was it. All they wanted you to do was play ball." Ernest Hawkins's only "employment" at Lyman was opening Howard's daily mail. Interviews wtih Jasper DeYoung, Mae DeYoung, and Ernest C. Hawkins (quotation).

61. Interview with Elbert J. Pye.

62. Hall et al., *Like a Family,* 124–26, 175–80. Tullos, in *Habits of Industry,* gives even greater weight to Christianity's importance in mill-village life as recorded in the words of his informants, but the definitive study of mill-village religion remains Pope's *Millhands and Preachers.*

63. Interviews with Jasper DeYoung, Mae DeYoung, Herman Bagwell, and A.

Beatrice Norton. Aaron Thornton, a neighbor of Bagwell's, agreed with his assessment of the Cliftons: "The community was built mostly on people's beliefs. My mother was a Baptist, and every time the doors was opened she was there." Interview with Aaron Thornton.

64. Pope, *Millhands and Preachers,* chapter 7. Wesleyans in Spartan Mills, for example, "were regarded as a little bit more strict in their beliefs. The women didn't wear jewelry." Interview with Vernon Foster. At Tucapau, the small Church of God congregation formed in 1933 outdid Methodists, Baptists, and Wesleyans. All three groups told their members to stay away, according to a founding member. Interview with Millard C. Freeman. In upcountry South Carolina, all such sectarian groups remained miniscule in or adjacent to mill villages before 1940.

65. Interviews with Howard Croxdale, Abbie Lee Croxdale, John Roland Brown, Helen (Cash) Brown, and Aaron Thornton.

66. Interviews with J. Luther Campbell and Vernon Foster.

67. Interview with Clayton Faulkner. The actual level of mill worker participation in church life remains problematic. Clement Riddle recalled that "pretty well" all of Arkwright's residents attended either Arkwright Baptist or El Bethel Methodist, but according to Marie Jones, who lived in the village during the same period, people "just didn't go. This just wasn't a church-going community." Part of the discrepancy in perceptions may stem from whether one was or was not a churchgoer. As Beatrice Norton, a Saxon resident, noted, "We had a few that lived here that would not go to church, would not attend any kind of a meeting—but they kept to themselves." Interviews with Clement Riddle, Hoyt Jones, Marie Jones, and A. Beatrice Norton.

68. Interview with J. E. Blackwell and Lucille Blackwell. Revivals as social occasions are discussed in interviews with Delbert Willis, Nell Willis, and Homer Lee Harrison.

69. As a Clifton resident noted, "I think the company kind of controlled all that was done in the churches, to a certain extent, because most of their supervisors and things had a position in the churches." Interview with Aaron Thornton.

70. Interview with A. Beatrice Norton.

71. Interview with J. E. Blackwell and Lucille Blackwell.

72. Quotations, respectively, from interviews with Marie (Vaughan) Coggins, Joe Love, J. Luther Campbell, and Carlton Seals, in interview with Georgia Seals and Ibera Holt.

73. For example, in Spartanburg, "The people on the mill hill, they were all just like one family," and "we were just one big family." Interviews with Homer Lee Harrison (Arkwright) and Ibera Holt (Cliftons). As its title implies, Hall et al.'s *Like a Family* emphasizes this simile for mill-village community life. For an intriguingly different take on the "family metaphor," emphasizing the parallels between patriarchal family structure and hierarchical social structure in the mills and villages, see Tullos, *Habits of Industry,* 8–12.

74. Although this ethic of mutuality was linked to the mill system, its roots in a shared rural past were not lost on workers. The pattern of mutual aid "just kind of boiled over" from farms into the mill villages. As Hall et al. have noted, rural southerners spun ties of obligation and neighborliness into "a dense web of reciprocity and exchange" that accompanied workers to the mills as the most useful portion of their "cultural baggage." Interview with Clayton Faulkner; Hall et al., *Like a Family,* 4, 43.

75. By the 1930s, many villages were united as much by consanguinity as by co-residency. At Arkwright, "Used to be a whole side of there, where nearly everybody were kin to one another. They were related somehow or another on that whole mill village," while at Saxon, Ruby Bevill recalled, "a lot of the families were connected. And those that weren't connected were real good friends." Interview with Hoyt Jones and Marie Jones; interview with Ruby Bevill. Marjorie Potwin found "at least eighty families" out of 168 "related to each other by various bonds of kinship" in 1926. Potwin, *Cotton Mill People of the Piedmont,* 74.

76. Interview with Elbert Stapleton. This emphasis on caring for the sick reverberates through many accounts of mill-village life. "There was one thing about these small communities: everybody loved each other. And if anybody got sick . . . the neighbors would go in and sit with 'em all night, take turns," according to Louise Mabry of Clifton. Interview with Furman Mabry and Louise (Vaughn) Mabry; interviews with George McCarley, Clayton Faulkner, and Paul O. Taylor.

77. Interview with Homer Lee Harrison. As Hall et al. have noted, "Group solidarity served as a buffer against poverty and, above all, represented a realistic appraisal of working people's prospects." *Like a Family,* 172.

78. Interview with Willie Mae Shepherd.

79. Ibera Holt, in interview with Georgia Seals and Ibera Holt.

80. Georgia Seals, in interview with Georgia Seals and Ibera Holt; interview with Willie Mae Shepherd.

81. Interview with Zelia Ann (Chapman) Mabry.

82. Interview with Paul O. Taylor.

83. Asa Spaulding, quoted in Hall et al., *Like a Family,* 21.

84. Interview with Paul O. Taylor.

85. The most subtly nuanced examination of these twin themes is Mary Wingerd's examination of life, labor, and unionism in Cooleemee, North Carolina. Although the achievements of Cooleemee's workers—who pioneered a dynamic form of "community unionism" rooted in the culture and preexisting power relationships of the mill village—were very real, they could only go so far. Cooleemee workers never entirely eliminated the so-called stretch-out, and their form of community unionism was impotent in addressing such major issues as the mill's very operation, unilaterally terminated in 1969 after a major textile chain purchased the plant. Wingerd, "Rethinking Paternalism," 40 and passim.

86. What I call an accommodation has also been examined under the term *ne-*

gotiated loyalty by Gerald Zahavi and Mary Wingerd: a relationship predicated upon "an understanding of rights and obligations on both sides." As Wingerd explains, "When the rules of the game were transgressed by either side 'family' loyalties quickly evaporated and the players realigned themselves along other, more class-based lines." That is precisely what happened in southern textiles after the coming of the stretch-out (chapter 2). Zahavi, *Workers, Managers, and Welfare Capitalism*, 99–119; Wingerd, "Rethinking Paternalism," 17–18.

87. As noted in Hall et al., *Like a Family*, 86–90.

88. Interviews with Jasper DeYoung, Mae DeYoung, and Aaron Thornton.

89. Public protest against the mill system was comparatively rare before the 1920s. For examples, see McLaurin, *Paternalism and Protest*, and Tippett, *When Southern Labor Stirs*.

90. Interview with Furman Mabry and Louise (Vaughn) Mabry.

CHAPTER 2: HOPE RISING

1. Interview with Georgia Seals and Ibera Holt. In addition to the relevant portions of *Like a Family*, Tullos's *Habits of Industry*, Flamming's *Creating the Modern South*, and Irons's *Testing the New Deal*, the key historiographical account of southern textiles and the New Deal is Hodges, *New Deal Labor Policy and the Southern Cotton Textile Industry*. In the absence of a satisfactory general account of the Roosevelt years incorporating both high politics and worker activism, see Cohen, *Making a New Deal*, and Gordon, *New Deals*.

2. Exactly how common these conflicts were has not yet been determined by historians, although anecdotal evidence suggests they were much more frequent occurrences than even period observers realized. McLaurin, *Paternalism and Protest*, 69; Hall et al., *Like a Family*, 100.

3. The Knights of Labor and NUTW interludes are treated in detail in McLaurin, *Paternalism and Protest*, chapters 4–7. The 1919–21 strike wave is summarized in Hall et al., *Like a Family*, 187–95, and Mitchell, *Textile Unionism in the South*, 42–49. Other pre–1929 conflicts, including the spectacular 1915 general strike at Anderson, still await their historians.

4. The stretch-out's origins and deployment are well summarized in Hall et al., *Like a Family*, 195–212.

5. At the Cliftons, the comparatively relaxed pace of work had traditionally allowed operatives time to rest and socialize among themselves. "And then . . . them minute men. . . . they come in: what we called the stretch-out system. And they called it a cost measure. As that went into effect, more jobs were cut out, more people were eliminated. They always . . . picked out the best worker, the best operator, to check. . . . And then that made the other people lower down not able to keep up with the top people." Interview with Aaron Thornton.

6. Interview with J. Luther Campbell.

7. Interview with Furman Mabry and Louise (Vaughn) Mabry. The stretch-out scandalized experienced operatives who felt they knew the appropriate machine loads for their jobs. See, for example, transcript of CTLRB hearing, 11 April 1934 (Gertrude Johnson testimony), RG 9, entry 398, box 30, Spartan Mills folder; "A Weaver from Drayton Mill" to Hugh S. Johnson, 11 Nov. 1933, RG 9, entry 398, box 12, Drayton Mills folder; and Wingerd, "Rethinking Paternalism," 27–28.

8. Interviews with Herman Bagwell (for the Cliftons) and J. Luther Campbell (for Arcadia).

9. Interview with J. Luther Campbell.

10. All the strikes are summarized in Hall et al., *Like a Family* but examined in considerably greater detail by a contemporary observer, Tom Tippett, in *When Southern Labor Stirs*.

11. "A Mother" to Franklin D. Roosevelt, 17 Feb. 1934, RG 9, entry 398, box 30, Spartan Mills folder.

12. The most comprehensive account of the NRA remains Colin Gordon's in *New Deals,* chapter 5.

13. "With the owners in charge the Code Authority became synonomous with the Cotton-Textile Institute," the industry's main lobby group. As James Hodges makes clear throughout his study, "At every turn failure awaited those in the southern cotton textile industry who struggled to use the swiftly changing New Deal labor policy to achieve unionization. . . . To understand the loosing struggle . . . is to gain new insight into the limits of reform that shackled the New Deal and to understand better why the New Deal failed as often as it succeeded." *New Deal Labor Policy and the Southern Cotton Textile Industry,* 54, 7.

14. Hall et al., *Like a Family,* chapter 6; Irons, "Testing the New Deal," chapters 5–9, especially 212–20, 254–64; Hodges, *New Deal Labor Policy and the Southern Cotton Textile Industry,* chapters 4–6 (quotation on 6). The broader context—the NRA's inability to regulate key industries effectively—is covered in Gordon, *New Deals,* 173–94.

15. Irons, "Testing the New Deal," 180, 211–12.

16. A. W. Hammond to Hugh S. Johnson, 28 Aug. 1933, RG 25, entry 398, box 25, Pelham Mfg. Co. folder.

17. W. H. Fowler to Hugh S. Johnson, 26 July 1933, RG 9, entry 398, box 3, Apalache Mill folder; Irons, "Testing the New Deal," 183–90ff. Workers experienced the stretch-out through both the lower wages on their pay tickets and their own physical exhaustion. Complaints of having "to produce as much in eight hours as they formerly did in ten" were received, and dismissed, from Drayton, Tucapau, and other mills. According to one weaver at Spartan Mills, the bare financial evidence of maintaining the same production in fewer hours was ample evidence that the stretch-out really existed. Report of investigator Lewis F. Sawyer, 3 Oct. 1933, RG 9, entry 398, box 12, Drayton Mills folder; Lottie Gardner to Roosevelt, 21 March 1934, and complaint of G. Walter Moore, 24 April 1934, RG 9, entry 398, box 32, Tucapau Mills folder (and,

indeed, most of the contents of entry 398); Mrs. Myrtle McPherson to Francis J. Gorman, 14 April 1934, RG 9, entry 398, box 30, Spartan Mills folder.

18. W. H. Fowler to Hugh S. Johnson, 26 July 1933, and Dee M. Dye to Roosevelt, 24 Aug. 1933. Both in RG 9, entry 398, box 3, Apalache Mill folder.

19. Simon, "A Fabric of Defeat," 182–84.

20. Mrs. Carl Langford to James F. Byrnes, 27 July 1933, RG 9, entry 398, box 28, Riverdale Mills folder.

21. S. E. Knightson to Hugh S. Johnson, 22 July 1933, RG 9, entry 398, box 3, Arkwright Mills folder.

22. From Cowpens Mill came a stream of stretch-out-related complaints in early 1934, nearly all of them mentioning substandard wages. W. R. Crawford, a quill-skinner, complained that his weekly wages ranged from only $7.20 to $8.20 under the code; when he complained, his foreman fired him almost immediately. When Connie Bell Largent, a cleaner in the card room, filed a similar complaint, her foreman reportedly threatened to lower her pay by yet another dollar in retaliation. Complaints of W. R. Crawford and Connie Bell Largent, 7 May 1934, RG 9, entry 398, box 11, Cowpens Mfg. Co. folder.

23. A warp-doffer at Saxon complained that he had been dropped from $16.60 a week to $12.01 in the early days of the code. When he complained to his supervisor, he was briefly raised back to his former wage, but within a short time he had fallen back to $13.02. Anonymous complaint, 12 Jan. 1934, RG 9, entry 398, box 29, Saxon Mills folder.

24. "A Weaver from Drayton Mill" to Hugh S. Johnson, 11 Nov. 1933, RG 9, entry 398, box 12, Drayton Mills folder. The same system prevailed at Tucapau: "The skilled weavers with years of experience are only making $12.00 per week. . . . when they don't make production . . . the company pays them $12.00 and when they make over, the company takes out enough to make up the company loss." "M.A.M." to Hugh Johnson, RG 9, entry 398, box 32, Tucapau Mills folder.

25. Gertrude Johnson, a weaver at Spartan Mills, complained that she was being charged more to buy back defective cloth than she paid for first-class cloth at nearby retail stores. She noted angrily that "the operators are required to run so many looms that it is impossible not to make a few 'seconds.'" Johnson's superintendent later admitted to this practice but argued that very few workers suffered unduly from it. As he sharply noted, however, "This policy is taken up rather than a policy of firing." CTLRB decision in case of Spartan Mills, 26 May 1934, and hearing transcript in the case, 11 April 1934. Both in RG 9, entry 398, box 30, Spartan Mills folder.

26. "They just pay ten dollars a week to the sweepers, is that what they should have? I understood the papers and over the radio no one got less than twelve dollars per week," wrote a confused worker from Apalache mill. Sweepers traditionally performed production work as needed. At Pacolet Mills, for instance, they were also expected to take down spools, pour up yarn, pour up quills, roll yarn and quills to

and from the elevator, and roll spools from the spooler to the warper. All those extra jobs were covered by the code, but the men performing them remained classified as "sweepers." Pacolet workers later charged that management was deliberately placing more nonsweeping work on sweepers at noncode rates so they could eliminate jobs covered by the code. Similar doubling up of jobs for substandard wages occurred on night shifts, traditionally staffed with a smaller work force than day shifts. Dee M. Dye to Franklin D. Roosevelt, 24 Aug. 1933, RG 9, entry 398, box 3, Apalache Mill folder, W. J. Lloyd to Sen. J. F. Byrnes, 2 Nov. 1933, RG 9, entry 398, box 30, Spartan Mills folder, and complaints of Douglas Millwood, L. D. Bonner, Jim Brackins, Mat James, A. R. Pack, Cole L. Petty, Zelmer Banks, and George Kanipe, all dated 1 June 1934, as well as J. E. Hughes to L. R. Gilbert, 28 July 1934. All in RG 9, entry 398, box 25, Pacolet Mfg. Co. folder. See also P. F. Cox to Gus Smith, 21 Aug. 1934, RG 9, entry 398, box 3, Arkwright Mills folder, and Ansel Lyon to Hugh S. Johnson, 12 Jan. 1934, RG 9, entry 398, box 20, Jackson Mills folder.

27. J. T. Whitaker to Hugh Johnson, 31 July 1933, RG 9, entry 398, box 30, Spartan Mills folder. See also anonymous complaints, 3 Oct. 1933 and 21 Feb. 1934, RG 9, entry 398, box 26, Powell Knitting folder; affidavit of Kate Owens, 14 March 1934, RG 9, entry 398, box 32, Tucapau Mills folder; W. H. Fowler to Hugh S. Johnson, 26 July 1933, and Dee M. Dye to Roosevelt, 24 Aug. 1933, RG 9, entry 398, box 3, Apalache Mill folder; Miss Bertie Bailey to Hugh S. Johnson, 18 Aug. 1933, RG 9, entry 398, box 20, Jackson Mills folder; and J. H. Tillotson to Hugh S. Johnson, undated [Aug. 1934], RG 9, entry 398, box 5, Beaumont Mfg. Co. folders (first folder).

28. "That as we all believe is wrong," she added. Mrs. W. C. Bryant to Hugh S. Johnson, 12 Aug. 1933, RG 9, entry 398, box 26, Powell Knitting folder.

29. Clyde Rogers to Hugh S. Johnson, 9 Aug. 1933, RG 9, entry 398, box 29, Saxon Mills folder. As Rogers implied, code-prompted layoffs were even more difficult for textile workers to stomach because workers conceived of the NIRA as first and foremost a device to create and conserve jobs. "You all said in the Code that this was to put more hands to work," complained a weaver from Drayton in late 1933. Anonymous to Board, 2 Oct. 1933, RG 9, entry 398, box 12, Drayton Mills folder; J. E. Hughes to L. R. Gilbert, 28 July 1934, RG 9, entry 398, box 25, Pacolet Mfg. Co. folder.

30. R. S. Kirby of Pacolet Mills charged that his mill was doing precisely that in early 1934: "I know Mill No. 3 has been speeded up, because I helped carry the larger pullies to the spinning dept. myself." Management at Arcadia Mills actually admitted to having raised the pulley speeds in their spinning room by 1.5 percent, but like so many acts contributing to the overall stretch-out, this was not in and of itself a violation of the code. R. S. Kirby and Mrs. M. S. James to H. S. Johnson, 5 Feb. 1934, RG 9, entry 398, box 25, Pacolet Mills folder; report of investigator A. S. Thomas, 9 May 1934, RG 9, entry 398, box 3, Arcadia Mills folder.

31. L. B. Painter to Robert W. Bruere, 11 June 1934, RG 9, entry 398, box 15, Fair-

mont Mfg. Co. folder; John W. Califf to Robert Bruere, 5 July 1934, RG 9, entry 398, box 32, Valley Falls Mill folder. See also anonymous complaint, 7 Aug. 1934, RG 9, entry 398, box 29, Saxon Mills folder; Mrs. Myrtle McPherson and Paul Stephens to Francis J. Gorman, 25 July 1934, RG 9, entry 398, box 30, Spartan Mills folder; "Decision of the Cotton Textile Industrial Relations Board for S.C., Employees vs. Clifton Mfg. Co.," Mill No. 2, RG 9, entry 398, box 10, Clifton Mfg. Co. folder; and anonymous complaint, 12 Feb. 1934, RG 9, entry 398, box 11, Cowpens Mfg. Co. folder.

32. R. S. Kirby and Mrs. M. S. James to H. S. Johnson, 5 Feb. 1934, RG 9, entry 398, box 25, Pacolet Mfg. Co. folder.

33. Annie Laura West to [Thomas McMahon? forwarded to national CTLRB], 18 April 1934, RG 9, entry 398, box 29, Saxon Mills folder.

34. Anonymous complaint of a Clifton No. 1 spooler read into the transcript of a CTLRB hearing at Clifton No. 1. Hearing transcript, 13 April 1934, RG 9, entry 402, box 27, Clifton Mfg. Co. folders (first folder).

35. "Speedy" [Dorthy Sprouse] to CTLRB, 12 Feb. 1934, RG 9, entry 398, box 11, Cowpens Mill folder. See also Anonymous to Board, 2 Oct. 1933, RG 9, entry 398, box 12, Drayton Mills folder (for isolation), and G. W. Smith to Lawrence Pinkney, 26 Dec. 1934, RG 9, entry 402, box 98, Pelham Mill folder (sanitation). See also Anonymous to Franklin D. Roosevelt, 24 June 1934 (company store again), and Thomas F. McMahon to L. D. Tindall, 23 March 1934, also affidavit of Mamie White, 11 April 1934 and attached affidavits (sexual harassment). All in RG 9, entry 402, box 27, Clifton Mfg. Co. folders (first folder).

36. See, for example, report of investigator R. F. Howell, 15 Dec. 1933, on complaint of W. J. Lloyd, RG 9, entry 398, box 30, Spartan Mills folder.

37. Mrs. N. R. Wheatley to Hugh S. Johnson, 28 Dec. 1933, RG 9, entry 398, box 29, Saxon Mills folder.

38. Report of investigator A. S. Thomas, 27 June 1934, RG 9, entry 398, box 15, Fairmont Mfg. Co. folder.

39. Robert W. Bruere to James F. Byrnes, 7 May 1934, RG 9, entry 398, box 11, Cowpens Mfg. Co. folder.

40. Original complaint (anonymous), 12 Jan. 1934, and investigation report of R. F. Howell, 9 April 1934, RG 9, entry 398, Saxon Mills folder. In subsequent months, Howell investigated—and dismissed out of hand—two other complaints from Saxon; his reports of 26 July and 17 September are in the same folder.

41. Thus, management's response to CTLRB inquiries ran the gamut from denial to dismissal. When workers reported violations at Whitney, management excused themselves by stating that "they are curtailing their operations." Arcadia's owner appealed to local "custom" when it dismissed a worker's complaint that he was being forced to perform fireman's work as unpaid overtime. Chesnee Mill's superintendent successfully sidestepped accusations of discriminatory discharge by personally assuring an NLRB investigator "that no one had ever been discharged

from this mill where their membership or nonmembership in a labor organiza-tion had been a governing factor." When workers complained that Riverdale Mills was doubling up battery-fillers' job assignments in order to eliminate po-sitions, an Enoree manager stated that loom assignments were "standardized" according to individual worker proficiency. During a previous "work sharing policy" that standard had been ignored, but as soon "as the minimum wage be-came effective" it was conveniently reinaugurated. L. R. Gilbert to W. C. Goforth, undated [summer 1934], RG 9, entry 398, box 33, Whitney Mfg. Co. folder; H. A. Ligon to H. H. Willis, 17 April 1934, RG 9, entry 398, box 3, Arcadia Mills folder; report of investigator E. O. Fitzsimons, 19 Dec. 1933, RG 9, entry 398, box 9, Chesnee Mills folder; report of investigator Lewis F. Sawyer, 6 Oct. 1933, RG 9, entry 398, box 28, Riverdale Mills folder; see also report of "LRG," RG 9, entry 398, box 15, Fairmont Mfg. Co. folder; and report of R. F. Howell, 26 July 1934, RG 9, entry 398, box 29, Saxon Mills folder.

42. This history of the Saxon Mills hearing before the CTLRB is largely drawn from the following documents (all in RG 9, entry 398, box 29, Saxon Mills folder): Thomas McMahon to L. R. Gilbert, 27 Feb. 1934; official transcript of the Saxon hearing, 16 Feb. 1934; "Decision of the Cotton Textile Industrial Relations Bord for S.C., Employees vs. Saxon Mill," 21 May 1934; memorandum, "Review of the mat-ter of Employees vs. Saxon Mills," 11 July 1934 and addended items; and Annie Laura West to Robert W. Bruere, 7 May 1934.

43. The workers who testified included W. J. Fowler, who charged that he had been laid off and a nonunion man placed on his job; Blanche Wheatley, who al-leged that she had been fired—and told so by her supervisor—for alleged miscon-duct on the part of her father; Algie Reid, who charged the company with stretch-ing out the doffers; Montine Grimsley, who maintained that her supervisor had demoted her in order to make room for his nonunion sister-in-law; and G. E. Hen-derson, who described the speedup in the cardroom.

44. In four cases, the complainants—out of work for four to six months by this time—had given up and left for employment elsewhere, and so the board declined to rule either way on three of them. In the case of the fourth, the board ruled that C. A. Loftis's job laying up roving in the basement "was discontinued on account of these machines being discarded" and therefore not a CTLRB concern. In the case of Blanche Wheatley, the board used a stray remark she had made during the hear-ing—that she did not know whether she "cared to work" for Saxon any more—to sidestep having to make any decision. W. A. Norton was summarily judged to be "not an efficient card grinder," even though he had been employed in that capac-ity for more than a decade. In the case of Montine Grimsley, the board intoned that "the mill has the right to transfer help as it sees fit, providing the employee is giv-en fair treatment and reasonable work," which the board ruled she was being giv-en despite her claims to the contrary. In no case did the board even refer to the

question of antiunion discrimination, which members of UTWA Local 1882 had charged.

45. "Review of the Matter of Employees vs. Saxon Mills," (reported date 11 July 1934), entry for 23 May, in RG 9, entry 398, box 29, Saxon Mills folder.

46. Ibid., entry for 25 June.

47. Robert W. Bruere to Sen. James F. Byrnes, 2 July 1934; see also Hugh S. Johnson to J. J. McSwain, 21 Feb. 1934. Both in RG 9, entry 398, box 29, Saxon Mills folder.

48. Annie Laura West to Frances Perkins, 28 Aug. 1934 (telegram), RG 9, entry 398, box 29, Saxon Mills folder.

49. Annie Laura West to Robert W. Bruere, 7 May 1934, RG 9, entry 398, box 29, Saxon Mills folder.

50. R. S. Kirby to Roosevelt, undated [Oct. 1933], RG 9, entry 398, box 25, Pacolet Mfg. Co. folder. In a humbler vein, a discharged Spartan Mills worker appealed to Sen. J. F. Byrnes for help, admitting, "I do not understand the code of the Textile Industry." W. J. Lloyd to Sen. J. F. Byrnes, 2 Nov. 1933, RG 9, entry 398, box 30, Spartan Mills folder.

51. W. H. Fowler to Hugh S. Johnson, 26 July 1933, RG 9, entry 398, box 3, Appalache Mill folder.

52. J. E. Hughes to L. R. Gilbert, 28 July 1934, RG 9, entry 398, box 25, Pacolet Mfg. Co. folder.

53. Section 7(a) was ultimately more an "innocuous moral shibboleth" (in the words of New Deal bureaucrat Francis Biddle) than "labor's Bill of Rights" (as hailed by AFL president William Green). Hodges, *New Deal Labor Policy and the Southern Cotton Textile Industry,* 46.

54. Tippett, *When Southern Labor Stirs.* The 1929 strike wave in South Carolina is also summarized in Simon, "A Fabric of Defeat," 102–7ff.

55. The known Spartanburg County locals were 1332–Spartanburg, 1356–Converse, 1359–Spartanburg, 1372–Fairmont, and 1373–Whitney. UTWA Convention Proceedings, 1919, 36–37, and 1920, 35–37.

56. This campaign was idiosyncratic and highly localized. In some cases the UTWA actually "organized" mills, but in others the union merely gave face to preexisting worker organizations in varying stages of development. Irons provides an excellent account of southern organizing dynamics during 1933 and 1934 in "Testing the New Deal," 201–12.

57. Affidavit of John Binkley Gregory, RG 9, entry 398, box 9, Chesnee Mills folder; affidavit of D. B. Bledsoe, 13 Oct. 1933, RG 9, entry 402, box 27, Clifton Mfg. Co. folders (seventh folder); Hembree and Crocker, *Glendale,* 48. The point is also made by Irons, "Testing the New Deal," 205–6, and by Wingerd, "Rethinking Paternalism," 21–22. Wingerd's North Cooleemee boasted taverns, brawls, noncompany grocers, Pentecostals, and blacks—anyone and anything not welcome in the village proper. As such, "It had a subversive function that was both material and sym-

bolic. North Cooleemee provided the physical free space to interact independently, away from the company's watchful gaze." It was here that Cooleemee workers met to form their own union in 1937.

58. Taken from financial records of the UTWA, TWUA Papers (Mss. 396), box 674. Arcadia and the two Woodruff mills were still smarting from the strikes of 1932 and 1929, respectively. The four small mills—none employing more than two hundred workers—were Fingerville, Fairforest Finishing, Bobo Weaving (which had no village), and Crescent Knitting. The anomalous mill was Chesnee in the northeastern corner of the county, geographically isolated from the bulk of Spartanburg's textile population.

59. Local 2070 ledger book, Moore Papers.

60. In addition to John Peel, two other AFL organizers operated in Spartanburg County during 1933 and 1934: J. W. Nates and Furman B. Rogers. Nates, a railway car painter, was primarily responsible for chartering new locals. Rogers, a printer, was officially in charge of servicing established locals, but he spent the bulk of his time representing labor on the South Carolina CTLRB.

61. Local 2070 ledger book, Moore Papers.

62. Although not uncommon, discriminatory discharges before the General Strike were far from universal. One such case reached the CTLRB from Pacolet Mills, where loom-fixer Ernest Mabry was discharged on 24 May 1934. Mill superintendent D. W. Anderson personally assured the CTLRB that he had instructed overseers to ignore union activity; he even presented the board with four supervisory affidavits stating that Mabry's work as loom-fixer had never been "entirely satisfactory." Local 1994 countered with three affidavits from weavers in Mabry's section asserting his competency. In an anguished letter, Mabry told Franklin Roosevelt how he had been "mistreated . . . on account of the interest I took in the N.R.A." Mabry, forty-three, explained that he had worked for Pacolet since the age of nine and that his work had always been acceptable before. He faced eviction:

> I am now appealing to you to see that I am justly treted in this affair. I have five children who are solely dependent on my labour for food. And if I am forced out of this house my family will be out of doors. I am a good citizen, and can furnish affidavits from the best people in the town to this effect.
>
> I am honest and fair, I pay my bills and try to treat my fellowman right.
> . . . I am appealing to you for support.

Mabry's character and family needs, however, were no legal concern of either the CTLRB or the Code Authority. Apparently, he was never reinstated. Affidavit of D. W. Anderson, 23 June 1934 and enclosed affidavits, Shop Committee to H. H. Willis, 6 July 1934 and enclosed affidavits, and Ernest Mabry to Roosevelt, 23 Aug. 1934. All in RG 9, entry 398, box 25, Pacolet Mfg. Co. folder. Pre-strike discriminatory discharge cases also came from Spartan (CTLRB hearing transcript, 11 April 1934, and decision, 26 May 1934, RG 9, entry 398, box 30, Spartan Mills folder); Saxon (CTLRB hearing transcript, 16 Feb. 1934, and decision, 21 May 1934, RG 9, entry 398, box 29, Saxon Mills folder); Clifton ("review of events" up to July 1934, noting affidavits submitted on 30 March and 11 April 1934, RG 9, entry 402, box 27, Clifton Mfg. Co. folders [first folder]); Glendale (affidavit of D. B. Bledsoe, 13 Oct. 1933, misfiled in RG 9, entry 402, box 27, Clifton Mfg. Co. folders, seventh folder); and Chesnee (affidavits of Arthur O. Fowler and John Binkley Gregory, 30 Oct. 1933, RG 9, entry 398, box 9, Chesnee Mills folder).

63. Even after a mill was ostensibly organized, the UTWA frequently had to deal with widely varying levels of leadership and worker support inside the plant. According to some activists, the primary phenomenon undergirding union majorities at many mills was not commitment to the ideals of unionism but rather simple peer pressure. Robert Donnahoo, then president of the Inman Mills local, later claimed that the UTWA never did have a committed majority in most of Spartanburg's mills, although in practice the union could exercise influence far out of proportion with its actual dedicated membership. Interviews with Vernon Foster, Jasper DeYoung, Mae DeYoung, and Robert W. Donnahoo.

64. Ever since the 1890s, with the rise of Jim Crow segregation in the South, the de facto reservation of mill work for whites only, and the attempts by a few disgruntled southern manufacturers to operate mills with all-black work forces, the threat of blacks replacing whites in southern mills had been a potent one, although never realized in later years. McLaurin, *Paternalism and Protest,* 60–66; Carlton, *Mill and Town in South Carolina,* 158–60, 244–45; interview with Robert W. Donnahoo.

65. Interview with Robert W. Donnahoo; Local 2145 information taken from the 1934 Spartanburg city directory.

66. The mid–1934 strike wave is covered in Irons, "Testing the New Deal," 352–73.

67. In his first official statement concerning the strike, UTWA representative John A. Peel noted, "Labor deplores the necessity of a strike, but we have no other means of redress, now that Dr. Robert Bruere, chair of the National Cotton Textile Industrial Relations Board, made a definite statement to the American Cotton Manufacturers' Association that of more than two thousand cases before the board no decision has been rendered because of the disturbing influence that such decision might have on industry. If this is the attitude of the board set up to handle the complaints, then there is nothing left for the workers to do but strike when the manufacturers fail to make adjustments." James F. Byrnes to Robert W. Bruere, 5 May 1934, with clipping from *Greenville Piedmont* enclosed, and Robert W. Bruere to James F. Byrnes, 7 May 1934. Both in RG 9, entry 398, box 11, Cowpens Mfg. Co. folder.

68. According to the company, Cowpens Mill had manufactured sheetings until mid-December, when its orders had dried up. It then switched to seersucker, but orders for that fabric also dried up in mid-April, whereupon the company "under-

took certain experiments in the manufacture of print cloth . . . with the hope of obtaining orders for this type of fabric." Because seersucker was "fancier" work than basic print cloth, management added, weavers of print cloth would be expected to run more looms than they had for seersucker, necessitating the layoff of some employees. H. H. Willis, Cowpens Mill report (enclosure in Willis to Robert W. Bruere, 16 May 1934), RG 9, entry 398, box 11, Cowpens Mfg. Co. folder.

69. H. H. Willis, Cowpens Mill report (enclosure in Willis to Robert W. Bruere, 16 May 1934), RG 9, entry 398, box 11, Cowpens Mfg. Co. folder; *Spartanburg Herald,* 15, 16 May 1934. Willis's response was consistent with the board's earlier nonattempts to resolve the Horse Creek Valley controversy. Irons, "Testing the New Deal," 247.

70. See, for example, worker Mable Brown to Hugh S. Johnson, 18 June 1934, RG 9, entry 398, box 11, Cowpens Mfg. Co. folder.

71. F. B. Rogers to Robert W. Bruere, 16 July 1934, RG 9, entry 398, box 11, Cowpens Mfg. Co. folder.

72. This was also the case elsewhere in South Carolina. Although the South Carolina board was one of the few state boards that actually operated, the "momentum" of its decisions, as Janet Irons makes clear in the contemporaneous Horse Creek Valley strike, was that "while the Board did not openly embarace the mill managements' position, it would not reverse any actions already taken by the mills," thus eating away at unionization "on a piecemeal basis." In sum, "Because the Boards had no real power, they tailored their interpretations of events to correspond with actual power relationships in order that their decisions could appear to have authority. Bruere's entire Board structure was a mirage." "Testing the New Deal," 251, 253.

73. Cowpens Mill hearing transcript, 25 July 1934, "Recommendation in Case of Cowpens Mill," 2 Aug. 1934, and shop committee to Robert W. Bruere, 10 Aug. 1934. All in RG 9, entry 398, box 11, Cowpens Mfg. Co. folder.

CHAPTER 3: "IT'S NOW OR NEVER"

1. Hodges, *New Deal Labor Policy and the Southern Cotton Textile Industry,* 95.

2. Transcript of Cowpens Mill hearing, 25 July 1934, RG 9, entry 398, box 11, Cowpens Mfg. Co. folder.

3. The UTW's predicament—and the rising southern discontent that was its source—is detailed in Irons, "Testing the New Deal," chapters 7–9. As Irons notes, the UTW's position was inherently untenable. On the one hand, the thousands of southern workers joining its ranks forced it into the role "of being an interpreter of a plethora of new demands and grievances before the federal government." On the other, however, the UTW had obligated itself as a "partner" in two key Rooseveltian endeavors, the NRA and the Cotton Textile Code. Under Thomas McMahon, the UTW's course throughout 1933 and 1934 was primarily one of accommodation to the Roosevelt administration, urging southern workers to

trust the ineffective government-sponsored boards and discouraging strikes at every turn. "By the beginning of 1934, therefore, the union and the local southern membership were at very different places, conceptually speaking. Union locals, seeing their strength undermined by the inaction of the federal government and bad Board decisions, were growing increasingly angry and impatient with the NRA machinery. The UTW, meanwhile, was urging labor's co-operation and its full support of what it presumed were the NRA's best efforts to create industrial harmony in the southern mills." Only after the mid–1934 Alabama strikes forced the UTW's hand did the union agree, reluctantly, to a course of direct action. Irons, "Testing the New Deal," 266–67, 273–74ff.

4. This paragraph and subsequent ones concerning the SCFTW's July convention are drawn from articles in the *Spartanburg Journal,* 20–22 July 1934.

5. On Saturday morning, the convention also passed a number of other resolutions expressing solidarity and determination: asking the CTLRB and Code Authority to send investigators to Cowpens Mill; "being in full sympathy with the textile workers of the state of Alabama"; censuring Governor Blackwood for sending "armed guards" into the Piedmont strike areas when no violence or damage had been committed or threatened; petioning the CTLRB to investigate conditions at the closed Musgrove Mill at Gaffney; demanding a CTLRB investigation of the buy-back policy inflicted on weavers and loom-fixers at Spartan Mills; generally condemning "that a certain part of the employers in the industry have not abided by the code"; and demanding that the CTLRB take up cases of alleged discriminatory discharge immediately. The convention formed a legislative committee "to foster and urge the passage of labor bills in the South Carolina legislature and in the national Congress" and another committee to investigate charges that merchants in some textile towns were discriminating against union members.

6. *Spartanburg Journal,* 7 Aug. 1934.

7. Irons, "Testing the New Deal," 384–406.

8. *Spartanburg Journal,* 19 Aug. 1934.

9. *Spartanburg Journal,* 22, 30, 31 Aug. 1934.

10. *Spartanburg Journal,* 24–26 Aug. 1934.

11. *Spartanburg Journal,* 28 Aug. 1934; see also the *Journal's* editorial on 31 Aug.

12. *Spartanburg Journal,* 31 Aug. 1934. This was the only public acknowledgment from any source that black workers were indeed being organized by the UTWA in mid–1934.

13. *Spartanburg Journal,* 31 Aug. 1934.

14. RG 9, entry 398, box 5, Beaumont Mfg. Co. folders (first folder); P. D. Hughes to Hugh S. Johnson, 1 Sept. 1934 (telegram), RG 9, entry 398, box 25, Pacolet Mfg. Co. folder.

15. *Spartanburg Journal,* 30 Aug. 1934.

16. *Spartanburg Journal,* 1 Sept. 1994.

17. Ibid.

18. *Spartanburg Journal,* 3 Sept. 1934. Closed that morning were Fairmont, Beaumont, Tucapau, Saxon, Arkwright, Whitney, all three Cliftons, Drayton, Cowpens, Jackson, Spartan, Valley Falls, Enoree, and Inman. Still running were Glendale, Powell Knitting, Fairforest Finishing, Bobo Weaving, Crescent, Victor, Apalache, Mills Mill and Brandon Mill at Woodruff, Arcadia, Lyman, Chesnee, and Fingerville. With the exception of Glendale, this was an excellent summation of the state of union organizing in Spartanburg County. All of the mills that ran through Monday either had nonexistent or weak, recently organized locals.

19. *Spartanburg Journal,* 3 Sept. 1934.

20. Ibid. On Friday, 7 September, Sheriff Henry deputized twenty-two more special deputies, twenty of them for Victor Mill and two for Arcadia.

21. *Spartanburg Journal,* 4, 5, 7, 10 Sept. 1934.

22. Interview with Clement A. Riddle.

23. *Spartanburg Journal,* 5 Sept. 1934. An account of Honea Path is contained in the interview with Vivian Duncan, whose brother was one of the Guardsmen there.

24. Interview with Ernest C. Hawkins.

25. Interview with Fred Jewell.

26. *Spartanburg Journal,* 7, 8 Sept. 1934.

27. See, for example, *Spartanburg Journal,* 2, 6 Sept. 1934.

28. Only a few locals were large enough to have the financial resources for comprehensive relief work. Unfortunately, a membership base large enough to have generated a sizable bank account was also large enough to eat it away. The expense of feeding so many for a month bankrupted locals. At Tucapau, for instance, Local 2070 paid out $210.04 for groceries and $29.51 for fuel during the strike, virtually its entire treasury. Local 2070 ledger book, G. Walter Moore Collection.

29. *Spartanburg Journal,* 3, 4 Sept. 1934.

30. See *Spartanburg Journal,* 5, 6 Sept. 1934.

31. *Spartanburg Journal,* 5 Sept. 1934. The "expansion" of the squadron's effective territory is covered in the interview with Vernon Foster, and an excellent description of the squadron's Greenville activities at Dunean, Judson, and Woodside is included in the interview with Furman Mabry and Louise Mabry.

32. *Spartanburg Journal,* 5 Sept. 1934.

33. *Spartanburg Journal,* 6, 7 Sept. 1934; interview with Vernon Foster.

34. *Spartanburg Journal,* 5, 6, 7 Sept. 1934. A discussion of the role of the squadron in organizing Woodside Mill is in the interview with Vernon Foster.

35. The same point is made in Irons, "Testing the New Deal," 425–42, esp. 440.

36. *Spartanburg Journal,* 7, 10, 11 Sept. 1934. The degree to which top UTWA leadership supported the flying squadrons at any point in the strike is debatable. The decision to disband must have come from higher up than John Peel. While the Spartanburg squadron was operating in Greenville, however, the UTWA kept them supplied with food ("they sent over a few loaves of bread and some baloney"), a

level of support possible only with Peel's knowledge and blessing. Interview with Vernon Foster.

37. *Spartanburg Journal,* 6 Sept. 1934. The days were Wednesday through Friday, 5–7 September 1934, and Monday, 10 September.

38. Hall et al., *Like a Family,* 343. The double-edged nature of mill-village community is well portrayed by Douglas Flamming, who recounts a 1939 strike in Dalton, Georgia: "The millhands' own culture was geared more toward mutual interdependence than individualism, but the tradition of unity could cut two ways. It could nourish a vibrant community of workers and contribute to successful unionization, but it could also lead to severe polarization within the mill village." *Creating the Modern South,* 228–29.

CHAPTER 4: "GETTING OUR THROATS CUT"

1. As Janet Irons notes, "Fragile outposts of unionism or nonunionism in 'enemy' territory sometimes survived and sometimes succumbed to the organized strength of the opposite side. It was in such disputed territories that tension between the two sides heightened and threatened to erupt into violence." Irons gives the key examples of Greenville's Dunean mill (an island of prounion sentiment in an overwhelmingly antiunion environment) and Gastonia's Loray Mill (the reverse). "Testing the New Deal," 443–45.

2. Smith's testimony in UTWA Emergency Committee minutes, 20–21 Nov. 1934 (special Greenville meeting), TWUA Papers, box 674.

3. *Spartanburg Journal,* 10, 11, 12 Sept. 1934.

4. *Spartanburg Journal,* 15, 18 Sept. 1934.

5. Affidavits of Miss Cleo Linder and George M. Garland, 13 Oct. 1934, RG 9, entry 402, box 34, Cowpens Mfg. Co. folders (third folder).

6. Affidavit of Horace Waddell, 13 Oct. 1934, RG 9, entry 402, box 34, Cowpens Mfg. Co. folders (third folder).

7. At the Cliftons, where the plants remained closed for the duration of the strike, the main entertainment was walking the three miles to Cowpens to gawk at the National Guardsmen and their machine guns at Cowpens Mill. According to one young man who made the trip, hundreds of Clifton residents—men, women, and children—took in the spectacle. Interview with Aaron Thornton.

8. Cowpens Mill to "Our Operatives," 10 Sept. 1934, RG 9, entry 402, box 34, Cowpens Mfg. Co. folders (third folder).

9. Affidavit of W. A. Hicks, 13 Oct. 1934, RG 9, entry 402, box 34, Cowpens Mfg. Co. folders (third folder).

10. *Spartanburg Journal,* 10, 11 Sept. 1934.

11. Group affidavit of John Robbins, Newton Largent, Lloyd Linder, and Dock Johnson, 13 Oct. 1934, and affidavit of Jim Eldridge, 13 Oct. 1934. Both in RG 9, entry 398, box 34, Cowpens Mfg. Co. folders (third folder).

12. M. E. Jackson and C. H. Darman to Lawrence W. Pinkney, 12 Sept. 1934, RG 9, entry 398, box 11, Cowpens Mfg. Co. folder.

13. *Spartanburg Journal,* 13 Sept. 1934.

14. *Spartanburg Journal,* 17, 18 Sept. 1934.

15. *Spartanburg Journal,* 19 Sept. 1934.

16. *Spartanburg Journal,* 10, 13, 17 Sept. 1934.

17. UTWA partisans continued to rally behind the strike banner. On Monday night of the strike's second week, Spartanburg's Central Labor Union had a mass meeting (even the hostile *Journal* reported attendance at around a thousand) to review the strike situation, receive reports from the locals, and discuss relief options. *Spartanburg Journal,* 18 Sept. 1934.

18. *Spartanburg Journal,* 13, 14, 20 Sept. 1934. The WPA also reopened old projects, such as improvements on Spartanburg city's Cleveland Park, in order to give strikers work.

19. *Spartanburg Journal,* 16 Sept. 1934. Ironically, the only major occurrence of strike violence in Spartanburg came at this devolving juncture. On Tuesday, 19 September, six young women entered Powell Knitting and spent the day working in the stockroom, possibly preparing for a resumption of work. Word spread through the Powell and neighboring villages, and around 6:30 A.M. on the following morning a crowd estimated by the press at "several hundred" gathered outside Powell Mill to prevent their return. Ten of Sheriff Henry's "special deputies" were on hand and turned fire hoses on the crowd after repeatedly commanding it to disperse. Some in the crowd began to pelt the officers with stones in response, whereupon the deputies escalated the situation by exploding two tear gas bombs. The crowd scattered, but the Powell plant thereafter remained idle until the end of the strike. In what may have been a revenge attack, two dynamite bombs exploded on the Powell mill property the following Saturday night but no damage was done. *Spartanburg Journal,* 19, 24 Sept. 1934.

20. *Spartanburg Journal,* 21 Sept. 1934; Irons, "Testing the New Deal," 473–77.

21. Less sanguine, local strike leaders H. M. Branch of Clifton and H. C. Godfrey of Spartanburg sent Francis Gorman a guarded telegram on Friday afternoon: "The sentiment of locals in this vicinity is to accept proposal of president of the United States." *Spartanburg Journal,* 21 Sept. 1934.

22. Johnston's life story is told, glowingly, in Huss, *Senator for the South.* For more critical examinations of his tumultuous years as governor of South Carolina, see Carpenter, "Olin D. Johnston," and Simon, "A Fabric of Defeat."

23. *Spartanburg Journal,* 23 Sept. 1934.

24. "Moreover," the union leaders added, "we cannot refuse to cooperate with the President, as he has asked us to do." UTWA Emergency Committee minutes, 22 Sept. 1934, TWUA Papers, box 674.

25. Ibid.

26. Irons, "Testing the New Deal," 478–86.

27. *Spartanburg Journal,* 24 Sept. 1934. At Powell Knitting, superintendent J. H. Dupre even began issuing arrest warrants for selected strike participants. He ultimately had thirteen men and eleven women arrested for alleged "violations of section 1380 of the state code relative to obstructing citizens of Powell Knitting Company from enjoying the rights secured to them by the Constitution." *Spartanburg Journal,* 25 Sept. 1934.

28. Glendale was the only Spartanburg mill to reopen on Monday, 23 September. Drayton, Whitney, and Valley Falls all reopened on 26 September; Pacolet opened the following morning, Enoree in the afternoon, and Saxon on Friday morning. The last National Guardsmen left Woodruff and Lyman on Thursday and Friday, respectively. On Monday, 1 October, nine plants reopened: Powell Knitting, Spartan, the Cliftons, Beaumont, Tucapau, Inman, and Jackson Mill. The next day, Fairmont and Arkwright resumed operations, marking, as the *Journal* noted, "an end, insofar as Spartanburg County is concerned, to the most serious textile strike in history." *Spartanburg Journal,* 27 Sept.–2 Oct. 1934.

29. UTWA Emergency Committee minutes, 26–27 Oct. 1934, TWUA Papers, box 674.

30. UTWA Emergency Committee minutes, 20–21 Nov. 1934 (special Greenville meeting), TWUA Papers, box 674.

31. The CTLRB's ignominious fate is covered in Irons, "Testing the New Deal," 488–92.

32. Ibid., 493–500. Eloquent local testimony came from Whitney, where unionists reported in late December that "our stretch-out system in our mill is bad in all departments"; from Glendale, where as late as May 1935 management had yet to even post copies of the code, as required by law; and from Fairmont, whence unionist F. J. McAbee wrote the UTWA's Francis Gorman in early February that "things are in bad shape here. Our members are getting discouraged. Something has got to be done. They have speeded up the machinery in the card room and the spinning room. . . . In the weave room . . . the work runs so bad you can never get it started up." Talmadge Richards to Francis Gorman, undated [Dec. 1934], RG 9, entry 402, box 139, Whitney Mfg. Co. folders (first folder); F. J. McAbee to Francis Gorman, 6 Feb 1935, RG 9, entry 402, box 134; Union–Buffalo Mills Co., Fairmont plant folders (first folder, see also McAbee to Gorman, 10 Dec. 1934 and 16 May 1935); Francis J. Gorman to W. J. Taylor, 8 May 1935, RG 9, entry 402, box 31, D. E. Converse Co. folder. Other post-strike stretch-out complaints came from Chesnee Mill (anonymous complaint, 28 March 1935, RG 9, entry 402, box 25, Chesnee Mills folder); Enoree (documents in RG 9, entry 402, box 109, Riverdale Mills, both folders); Jackson Mill (memorandum of telephone conversation, J. L. Bernard to Samuel R. McClurd, 12 Jan. 1935, RG 9, entry 402, box 69, Jackson Mill folder); and Valley Falls (series of complaints filed by the UTWA on 31 Oct. 1934, RG 9, entry 402, box 80, Martel Mills of Valley Falls [third folder]). In the Valley Falls case, someone on the CTLRB office staff scrawled "not investigated" at the bottom of each sheet and let them go.

33. H. M. Branch to Francis Gorman, 17 Nov. 1934, RG 9, entry 402, box 27, Clifton Mfg. Co. folders (third folder).

34. H. M. Branch to CTLRB, 30 Jan. 1935, RG 9, entry 402, box 27, Clifton Mfg. Co. folders (second folder).

35. As Branch warned the CTLRB, "The workers here are becoming very restless and discouraged about no action being taken in our case by the Work Assignment Board." H. M. Branch to W. A. Mitchell, 14 March 1935, RG 9, entry 402, box 27, Clifton Mfg. Co. folders (third folder).

36. John Peel to W. A. Mitchell, 14 March 1935, RG 9, entry 402, box 27, Clifton Mfg. Co. folders (third folder).

37. One Spartan striker was not rehired. That man, mill owner Walter Montgomery noted, had been convicted of criminal misconduct while on strike and would have been dismissed on that account anyway. Local 1881 even backed the company in its decision to fire and evict a family deemed responsible for a brief wildcat strike in late November, Pollard admitting that the Lawters were indeed "more or less a disturbing and influence." Other mills from which discrimination cases were conspicuously absent after the strike included the three Clifton plants. Walter S. Montgomery to Samuel R. McClurd, 10 Dec. 1934, and Walter R. Taliaferro Jr. to Samuel R. McClurd, 11 Dec. 1934 (quotation). Both in RG 9, entry 402, box 123, Spartan Mills folders (third folder). For the Lawter case, see documents in RG 9, entry 402, box 123, Spartan Mills folders (second and third folders), and J. C. Pridmore to Francis J. Gorman, 31 Oct. 1934, RG 9, entry 402, box 69, Jackson Mills folder.

38. Documents in RG 9, entry 402, box 134, Union–Buffalo Mills Co., Fairmont plant folders (third folder). CTLRB investigator Dudley Harmon was able to get the strikers to return to work, whereupon she convinced plant owner F. W. Symmes to take back not only them but also the nine cases of alleged discrimination.

39. Dudley Harmon repeatedly negotiated favorable settlements on these points with plant owner Ralph Powell, all of which Powell repeatedly broke. At one point she cabled the board's Washington office to beg for immediate advice, because she was "going mad" from her Orwellian dealings with Powell and other area mill executives. Documents in RG 9, entry 402, box 103, Powell Knitting Co. folder, especially Harmon's initial investigation report of 15 Oct. 1934 and Dudley Harmon to Samuel R. McClurd, 26 Nov. 1934 (quotation).

40. The quotation is from P. D. Hughes to Francis J. Gorman, 22 Nov. 1934, RG 9, entry 402, box 95, Pacolet Mfg. Co. folders (first folder), but see also the other documents in this folder, all of which pertain to alleged discrimination cases at Pacolet. Other post-strike discrimination cases emanated from Drayton (documents in RG 9, entry 402, box 39, Drayton Mills folder); Beaumont (complaint of J. F. Laughter, 6 Oct. 1934, RG 9, entry 402, box 12, Beaumont Mfg. Co. folders); Inman (complaint of R. W. Donnahoo, 18 Oct. 1934, and report of Peter A. Carmichael, 3 Nov. 1934, RG 9, entry 402, box 68, Inman Mills folders); Arkwright (complaint of Ira Boozer, 11 Dec. 1934, RG 9, entry 402, box 8, Arkwright Mills

folders); and Enoree (complaint filed by J. W. Nates, 3 Oct. 1934, RG 9, entry 402, box 109, Riverdale Mills folders).

41. For the tally, see memorandum on Pacific Mills situation, undated, RG 9, entry 402, box 95, Pacific Mills folders (first folder, 1).

42. Peter A. Carmichael to H. L. Kerwin, 3 Oct. 1934, RG 9, entry 398, box 95, Pacific Mills folders (first folder). Hayes's position was upheld by Pacific Mills president A. E. Colby of Boston. A. E. Colby to CTLRB, 8 Oct. 1934, RG 9, entry 398, box 95, Pacific Mills folders (first folder).

43. Being careful to heap praise on the company, its village, and C. B. Hayes, Carmichael noted that the remaining Lyman strikers had been guilty of no strike disturbances and that "they are afraid they will suffer painfully as the weather grows colder, if they are not able to get back to their jobs." Peter A. Carmichael to Irving Southworth, 17 Oct. 1934, RG 9, entry 402, box 95, Pacific Mills folders (first folder).

44. See B. M. Squires to A. E. Colby (telegram) and also A. E. Colby's reply, both 17 Oct. 1934, RG 9, entry 402, box 95, Pacific Mills folders (first folder).

45. Bruce Sheriff to Frances Perkins, 22 Oct. 1934, RG 9, entry 402, box 95, Pacific Mills folders (first folder).

46. J. O. Ivester to Frances Perkins, 23 Oct. 1934, RG 9, entry 402, box 95, Pacific Mills folders (first folder).

47. H. A. Wooten to Frances Perkins, 1 Nov. 1934, RG 9, entry 402, box 95, Pacific Mills folders (fifth folder).

48. Ralph Mullinax to B. M. Squires, 7 Nov. 1934, RG 9, entry 402, box 95, Pacific Mills folders (fifth folder).

49. Mrs. G. W. Lankford to Frances Perkins, 7 Nov. 1934, RG 9, entry 402, box 95, Pacific Mills folders (fifth folder).

50. Mrs. Edna Atkins to B. M. Squires, 13 Nov. 1934, RG 9, entry 402, box 95, Pacific Mills folders.

51. N. J. Sheriff to Frances Perkins, 23 Oct. 1934, RG 9, entry 402, box 95, Pacific Mills folders (first folder).

52. Annie Morgan to Franklin D. Roosevelt, 18 Oct. 1934, RG 9, entry 402, box 95, Pacific Mills folders (first folder).

53. Mrs. Clora Leonard to B. M. Squires, 31 Oct. 1934, RG 9, entry 402, box 95, Pacific Mills folders (fifth folder).

54. A. L. Millwood to B. M. Squires, 31 Oct. 1934, RG 9, entry 402, box 95, Pacific Mills folders (fifth folder).

55. J. M. Brown to B. M. Squires, 3 Nov. 1934, RG 9, entry 402, box 95, Pacific Mills folders (first folder).

56. J. H. Stone and Furman Garrett to B. M. Squires, 30 Oct. 1934, RG 9, entry 402, box 95, Pacific Mills folders (first folder).

57. Mrs. Clora Leonard to B. M. Squires, 19 Nov. 1934, RG 9, entry 402, box 95, Pacific Mills folders (first folder).

58. Mrs. Clora Leonard and Annie Morgan to Judge Stacey, 17 Jan. 1935, RG 9, entry 402, box 95, Pacific Mills folders (first folder).

59. According to investigator J. L. Bernard, of the 357 discrimination cases registered with him, 296 workers had been rehired by the company as of 9 January, but only forty-four had been rehired back onto their old jobs. Some sixty-one were still completely out of work. Memorandum of telephone conversation, J. L. Bernard to Samuel R. McClurd, 9 Jan. 1935, RG 9, entry 402, box 95, Pacific Mills folders (first folder).

60. John Peel to Col. Frank P. Douglas of CTLRB, 31 Jan. 1935 (telegram), RG 9, entry 402, box 95, Pacific Mills folders (first folder).

61. Telfair Knight to Henry L. Stevens, 9 Feb. 1935, J. L. Bernard to Samuel R. McClurd, 12 Feb. 1935 (telegram), and J. L. Bernard to Samuel R. McClurd, 16 and 27 Feb. 1935. All in RG 9, entry 402, box 95, Pacific Mills folders (first folder).

62. J. L. Bernard to Samuel R. McClurd, 16 Feb. and 15 June 1935, RG 9, entry 402, box 95, Pacific Mills folders (first and third folders).

63. Local 2191 even threatened to take a strike vote if Hayes moved forward with his eviction plans, and although J. L. Bernard judged the threat to be hollow, he admitted that in such a touchy situation "you cannot say what is liable to occur twenty-four hours in advance." J. L. Bernard to Samuel R. McClurd, 27 Aug., 27 Sept., and 6 Nov. 1935. All in RG 9, entry 402, box 95, Pacific Mills folders (third folder).

64. George Kamenow to Samuel R. McClurd, 21 Dec. 1935, RG 9, entry 402, box 95, Pacific Mills folders (third folder).

65. For the NLRB portion of this case's history—including hundreds of pages of hearing transcripts—see RG 25, entry 155, box 250, Pacific Mills folders.

66. Una News-Review, 18 June 1937.

67. Furman Garrett to Franklin D. Roosevelt, 19 Jan. 1935, RG 9, entry 402, box 95, Pacific Mills folders (fifth folder).

68. Testimony of Jack Kirby, Cowpens Mill hearing transcript, 22 March 1935, RG 9, entry 402, box 34, Cowpens Mfg. Co. folders (fourth folder, 15–16).

69. Complaint/affidavit of George Garland, 4 Oct. 1934, RG 9, entry 402, Cowpens Mfg. Co. folders (third folder).

70. H. W. Kirby to B. M. Squires, 5 Oct. 1934, RG 9, entry 402, box 34, Cowpens Mfg. Co. folders (third folder).

71. Investigation report of Dudley Harmon, 22 Oct. 1934, RG 9, entry 402, box 34, Cowpens Mfg. Co. folders (third folder).

72. Ibid.

73. Superintendent D. G. Floyd told Lula Fisher that "he was filled up and couldn't use her family." Floyd told Billy Bishop that he had hired another man on his job and that "it wouldn't be fair to turn the man off and put him back to work." Eunice Maynor was told that the mill had "nothing for her to do at present." H. W. Kirby himself told C. C. and Sara Lou Keener that "it would be unpleasant for the hands

here to work with them, best to go somewhere else." Investigation report of Dudley Harmon, 31 Oct. 1934, and Dudley Harmon to B. M. Squires, 6 Nov. 1934 and attached affidavits. All in RG 9, entry 402, box 34, Cowpens Mfg. Co. folders (third folder).

74. Dudley Harmon to Samuel R. McClurd, 24 Nov. 1934, and her investigation report of 26 Nov. 1934. Both in RG 9, entry 402, box 34, Cowpens Mfg. Co. folders (third folder).

75. Memorandum, Samuel R. McClurd to Telfair Knight, undated [March 1935], and memorandum of telephone conversation, J. L. Bernard to McClurd, 26 Jan. 1935. Both in RG 9, entry 402, box 34, Cowpens Mfg. Co. folders (third folder).

76. John A. Peel to Samuel R. McClurd, 6 March 1935, RG 9, entry 402, box 34, Cowpens Mfg. Co. folders (third folder).

77. During this time, the Cowpens case acquired a distinctive twist when, on 5 January 1935, H. W. Kirby fired his superintendent, D. G. Floyd. Floyd claimed that he had angered Kirby in mid-December by quietly rehiring a few blacklisted workers. There was indeed a blacklist, according to Floyd, who switched sides three days after his discharge and filed his own complaint with the CTLRB. "Fully 95 percent of those who are out of work here are good people," he wrote, "and they are suffering for the necessities of life. Some of them have done no other wrong than make remarks about the President of the Company 'keeping' a Widow woman who works in the Weave Room and they were justifiable in such remarks."

Realizing that his testimony would end his career in textiles, Floyd nevertheless promised to tell all about Kirby's eight-month campaign against the union, including behind-the-scenes details of the April strike and the company's subsequent efforts to misinform and circumvent the CTLRB. The CTLRB kept Floyd's case separate and did not permit him to testify at the hearing. Investigator R. F. Howell later sustained Floyd's allegations that the mill had violated both the code's wage and hour provisions, doctoring its books to hide the fact, but even so Howell concluded that "it is difficult to place the blame." Floyd himself was left writing the same kind of poignant but useless letters to Washington as had his former employees. D. G. Floyd to Franklin D. Roosevelt, 8 Jan. 1935, report of R. F. Howell, 1 Feb. 1935, and D. G. Floyd to CTLRB, 29 Jan. 1935. All in RG 9, entry 402, box 34, Cowpens Mfg. Co. folders (third and second folders).

78. Testimonies of Mrs. George Garland and George Garland. Both in hearing transcript, United Textile Workers of America vs. Cowpens Mfg. Co., RG 9, entry 402, box 34, Cowpens Mfg. Co. folders (fourth folder, 10–11, and 40, for Annie Bell Barnett's discharge).

79. Cowpens Mfg. Co. brief, RG 9, entry 402, box 34, Cowpens Mfg. Co. folders (third folder).

80. Wettach noted circumspectly that "the officials who testified were fairly narrow and restricted in their views," somewhat less circumspectly that "there was no one person of outstanding calibre such as your examiner has had the pleasure

of dealing with in other hearings." Report of examiner Robert H. Wettach, United Textile Workers of America vs. Cowpens Mfg. Co., and "Supplementary Report." Both in RG 9, entry 402, box 34, Cowpens Mfg. Co. folders (third folder).

81. Ibid.

82. Samuel R. McClurd to John Peel, 1 June 1935, RG 9, entry 402, box 34, Cowpens Mfg. Co. folders (third folder).

83. News clippings, *Gaffney Ledger,* 27 Aug. 1935, and *Daily News Record,* 11 June 1936. Both in RG 9, entry 402, box 34, Cowpens Mfg. Co. folders (first folder).

84. B. B. Fowler to Franklin D. Roosevelt, 20 June 1935, RG 9, entry 402, box 34, Cowpens Mfg. Co. folders (first folder). In another letter to Roosevelt, Fowler detailed what he perceived as the violation of Cowpens's moral economy that the employment of farmers represented: "I believe in helping the farmer when he is due help, and when he does receive gov't aide make him stay with his Crop, not running two jobs at once at the other mans expense. That is the case here, when the General Strike occurred the mill company ran it over the people by hiring all the farmers in the district. Many farmers let their farms lay idle. While others, the heads of the familys would pretend to farm or hire hands at a cheap rate of labor and the children went to the mill." B. B. Fowler to Franklin D. Roosevelt, 22 July 1935, RG 9, entry 402, box 34, Cowpens Mfg. Co. folders (first folder). The issue of "farmers"—which could mean any rural-dweller living outside of a mill village, regardless of textile experience—versus bona fide textile mill workers remained an undercurrent in virtually every southern strike of the period. Simon, "Rethinking Why There Are so Few Unions in the South," 480–81.

85. B. B. Fowler to Franklin D. Roosevelt, 20 June 1935, RG 9, entry 402, box 34, Cowpens Mfg. Co. folders (first folder). Iris Henderson, former secretary of Local 1934, described her version of this aftermath: "After we found we had completely lost the strike and the union had finally dispersed, I started the slow, monotonous grind of looking for a job. To my horror I found that I, along with the others, had been blacklisted. I went continuously from one plant to another. Besides that, I tried the shops, stores, and cafes, but business being slack, it was impossible to get on." Through the graces of her aunt, Henderson was eventually able to get a job at the Alma Mill in nearby Gaffney but worked there only six months before she lost that job in yet another strike. Henderson, "The Recommendation," in the 1936 annual of the Southern Summer School for Workers, Moore Papers.

86. B. B. Fowler to Franklin D. Roosevelt, 22 July 1935, RG 9, entry 402, box 34, Cowpens Mfg. Co. folders (first folder).

87. *Spartanburg Journal,* 23 Sept. 1934.

88. A union member later charged that Walter Montgomery—proud of his paternalistic reputation as a responsible and humane mill official—never "saw what the union really meant, or what it foretold." Interview with Vernon Foster.

89. The Drayton local was built around only a handful of talented and dedicated leaders like J. O. Blum. After the collapse of the strike and the departure of Blum,

the local disintegrated. The Arkwright local, however, never had firm support from the mill's workers. In mid–1934, for instance, Arkwright had hired textile baseball star Ernest Hawkins to coach its team. Hawkins proved a dependable company man; for his "job," the company assigned him to push the snack wagon through the mill. On his first day, one of Local 2119's officers informed Hawkins that he would have to buy a union sticker for his wagon. Hawkins refused, and the local called a boycott against him. For two or three days the boycott held. The company store manager told Hawkins to continue pushing the wagon through the mill anyway. Clearly using Hawkins to test the overall strength of the UTWA at their mill, the company got its answer quickly: "In about a week I was selling as much as I had, or more," Hawkins later recalled: "And that's the way the union stuck together." Interviews with various former Drayton employees; interview with Ernest C. Hawkins.

90. But they all blend together, as Janet Irons has noted. "As told by the southern workers themselves, the history of textile unions in the South possesses a timeless quality. Workers find it difficult to recall in which strike a particular incident occurred; the stories of different strikes inevitably run together. Specific causal details blur into a larger truth, one which seems to apply whatever strike, or whatever union is being discussed." "Testing the New Deal," 541.

The Spartanburg workers whom I interviewed almost inevitably conflated the General Strike with other conflicts during 1930s. Only those who had been particularly active in the labor movement at the time, or who had experienced a major life event during the General Strike, could make clear distinctions. Even they agreed that, what with the strength of Spartanburg's local unions and the fact that so much strike action occurred elsewhere, "It was peaceful here. . . . In '34 it went smooth in Spartanburg." Interviews with Paul O. Taylor and Joe Love.

91. Irons, "Testing the New Deal," 501. Timing was critical. "No argument is being made here that the union would have eliminated the stretch-out had the workers only convinced them to let them stay on strike a few more weeks, or even a few more months, than they did. Had they done so, the integrity of the relationship between the workers and the union would have been better maintained, but the workers still might have lost. What would have been preserved, however, was an unfinished agenda for the labor movement." Ibid., 543–44.

92. As Irons has noted, workers she interviewed "who clearly remembered the '34 strike recalled not the reasons for the strike but its impact. They remembered the machine guns posted on the mill towers, the national guard armed with guns ready to shoot, the battles between striking and non-striking workers." Although Irons rightly emphasizes that such responses reveal a devastating collective and selective loss of memory, they also reveal the nature of the scarring itself. Ibid., xx–xxi.

93. Interview with Aaron Thornton.

94. Interview with Hoyt Jones and Marie Jones. Jones was, of course, correct, as

elucidated brilliantly in Hodges, *New Deal Labor Policy and the Southern Cotton Textile Industry.*

95. "The UTW's real mistake in fall 1934 was insisting that the strike and its inconclusive settlement were a success rather than the opening round in a continuing offensive," as James Hodges notes. "The workers perceived that the new array of boards and studies had really gained them little in immediate terms, and they were bitter over UTW claims of victory." Ibid., 117–18.

96. Mollie Dowd letter, 8 Oct. 1934, quoted in Irons, "Testing the New Deal," 483.

97. Hall et al., *Like a Family,* 353.

CHAPTER 5: DEALT OUT

1. Irons, "Testing the New Deal," 541–42.

2. Seven of the nine were weak locals formed just before the strike: 2190–Victor, 2218–Apalache, 2232–Woodruff, 2236–Enoree, and the black locals at Beaumont–2219, Pacolet Mills–2266, and Fairmont–2275. The other two were Whitney Local 2017 and the black local at the Cliftons, 1884.

3. The strongest Spartanburg local to emerge from the General Strike was Local 2070 at Tucapau. Because they spent most of 1935 and 1936 embroiled in bitter strikes of their own, Tucapau's workers consistently kept their local's membership at around four hundred.

4. Una *News-Review,* 8 May, 5, 26 June, 5 July 1936.

5. Una *News-Review,* 24 July 1936.

6. Una *News-Review,* 10 July 1936.

7. The same point is made by Irons in "Testing the New Deal," 505–6.

8. Una *News-Review,* 19 June 1936.

9. At the Cliftons, for instance, a functioning interplant shop committee—led by union veteran H. M. Branch—continued to meet. They even petitioned J. Choice Evins, the company's president, for recognition and a contract in the fall of 1935, but there is no evidence that Evins ever met with Branch and his committee or even issued a formal reply. "Employees of Clifton Mills" to J. Choice Evins, 1 Oct. 1935, Clifton Papers, series 6, box 10, folder 136.

10. Of the four unions, only the Fairmont local won its strike and survived. For Powell Knitting, see G. W. Smith to Francis J. Gorman, 27 March 1935, RG 9, entry 402, box 103, Powell Knitting Co. folder. For Fairmont, see J. L. Bernard to Samuel R. McClurd, 5 March 1935, RG 9, entry 402, box 134, Union–Buffalo Mills (Fairmont plant) folder. For Jackson Mill, see J. L. Bernard to Samuel R. McClurd, 29 Jan. 1935 (telegram), RG 9, entry 402, box 69, Jackson Mill folder, and Gordon L. Chastain to Samuel R. McClurd, 7 Dec. 1935 (telegram), RG 9, entry 402, box 8, Arkwright Mills folders (first folder). For Arkwright, see George Kamenow and John L. Conner to Samuel R. McClurd, 11 Dec. 1935, and George Kamenow

to Samuel R. McClurd, 8 June 1936. Both in RG 9, entry 402, box 8, Arkwright Mills folders (first folder).

11. In this exceptional instance the workers won a clear-cut victory. See documents in RG 9, entry 402, box 134, Union–Buffalo Mills (Fairmont plant) folder, especially reports of J. L. Bernard, 27 and 28 Oct. 1935, J. L. Bernard to Samuel R. McClurd, 17 Nov. 1935 (telegram), and John L. Conner and George Kamenow to TLRB, 6 Dec. 1935. The "official" union account of the strike may be found in *The Textile Worker*, 16 Nov. 1935.

12. The documentation for the post–General Strike fight against the stretch-out at Clifton takes up seven thick folders in RG 9, entry 402, box 27. For the sit-down strike itself, see John A. Peel to Samuel R. McClurd, 13 Dec. 1936 (second folder), and the Una *News-Review*, 19 June 1936.

13. Gordon, *New Deals*, 200–203.

14. The Wagner Act and the NLRB's early history are both covered in Gordon, *New Deals*, chapter 6.

15. Summarized in *Textile Labor Banner*, 10 Aug. 1935.

16. Report of NLRB regional director Charles N. Feidelson, 28 Oct. 1935, RG 25, entry 155, box 287, Saxon Mills case; substantiated by Annie Laura West, "The Eight Months' Strike," in the 1936 annual of the Southern Summer School for Workers, Moore Papers. The UTWA's "official" account differed somewhat: "The 'stretch-out,' coupled with a threatened reduction in wages, has precipitated a strike at the Saxon mills. The wage reduction affected weavers and slubber operatives, and [was] looked upon as an entering wedge for a general wage cut throughout the mill. The plant was idle following the start of the strike in the carding and spinning departments. Weavers walked out an hour later." *Textile Labor Banner*, 10 Aug. 1935.

17. Report of NLRB regional director Charles N. Feidelson, 28 Oct. 1935, and summary transcript of discussion between Law and shop committee, undated. Both in RG 25, entry 155, box 287, Saxon Mills case. For a very complimentary portrait of Law along these lines, see Camak, *Human Gold from Southern Mill Hills*.

18. I use the term *paternalism* guardedly and largely because Law himself defined his role paternalistically. As Mary Wingerd has noted, "The term paternalism presents a descriptive problem since it has been used to describe systems as widely variant as southern slave society and forms of systematized, industrial welfare capitalism. In characterizing the particular and highly personalized character of southern textile labor relations, scholars have drawn from both ends of this spectrum." Yet, Wingerd argues, paternalism as it existed in southern textiles was a discrete and distinctive phenomenon: "Neither analogous to slavery nor to articulated welfare capitalism, textile paternalism represents an economic and social system in transition." The Saxon experience further illuminates what Wingerd, drawing on the work of James Scott, terms "the infrapolitics of paternalism": the extent to which daily, less visible struggles among subordinate groups exist and the powerful shape manifest-

ed by the more public options for change available to subordinate groups. "Rethinking Paternalism," 1-4.

19. Report of NLRB regional director Charles N. Feidelson, 28 Oct. 1935, RG 25, entry 155, box 287, Saxon Mills case.

20. Ibid.

21. Ibid.

22. Ibid.

23. Report of Mortimer Kollender, 18 Oct. 1935, and transcript of election hearing, 21-22 Nov. 1935. Both in RG 25, entry 155, box 287, Saxon Mills case.

24. Weekly report for 1 Feb. 1936, and Melvin C. Smith to Nathan Witt, 31 Jan. 1936 (quotation). Both in RG 25, entry 155, box 287, Saxon Mills case.

25. John A. Peel to J. Warren Madden, 9 Oct. 1936, RG 25, entry 155, box 287, Saxon Mills case; and J. L. Bernard to CTLRB, 25 Sept. 1935, and John L. Conner to CTLRB, 26 Sept. 1935. Both in RG 9, entry 402, box 117, Saxon Mills folders (second folder). Law's manipulation of Chesnee Mill is covered (from a nonunion worker's point of view) in the interview with Fred Jewell and (from the union perspective) in West, "The Eight Months' Strike." As for Saxon, Law allegedly remarked at the beginning of the strike that "he was 'glad to be relieved of responsibility of operating the mill under present marketing conditions.'" *Textile Labor Banner,* 10 Aug. 1935.

26. Unidentified news clipping, 4 Oct. 1935, *Greenville News,* 31 Oct. 1935, and J. L. Bernard (quoting Law) to Samuel R. McClurd, 16 Nov. 1935. All in RG 9, entry 402, box 117, Saxon Mills folders (second folder). In the most serious incident, a few days after Law had machine guns placed on the mill's roof, small boys began heckling and throwing rocks at a nonunion guard inside the gate. The guard allegedly pulled a gun and began firing into the nearby crowd of pickets; several returned the fire with arms of their own, severely injuring the guard. As Annie West later told the story, "Fifteen of our men were arrested including our shop committee and relief chairman, who had been fired off the job that the scab guard was on. These four men were eleven miles away cutting a tree for the CLU Christmas program. They were released. But seven of these men were tried in magistrate's court and four of them freed while five were bound over to the next term of Sessions Court. When the trial came up twenty-nine witnesses were placed on the stand for them, but in spite of that three of them were sentenced to two and a half years in the State Penitentiary." This incident, as well as the boxcar sit-down, is covered in more detail in West, "The Eight Months' Strike."

27. Law's insistence on being able to discipline—that is, fire and evict—strikers he deemed responsible for strike violence is evident in J. L. Bernard to Samuel R. McClurd, 16 Nov. 1935, George Kamenow and John L. Conner to Samuel R. McClurd, 6 Dec. 1935, and George Kamenow to Samuel R. McClurd, 8 Feb. 1936. All in RG 9, entry 402, box 117, Saxon Mills folders (second folder). Concerning discontent among Law's stockholders, see George Kamenow to Samuel

R. McClurd, 1 March 1936, RG 9, entry 402, box 117, Saxon Mills folders (second folder).

28. George Kamenow to Samuel R. McClurd, 30 March 1936, RG 9, entry 402, box 117, Saxon Mills folders (second folder). Johnston's role in ending the strike is reviewed in Carpenter, "Olin D. Johnston," 243–48.

29. J. M. Mills to Francis J. Gorman, 18 May 1936, RG 9, entry 402, box 117, Saxon Mills folders (fourth folder).

30. J. M. Mills to Frances Perkins, 16 July 1936, RG 9, entry 402, box 117, Saxon Mills folders (second folder); interview with Ruby Bevill. See also Claude A. Loftis to Frances Perkins, 13 Sept 1937, and Daniel H. Taft to J. R. Steelman, 7 Oct 1937. Both in RG 280, box 339, case 176–1885, Saxon Mills. For those eliminated, prospects in Spartanburg were bleak. When James Bevill, son of union stalwart and Methodist steward Jedediah Bevill, lost his job, "he had a right hard time finding another one, because they blackballed him. He went to Beaumont and got a job, went back the next day for an examination, and they told him something had come up, they didn't need him. He went to Spartan Mill . . . and worked one night, and they didn't need him. And he went to Valley Falls and he worked two or three nights, and they didn't need him. . . . They turned our lights off, cut our water off, there on the village." In desperation, the family moved to a tiny apartment downtown, from which an old friend obtained a job for Bevill at Drayton. He worked there for twenty-six years and never mentioned the union again. Interview with Ruby Bevill.

31. Documents in RG 9, entry 402, box 117, Saxon Mills folders (third folder); see also John A. Peel to J. Warren Madden, 9 Oct. 1936, RG 25, entry 155, box 287, Saxon Mills case.

32. For the strike's origins, see John H. Small to Telfair Knight, 18 March 1935, and J. L. Bernard to Samuel R. McClurd, 23 Feb. 1935. Both in RG 9, entry 402, box 132, Tucapau Mills folders (first and second folders).

33. G. W. Smith to Francis L. Gorman, 28 Jan. 1935 (telegram), J. L. Bernard to Samuel R. McClurd, 29 Jan. 1935 (telegram), and Daniel H. Taft to William A. Mitchell, 12 Feb. 1935. All in RG 9, entry 402, box 132, Tucapau Mills folders (first folder).

34. J. L. Bernard to Samuel R. McClurd, 23 Feb. 1935, RG 9, entry 402, box 133, Tucapau Mills folders (first folder).

35. The condition of the village was revealed in photographs taken by Spartan mills after that company purchased Tucapau from bankrupt New England Southern a year later. Photographs in possession of Junior E. West.

36. J. L. Bernard to Samuel R. McClurd, 23 Feb. 1935, RG 9, entry 402, box 133, Tucapau Mills folders (first folder).

37. G. W. Smith to John Peel, 23 Feb. 1935 (telegram, quotation); quotation in J. L. Bernard to Samuel R. McClurd, 27 Feb. 1935 (telegram). Both in RG 9, entry 402, box 133, Tucapau Mills folders (first folder).

38. J. L. Bernard to Samuel R. McClurd, 7 March 1935 (telegram), and undated news clipping announcing formation of the "Good Will Association." Both in RG 9, entry 402, box 133, Tucapau Mills folders (first folder).

39. J. L. Bernard to Samuel R. McClurd, 9 April 1935, RG 9, entry 402, box 133, Tucapau Mills folders (first folder).

40. Interviews with Willie Mae Shepherd and Laura Daugherty (quotation).

41. J. L. Bernard to Samuel R. McClurd, 15 May 1935, J. L. Bernard to Samuel R. McClurd, 2, 6, 10, 15 June 1935, and unidentified news clipping ("Officer Halts Tucapau Crowd"). All in RG 9, entry 402, box 133, Tucapau Mills folders (first and second folders).

42. J. L. Bernard to Samuel R. McClurd, 22 June 1935, L. W. Perrin to Samuel R. McClurd, 2 July 1935, Samuel R. McClurd to Allan McNab, 6 July 1935, and assorted news clippings. All in RG 9, entry 402, box 133, Tucapau Mills folders (second folder). Governor Johnston's pivotal role in the Tucapau strike is also reviewed in Carpenter, "Olin D. Johnston," 248–53, and Simon, "A Fabric of Defeat," 315–21. As both Carpenter and Simon show, Johnston adopted a generally prounion stance in the wake of the General Strike and also intervened in equally nasty conflicts at Pelzer, Union, and Clinton.

43. *Daily News Record,* 2, 4 April 1936.

44. Thompson, "A Managerial History," 140–47.

45. George Kamenow to Samuel R. McClurd, 22 July 1936, RG 9, entry 402, box 124, Startex Mills folder.

46. During the shutdown of the print cloth mill, Montgomery promised that the complex's other two components—the crash mill, where flax was processed and woven, and the bleachery—would continue to operate. Complaint, 18 July 1936, and copy of Montgomery's memorandum, 10 Aug. 1936. Both in RG 9, entry 402, box 124, Startex Mills folder.

47. George Kamenow to Samuel R. McClurd, 20 Aug. 1936, amended complaint, 13 Aug. 1936, John A. Peel to Samuel R. McClurd, 15 and 17 Sept. 1936 (telegrams), and George Kamenow to Samuel R. McClurd, 26 Sept. 1936 (quotation). All in RG 9, entry 402, box 124, Startex Mills folder.

48. Preliminary report of Charles N. Feidelson, undated [mid-Nov. 1936], RG 25, entry 155, box 1122, case C-1224, Startex Mills.

49. The quotation is from E. C. Curtis, "informal report" appended to weekly report of 12 Dec. 1936; see also weekly report for 28 Nov. and undated account by Charles Feidelson of his meeting with John Peel on 26 Nov. All in RG 25, entry 155, box 1122, case C-1224, Startex Mills.

50. Weekly reports of 26 Dec. 1936, 2, 9, 23 Jan., 6, 13 Feb., 10 April 1937 (quotation), and Charles N. Feidelson's monthly report of 25 Jan. 1937. All in RG 25, entry 155, box 1122, case C-1224, Startex Mills.

51. Speaking also for the Textile Workers Organizing Committee, Cloyd Gibson urged the NLRB to hold a hearing in the Tucapau case but also admitted that TWOC

wanted to postpone definite action in any of South Carolina's Deering-Milliken plants until it was sure it held a majority in each. Weekly report of 1 May, RG 25, entry 155, box 1122, Startex Mills case. For more on the TWOC's involvement at Tucapau and elsewhere in Spartanburg County, see chapter 7.

52. Charles N. Feidelson to Estelle S. Frankfurter, 18 Aug. 1938, RG 25, entry 155, box 1122, case C-1224, Startex Mills. For the comments on the Monarch Mills case, see weekly report of 23 Jan. 1937, and also Benedict Wolf to Charles N. Feidelson, 30 Dec. 1936. Both in RG 25, entry 155, box 1122, case C-1224, Startex Mills.

53. In his attempt to mobilize every potential avenue of redress within the federal government, Local 2070 secretary G. Walter Moore turned back to President Franklin D. Roosevelt and Secretary of Labor Frances Perkins. Such direct appeals were routinely handed over to Federal Mediation. G. W. Moore to Franklin D. Roosevelt, 21 Sept. 1937, and G. W. Moore to Frances Perkins, 23 Sept. 1937. Both in RG 280, box 456, case 199–581, Startex Mills.

54. J. R. Steelman, memorandum to Henry Baker, Jr., 28 Sept. 1937, RG 280, box 456, case 199–581, Startex Mills.

55. Henry Baker Jr. to J. R. Steelman, 4 Oct. 1937, and Steelman to Baker, 5 Oct 1937, RG 280, box 456, case 199–581, Startex Mills.

56. D. Yates Heafner to J. R. Steelman, 10 Nov. 1937, RG 280, box 456, case 199–581, Startex Mills.

57. Gerhard P. Van Arkel, memorandum to file, 17 Nov. 1937, Warren Woods, memorandum to file, 31 Jan., 9 Feb. 1939, G. Walter Moore to J. Warren Madden, 11 Feb. 1939, and Gerhard P. Van Arkel to Nathan Witt, 17 Feb. 1939. All in RG 25, entry 155, box 1122, case C-1224, Startex Mills. Those to be rehired included all of Local 2070's officers but not many of the union's most ardent rank-and-file supporters.

58. Gerhard P. Van Arkel, memorandum to file, 14 March 1939, Nathan Witt to G. Walter Moore, 15 March 1939 (telegram), Nathan Witt to J. Warren Madden, 9 June 1939, Fred G. Krivonos to Nathan Witt, 21 July 1939, Thomas I. Emerson to Nathan Witt, 31 Aug. 1939, and closing notice, 31 Oct. 1939. All in RG 25, entry 155, box 1122, case C-1224, Startex Mills.

59. Weekly report, 7 Nov. 1936, RG 25, entry 155, box 1122, case C-1224, Startex Mills. As it happened, South Carolina did have a state law covering the situation. According to this statute, manufacturing companies were required to allow workers to remain in their houses rent-free during any extended shutdown. The evictees retained Robert J. Gantt, the prounion attorney responsible for the NLRB's Spartan Mills case, to defend their interests, but even this expert assistance failed.

60. Charles N. Feidelson to Nathan Witt, undated [late Jan. 1939], RG 25, entry 155, box 1122, case C-1224, Startex Mills.

61. Ibid.

62. Following this unexpected development, the South Carolina senate appointed a committee to investigate Johnston's actions concerning Hicks, which it over-

turned by a majority of one, thus setting the openly anti-Johnston tone in the state senate that abided for the remainder of Johnston's gubernatorial career. Charles N. Feidelson to Nathan Witt, undated [late Jan. 1939], RG 25, entry 155, box 1122, case C-1224, Startex Mills .

63. Charles N. Feidelson to Nathan Witt, undated [late Jan. 1939], RG 25, entry 155, box 1122, case C-1224, Startex Mills. In November 1936, a county police officer arrested four union members on charges of shooting out the company's floodlights on the front of the mill and then dynamiting the mill's electrical transformers. Later that month, three more union members were arrested for an alleged fight in Tucapau. They were kept in jail for seventeen days, during which time the warrant under which they had been arrested was changed three times. They were finally charged with "conspiracy to force Mr. Montgomery to sign a union contract at the point of the gun." According to the NLRB, both sets of charges were "frame-ups" engineered by the company, with the physical evidence in the dynamiting case proving decisively that it was engineered from the inside. All seven men were subsequently released and never tried, although court session after court session passed during 1937 and 1938. The NLRB's Feidelson concluded that the company was "holding the indictments over their heads as a weapon of intimidation for use in some future emergency," and indeed their cases merged into the larger list of individuals whom Montgomery was refusing to reemploy.

64. For examples of unionists' privation at this late date, see Mrs. Lois Thomason to J. Warren Madden, 27 Nov. 1938, and H. B. Hawkins to J. Warren Madden, 29 Nov. 1938. Both in RG 25, entry 155, box 1122, case C-1224, Startex Mills.

65. G. Walter Moore, B. C. Comer, and S. P. Caldwell to J. Warren Madden, 9 Feb. 1939 (telegram), RG 25, entry 155, box 1122, case C-1224, Startex Mills.

66. Walter R. Taliaferro (quoting Pollard) to Samuel R. McClurd, 11 Dec. 1934, RG 9, entry 402, box 123, Spartan Mills folders (third folder).

67. George Kamenow report, 22 June 1936, RG 9, entry 402, box 123, Spartan Mills folders (fourth folder); *Spartanburg Journal,* 11 May 1936; Una *News-Review,* 15 May 1936 (quotations). Pollard did admit to the *Journal* that "we also have an agreement with Gaffney Local No. 1804, United Textile Workers of America, that should one union strike and the strike remain unsettled for a period of four weeks, the other union will go on strike also."

68. *Spartanburg Journal,* 10, 11 May 1936.

69. Henry Baker, Jr., to Samuel R. McClurd, 11 May 1936, RG 9, entry 402, box 123, Spartan Mills folders (fourth folder).

70. *Spartanburg Journal,* 11, 12, 13 May 1936.

71. *Spartanburg Journal,* 11 May 1936.

72. L. S. Harding and George Kamenow to Samuel R. McClurd, undated [received 18 May 1936], RG 9, entry 402, box 123, Spartan Mills folders (fourth folder).

73. L. S. Harding and George Kamenow to Samuel R. McClurd, 22 May 1936, RG 9, entry 402, box 123, Spartan Mills folders (fourth folder).

74. L. S. Harding to Samuel R. McClurd, undated [mid-May 1936], RG 9, entry 402, box 123, Spartan Mills folders (fourth folder).

75. *Spartanburg Journal,* 11, 12, 13 May 1936 (quotation from 13 May); Una *News-Review,* 15 May 1936.

76. The men were incarcerated overnight without any formal warrants and later released. *Spartanburg Journal,* 13, 18 May 1936.

77. L. S. Harding to Samuel R. McClurd, undated [mid-May 1936], RG 9, entry 402, box 123, Spartan Mills folders (fourth folder).

78. George Kamenow and L. S. Harding to Samuel R. McClurd, 8 June 1936, RG 9, entry 402, box 123, Spartan Mills folders (fourth folder).

79. Charles N. Feidelson, report to NLRB, 13 July 1937, and amended charges filed by union, 19 July, 8 Nov. 1937, RG 25, entry 155, box 1108, case X-C-196, Spartan Mills.

80. Charles N. Feidelson to Benedict Wolf, 10 Nov. 1937 (telegram), then subsequent weekly report sheets. All in RG 25, entry 155, box 1108, case X-C-196, Spartan Mills.

81. J. M. Brown to George O. Pratt, 30 Jan. 1938, RG 25, entry 155, box 1108, case X-C-196, Spartan Mills.

82. Ibid.

83. Allen G. Rainwater to NLRB, 5 July 1939, RG 25, entry 155, box 1108, case X-C-196, Spartan Mills.

84. Intermediate report of trial examiner James M. Brown, 10 Sept. 1938, RG 25, entry 155, box 1108, case C-953, Spartan Mills.

85. See amended report of trial examiner, 17 Sept. 1938. Emil Rieve and Solomon Barkin of the TWOC immediately protested the change and were vaguely informed by administrative assistant B. M. Stern that "the deletion in this section . . . was made by the Trial Examiner to correct his recommendations as based on his findings of fact and conclusions." Emil Rieve to Nathan Witt, 6 Oct. 1938, Solomon Barkin to John Madden, 11 Oct. 1938, and Beatrice M. Stern to both Emil Rieve and Solomon Barkin, 13 Oct. 1938. All in RG 25, entry 155, box 1108, case X-C-196, Spartan Mills.

86. Charles N. Feidelson to Beatrice M. Stern, 1 Dec. 1938, RG 25, entry 155, box 1108, case X-C-196, Spartan Mills.

87. Walter S. Montgomery to Charles N. Feidelson, 27 Feb. 1939, and Charles N. Feidelson to Nathan Witt, 28 Feb. 1939. Both in RG 25, entry 155, box 1108, case X-C-196, Spartan Mills.

88. S. P. Brewer to Gerhard P. Van Arkel, 3 March 1939, RG 25, entry 155, box 1108, case X-C-196, Spartan Mills.

89. Nathan Witt to John W. Pollard, 7 April 1939, RG 25, entry 155, box 1108, case X-C-196, Spartan Mills.

90. Allen G. Rainwater to NLRB, 5 July 1939, RG 25, entry 155, box 1108, case X-C-196, Spartan Mills.

91. John W. Pollard, Vernon Balentine, and A. G. Rainwater to Warren G. Madden [*sic*], 1 April 1939, RG 25, entry 155, box 1108, case X-C-196, Spartan Mills.
92. Ibid.

CHAPTER 6: SOUTHERN TEXTILE UNIONISM AND THE 1930S

1. This idea of "community unionism" is elaborated both here (chapters 5 and 7) and by Wingerd in "Rethinking Paternalism."
2. *Spartanburg Journal,* 16 June 1932.
3. Resolutions of Local 2070, 28 Nov. 1936, Moore Papers.
4. West, "Southern Cotton Mills."
5. As Hall et al. have generalized in reference to the 1929–30 strikes (*Like a Family* 222, see also 307), most local union leaders "had grown up in the mill villages or moved as children from the countryside. They did not see themselves as temporary sojourners, ready to beat a retreat to the land, or as destitute farmers for whom 'it was heaven to draw a payday, however small.' Their identities had been formed in the mill village; they had cast their fate with the mills."
6. For the Spartan defendents in the 1936 NLRB case, see intermediate report of trial examiner James M. Brown, 10 Sept. 1938, RG 25, entry 155, box 1108, Spartan Mills folder. Information on the tenure of Pollard, Stephens, and the Saxon union leaders comes from my ongoing database project of Spartanburg mill workers and village residents, drawn from the city directories and manuscript census returns between 1896 and 1940.
7. The institutional activity of the five Tucapau men, especially their lodge activities, is revealed in miscellaneous documents found in the Moore Papers. For Gault and Bevill, see the manuscript records of their respective churches. The list could go on and on: Norman Troxell, leader of the Arkwright local, was also the clerk of Arkwright Baptist Church at the time of the General Strike; Lloyd Kirby, officer in the Pacolet Mills local, headed the Baptist Young People's Union organization at the Baptist church there; and Charlie McAbee, Spartanburg's contribution to the UTWA's General Executive Board, was a respected lay preacher back home at Inman Mills.
8. Wingerd, "Rethinking Paternalism," 12–13.
9. To be sure, a few unionists in Spartanburg County saw the union struggle in purely Marxian terms. "The laboring people have built up large fortunes for capital. Yet capital denies the right of labor to demand a division of the profits created by it," a union member from Clifton No. 1 explained. Such practices would continue "until every person who labors decides to stop such unfair division of the wealth of this nation." John Pollard of Spartan Mills took the Marxian argument so far as to excuse the conduct of manufacturers: "It is only natural for them to want to make as much money as possible, and higher wages and shorter hours will substantially cut into their profits, therefore they fight our organizations. . . . This

is but to be expected." The burden of change, Pollard concluded, was on textile workers themselves, who would first have to understand their organic class position. Pollard's conception of the union struggle was atypical, however. Workers who emphasized economics would more likely have agreed with the homelier reasoning of another Clifton worker who declared, "When we fail to receive a just return for our labor we have been robbed as much so as if we are held up at the point of a gun and our money taken from us." Una *News-Review*, 29 May 1936 (Clifton No. 1) and 3 July 1936 (Pollard and second Clifton worker).

10. Una *News-Review*, 8 May 1936.

11. Una *News-Review*, 8, 15 May 1936 (Pacolet Mills), 5 June 1936 (Clifton), and 29 May 1936 (Inman quotations).

12. Examples are all drawn from the Una *News-Review*: 8 May, 22 May, 14 Aug. 1936 (Inman), 31 July 1936 (Glendale), and 17 July 1936 (Clifton). Mary Wingerd has observed a similar pattern whereby "the union rapidly became the social institution of the village as well as the structural vehicle for labor relations, involving the entire community in its many activities." "Rethinking Paternalism," 39.

13. Una *News-Review*, 10 July 1936. The writer's engrained racism—tellingly revealed in relation to his conception of American citizenship—was typical of white southern textile workers and inextricable from their understanding of just who would be included in their communities, both before and after the advent of unionism.

14. Una *News-Review*, 30 Oct. 1936; see also comments of the Clifton No. 2 correspondent (8 May 1936) and the Beaumont correspondent (3 July 1936). In trying to appropriate the language of patriotism—and of Americanism more generally—Spartanburg's workers were not, of course, unique. Gary Gerstle has explored the phenomenon in his study of working-class activism in Woonsocket, Rhode Island: *Working-Class Americanism*.

15. This was the preferred view of both Federal Mediation and Conciliation Service officials and the UTWA. The UTWA's official account of the strike termed it "the result of discriminatory methods of employing help." Even in that context, however, the UTWA could not entirely ignore the full ramifications of Fairmont workers' struggle: "It has been a policy of the superintendent to send out of the village and secure help rather than employ *those living in the village* who were members of the United Textile Workers of America, or whose relatives were members of the union." *Textile Worker*, 16 Nov. 1935 (emphasis added).

16. There was even a third level of righteous discontent at Fairmont, as revealed in a letter from CTLRB investigator George Kamenow. After all was said and done, Kamenow concluded, the cause of the strike had been that a certain family, the Morrows, had been selling bootleg whiskey in the village and that plant superintendent G. L. Gibson, who was friendly with the Morrows, refused to stop them, even after being contacted by both union and nonunion residents. Final report of John L. Conner and George Kamenow, 11 Dec. 1935, and report of George Kame-

now, 6 Feb. 1936. Both in RG 9, entry 402, box 124, Union–Buffalo Mills (Fairmont plant) folder. For Fairmont residents' embarrassment at the condition of their village, see Fairmont correspondent in the Una *News-Review,* 29 May 1936. As Mary Wingerd notes, "The expulsion of obstreporous elements from the village often supported the values of the settled cohort of workers," precisely those most likely to identify with the union. Wingerd, "Rethinking Paternalism," 14.

17. Una *News-Review,* 26 June 1936 (Clifton). This kind of reasoning put a southern twist on what Gerstle has labeled the "traditionalist" dimension of Americanist language, including racism and xenophobia generally. *Working-Class Americanism,* 11.

18. For blacks in the Spartan strike, see the Una *News-Review,* 22 May 1936; in the Saxon strike, see the *Greenville News,* 31 Oct. 1935. Accounts of the Tucapau murder are in interviews with Laura Daugherty and Willie Mae Shepherd. There is no evidence that Spartanburg manufacturers ever planned to hire black workers into production jobs previously held by whites, even during the strike. Yet because black workers traditionally held maintenance and boiler-firing jobs inside textile mills, any attempt by a mill company to reopen a plant required that these workers pass through the gates first (precisely the scenario that cost a life at Tucapau). Thus black "strikebreaking" was primarily symbolic, although the mere threat of hiring blacks remained potent to white workers all too knowledgeable of how precarious their employment really was.

19. Una *News-Review,* 8 May 1936 (first quotation), 15 May 1936 (second quotation), and 19 June 1936 (third quotation).

20. Una *News-Review,* 11 Dec. 1936. This extension of a community ethos was easier said than done, however, as the union's experience with downtown interests in the city of Spartanburg during the 1936 Spartan strike revealed. A group calling itself the "Hub City Business Leaders" passed resolutions condemning the strike (Una *News-Review* 15 May 1936). In response, union leaders from Spartan issued their own set of resolutions condemning Spartanburg's mercantile community. At issue was precisely how to define "community" in the city. As unionists pointed out, downtown merchants in the past had "called upon us to protect them against chain store methods in business," implying a local solidarity between mercantile and mill-village interests. Now, however, these same merchants "desert us in our fight to free labor from the stretch-out and chain gang methods of exploiting labor." The problem was the class divide. According to unionists, local merchants "know nothing of the conditions under which we labor and know nothing about the righteousness of our cause." The merchants had revealed how they really defined community: in ways that excluded textile workers, just as textile workers had always suspected. In this view, the merchants had betrayed the textile workers by "taking sides with 'the dollar' when it comes in conflict with human rights." As UTWA organizer Robert Donnahoo put it, "Instead of helping the workers win a justifiable fight—a fight for the betterment of all humanity—these so called business men chose to line up on the

side of the mill barons" (Una *News-Review*, 22 May 1936). "Like a prism, insurgency on the part of the southern textile worker refracted southern society into its constituent parts, revealing the roles of each in the shaping of southern economic and political power." Irons, "Testing the New Deal," xv.

21. For an example of Eugene Pettit's religion column, see the Una *News-Review*, 15 May 1936. For examples of the *Review*'s reporting on area religious events, see 20, 29 May 1936, 5 Nov. 1937, and 3 March and 5 May 1939.

22. Although the themes of dignity and redemption allowed the union movement to merge with elements of a preexisting Christian worldview, and specific local unions did frequently inherit the social and institutional functions previously performed by village churches, at no point did the union ever, in and of itself, function as a church. Despite all the rhetoric, textile workers seem to have maintained a clear distinction that only the churches, through faith in Jesus, could offer salvation in the traditional Christian sense. Although much of mill religion entered into the movement, significant strands thus remained outside.

23. Una *News-Review*, 8 May 1936 (first Clifton worker), 5 June 1936 (Spartan rally speaker), 19 June 1936 (Glendale), and 14 Aug. 1936 (Clifton No. 1).

24. Una *News-Review*, 8 May 1936 (Clifton) and 22 May 1936 (Glendale).

25. Una *News-Review*, 10 July 1936 (first Pacolet worker), 2 Oct. 1936 (Beaumont worker), and 15 May 1936 (second Pacolet worker, emphasis added).

26. Chastain's speech is reprinted in the Una *News-Review*, 21 Aug. 1936.

27. Irons, "Testing the New Deal," 419–20. The most detailed excavation of the religious themes characteristic of unionism, however, must remain Liston Pope's masterful account of Gastonia's Loray Mill strike of 1929: *Millhands and Preachers*, chapter 12.

28. Una *News-Review*, 12 June 1936.

29. Una *News-Review*, 10 July 1936.

30. West, "The Eight Months' Strike."

31. Unlike in Pope's Gastonia or many other southern textile centers, Christian sects that banned union membership as an issue of church polity—mainly Pentecostal—were comparatively rare in Spartanburg County. This strain of thinking, however, was present within existing denominations. Local mill owners sporadically tried to encourage it through carefully selected itinerant revivalists. Una *News-Review*, 1, 15 April 1938.

32. Carlton, *Mill and Town in South Carolina*, 161–70 and chapter 6 passim; Simon, "A Fabric of Defeat," 45–68; Grantham, *Southern Progressivism*, 57–59. All cover South Carolina textile workers at the ballot box during the early twentieth century, especially during the Cole Blease years. The specific and long-term political activism of Spartanburg County's textile workers is summarized in Potwin, *Cotton Mill People of the Piedmont*, 98–100.

33. Historians of the South since Reconstruction have consistently failed to recognize or explore one of the most important political components of the region:

the lack of local government. Except for a brief period under some Reconstruction state constitutions, the South has never had local or township-level government as in the North and Midwest. The only unit of government smaller than the county was the incorporated city or town, and, of course, most mill villages were unincorporated. Thus, even though southern textile workers participated in, even seemed to have an affinity for, formal politics, they almost always found their electoral presence diluted on the county level. In such a context, grass-roots political change was virtually impossible.

34. As Potwin noted, Spartanburg voters repeatedly sent former Saxon residents as their representatives to the state's general assembly. In 1926, four of the county's twelve representatives were former cotton mill workers. Potwin's implication that textile workers enjoyed direct electoral representation in these cases, however, is problematic. None of these men remained mill workers or mill-village residents, and most had been long gone from the textile world by the time they achieved electoral success, as the cases of the two Saxon men cited by Potwin reveal. W. Simpson Rogers, elected to the state general assembly as a representative in 1912 and 1914 and as a state senator from 1914 until his death in 1926, had spent time in the Saxon village as a youth but by 1912 was firmly esconced as a merchant with his father and uncle in Spartanburg's Arlington Street neighborhood. His legislative career was generally Progressive, but his work, other than a brief and unconsummated enthusiasm for a law to mandate shorter working hours, did not directly address any textile-related concerns. Dewey Foster, elected in 1924 and again in 1926, was the son of a Saxon supervisor and also left the village as a teenager. Potwin, *Cotton Mill People of the Piedmont*, 99–100; Waldrep, "Spartanburg Mill Workers Persistence Project" (database in process).

35. Simon, "A Fabric of Defeat," 117ff.

36. Ibid., 112–13.

37. Ibid., 143–45.

38. *Spartanburg Journal*, 5 Aug. 1934.

39. *Spartanburg Journal*, 29 Aug. 1934.

40. Simon, "A Fabric of Defeat," 276–77; Carpenter, "Olin D. Johnston," 162–64. Godfrey, for instance, introduced a bill that would have mandated a thirty-six-loom limit for weavers in the mills. It was endorsed by Governor Johnston and passed the house by a vote of 94-6. "Unfazed by the jam-packed gallery of boisterous mill workers sitting above them, however, the senate promptly killed the proposal." As Bryant Simon has concluded, "Laborers had put one of their own in the Governor's mansion, but this did not mean they could remake society." Simon, "A Fabric of Defeat," 277–78.

41. Una *News-Review*, 8 May 1936.

42. Una *News-Review*, 5 June 1936.

43. Una *News-Review*, 22 May 1936. For other local evidence of grass-roots po-

litical activism in the spring of 1936, see also the *News-Review*, 15 May 1936 (Fairmont and Beaumont) and 5 June 1936 (Clifton No. 2).

44. Una *News-Review*, 5, 12 June and 3, 10, 24 July 1936.

45. Una *News-Review*, 19 June 1936 (Donnahoo) and 10 July 1936 (Garrett).

46. The hopes engendeder by the 1936 campaign even overturned traditional strictures against women's political involvement in the textile villages. "You know, it is time we women began to take a part in politics if we ever expect to get the right men in the public offices," wrote textile worker Martha Crow just before the Democratic prpimary. "You men whose wives don't vote, will you just take a few minutes and explain to them how important it is that they cast their ballots at election time. The so-called 'big man's' wife always votes and if we don't do our part they will run things over us," Crow declared. "If we don't want to be slaves forever we had better begin voting now." Una *News-Review*, 5 June 1936.

47. Una *News-Review*, 31 July, 21 Aug. 1936.

48. Box totals are from election report of G. Walter Moore (one of the poll-watchers at Tucapau), Moore Papers.

49. Una *News-Review*, 2 Oct. 1936.

50. Una *News-Review*, 16 Oct. 1936. During late 1936 and early 1937, the labor movement in Spartanburg was too disorganized to make any formal protest against these renewed purges. The number of discharge cases later filed by the TWOC, however, gives some idea of how effective manufacturers actually were in disrupting the overall labor movement.

51. The impact of the 1936 defeats on textile worker politics in Spartanburg County was made abundantly clear in the general elections of 1938. Only two locally prominent unionists entered the races: William Fred Ponder for county probate judge and Paul Stephens for the state house. Both were defeated in the primaries, as was virtually every other prolabor candidate who ran in South Carolina, including incumbent Gov. Olin D. Johnston. Textile unionists continued to be active in local politics in 1938. The lists of election managers for the November balloting still included the names of at least nine known local union officers: Luke D. Tindall from Clifton No. 1, H. M. Branch from Clifton No. 2, L. A. Donald from Converse, L. B. Painter and J. C. Leister from Fairmont, R. B. Erskine and C. W. McAbee from Inman Mills, Hal Corn from Saxon, and Cloyd L. Gibson from Tucapau. Yet the politics of class in Spartanburg had disappeared. Una *News-Review*, 29 July, 2 Sept., 14 Oct. 1938.

52. *Textile Labor Banner*, 10 (quotation), 17 Dec 1934.

53. When an NLRB examiner asked Montgomery why he had chosen to enter the cases at Inman instead of Tucapau, Montgomery "gave the lame [but revealing] explanation that he was afraid Mr. O'Shields would have been embarrassed by the trial of cases involving personal friends of his." O'Shields's place in the textile workers' community is documented in Charles N. Feidelson to Nathan Witt, undated [late Jan. 1939], RG 25, entry 155, box 1122, Startex Mills folders.

54. See Hicks's letterhead for R. D. Hicks to Walter Moore, 16 March 1937, Moore Papers.

55. G. Walter Moore to Frances Perkins, 23 Sept. 1937, Moore Papers.

56. Hall et al., *Like a Family,* 320.

57. Interviews with Evelyn Neal Satterfield (quotation), A. Beatrice Norton, and Ruby Bevill.

58. Sifted from among various odd documents in Saxon's RG 9 and RG 280 files, chance (and, in the case of the school situation, veiled) remarks in the Una *News-Review,* and interviews and conversations with numerous former Saxon workers, particularly Ruby Bevill and A. Beatrice Norton. For the school controversy that grew out of the use of private guards for Potwin's residence during the 1935–36 strike and Law's subsequent attempts to obtain reimbursement from the school district for the same, see the Una *News-Review,* 22 May 1936 and 18, 25 Aug. 1939.

59. Interviews with Evelyn Neal Satterfield, A. Beatrice Norton, and Ruby Bevill.

60. Interview with Ruby Bevill.

61. Interview with A. Beatrice Norton. Among those victimized by Potwin's caprice was Norton's stepfather, Hamp Hamby. Hamby worked in the cardroom and by 1932 had come down with a classic case of byssinosis (brown lung). As Norton related, "He got coughing some, 'til he lost his breath. And he had to leave the job to go get air. They had windows in then, and he opened the window, and she happened to come through seeing him hanging his head out the window, she went over there and shook him! and told him to get back to work. And he cursed her. And she said, 'You're fired.' He said, 'No, I'm not fired. I quit two years ago and you didn't know it.' So he just come home and packed his things."

62. Village stories still abound concerning how Law carried flowers to Potwin while the rest of the village was in church, or (more generally) how he lavished attention on Potwin in the presence of his wife and children. Interviews with Ruby Bevill and A. Beatrice Norton.

63. Potwin's more magnanimous side was revealed in an anecdote told by Ruby Bevill: "There was a family that lived between me and Mama—I went through their backyard, going back and forth to Mama. I passed back through there, and she stopped me and she said, 'Ruby, do you know anybody that would want to buy a kitchen table, and chairs?' And I said, 'You're selling your kitchen table?' She said, 'Yeah, I've got to get something to eat.' Said her husband had been gone for a week hunting a job, and he hadn't been able to find anything, and she said that she was out of money and out of food and she just had to do something to get something to eat. She had three or four children. I said, 'No, I don't know of anybody.' I didn't know what to do about it, so I went up to the office and told Miss Potwin. Miss Potwin said, 'Oh my goodness, we can't have that!' She said, 'We'll have to do something about that.' So she went down to see about her. And to make a long story short, she found out that she had parents in Tennessee, that if she could get up there she could be taken care of. So she managed to find them enough clothes to

wear, she bought them tickets and everything. . . . She made all of their arrangements and got them on the train back to Tennessee."

64. Interview with Evelyn Neal Satterfield. Potwin even managed to offend the irenic Neal. "She wrote a book on the famous men of South Carolina" and brought the manuscript to Neal for typing. "I didn't want to do it—I knew it was for free, and I didn't want to do it. So I was very, very slow." Finally Potwin retrieved the manuscript and hired someone else to prepare it for publication. "And I just thought, if you'd have been smart, you would have paid me, and I would have done it. But I didn't say a word." Any other course would have been lethal insofar as employment at Saxon was concerned.

65. Interview with A. Beatrice Norton.

66. Interview with Polly Foster.

67. Interview with Ruby Bevill.

68. Annie Laura West to Francis J. Gorman, 1 Oct. 1940, undated [1941], and 15 April 1942. All UTWA Papers, box 385, folder 321.

69. Annie Laura West to Francis J. Gorman, 15 April 1942, UTWA Papers, box 385, folder 321.

70. Annie Laura West to Francis J. Gorman, 16 March 1942, UTWA Papers, box 385, folder 321.

71. Annie Laura West to Francis J. Gorman, 1 Oct. 1940, UTWA Papers, box 385, folder 321.

72. Annie Laura West to Francis J. Gorman, 15 April 1942, 27 June 1943, 24 July 1943, UTWA Papers, box 385, folder 321.

73. Annie L. West to J. R. Steelman, 24 Aug. 1943 (telegram), and closing report of Fred Beck, 6 Oct. 1943, RG 280, box 1124, case 301–3080, Warrior Duck Mills.

74. Annie Laura West to Francis J. Gorman, 1 Oct. 1940, undated [1941], 15 April 1942, 18 April 1944. All in RG 280, box 1124, case 301–3080, Warrior Duck Mills.

75. Annie Laura West to Francis J. Gorman, 18 April 1944, RG 280, box 1124, case 301–3080, Warrior Duck Mills.

76. Ibid. West's last years are described in the interview with William A. Bryant.

CHAPTER 7: THE POLITICS OF SURVIVAL

1. The best overview of these years remains Zieger, *The CIO*.

2. The TWOC-CIO "made no dramatic gains, especially in the South, and its performance, for all the vigor and purpose exuded by the CIO, seemed no better than that of the United Textile Workers, the AFL, and the NRA." Ibid., 74–78.

3. Carpenter, "Olin D. Johnston," 258.

4. Similarly, S. P. Caldwell understood that the ability to strike—if not striking itself—was the essential lever behind the NLRB mechanism, however much the mechanism itself was intended to prevent strikes. *Industrial Leader*, 22 (quotations), 29 July 1937.

5. The CIO's 1937 southern drive is examined in detail in Richards, "History of the Textile Workers Union of America," chapter 2.

6. *Industrial Leader,* 12 Aug. 1937. For Spartanburg workers' initial enthusiasm for the Textile Workers Organizing Committee and the CIO, see the Una *News-Review,* 16, 23, 30 April, 14 May, 11 June, and 9 July 1937.

7. Most of these points are reviewed in Richards's study of the TWUA during this period. Like the UTWA before it, TWOC leaders never understood that ending the stretch-out—not improved wages—remained the key southern concern. The evident condescension toward southern workers that TWOC officials such as Solomon Barkin displayed only exacerbated existing tensions. In the end, after the "premature and sudden end" of the 1937 organizing drive, the Textile Workers Organizing Committee "was no more prepared to cope with [the South's] problems than its predecessors had been." Richards, "History of the Textile Workers Union of America," especially 48–49, 57, 61–62, 133–38, 143–44. For TWOC's promise to handle pending NLRB cases, see the Una *News-Review,* 11 June 1937.

8. As Richards shows, TWOC tended to ignore the basic southern cotton textiles, focusing instead on the North and in other branches of the industry (synthetic fibers and dyeing and finishing), where it stood greater chances of success. This made TWOC "a northern-based organization laying siege to the southern anti-union fortress," like its predecessors, and thus set up the union for similar defeats and frustrations. Richards, "History of the Textile Workers Union of America," 83–84.

9. Ibid., 40–41ff.

10. In August 1937 Cloyd Gibson claimed (rather eliptically) that "all the mills under the Spartanburg Office either have a majority signed up or are making progress toward a majority." Despite such rhetoric, TWOC only petitioned for seven representation elections in Spartanburg County during 1937 and 1938. Of these, it withdrew one (at Tucapau, in light of the pending NLRB case) and narrowly won the remaining six (Beaumont, Spartan, Inman Mills, Fairmont, and Clifton No. 1 and No. 2). Other campaigns—including highly publicized drives at Drayton and Victor— never even led to petitions despite repeated assertions by TWOC's organizers that they were on the verge of filing. Such widening gulfs between rhetoric and reality only demoralized workers further. *Industrial Leader,* 12 Aug. 1937 (Gibson quotation); report of "B.M.W.," *Industrial Leader,* 22 July 1937 (Drayton); *Industrial Leader,* 22 July, 5, 26 Aug., and 16 Sept. 1937 (Victor).

11. TWOC's southern strategy is reviewed in Hodges, *New Deal Labor Policy and Southern Cotton Textile Industry,* chapter 9 (quotation from 152), and Irons, "Testing the New Deal," 533ff. It was also echoed by Judson Brooks, editor of the nonpartisan Una *News-Review* in Spartanburg, in the wake of the CIO's election at Inman Mills in late 1938 (Una *News-Review,* 21 Oct. 1938).

12. For management opposition—ranging from more direct forms of intimidation to enlistment of itinerant antiunion revivalists and the Ku Klux Klan—see

Industrial Leader, 12 Aug., 23 Sept., 11 Nov. 1937, and the Una *News-Review,* 25 Feb. and 15 April 1938.

13. Election report and supporting documents in RG 25, entry 155, box 448, case X-R-543, Beaumont Mfg. Co., and D. Yates Heafner to J. R. Steelman, 15 Oct. 1938 (quotation), RG 280, box 506, case 199–2499, Beaumont Mfg. Co.

14. Report of Clarence H. Williams, 18 July 1938, also intermediate reports of 21 July and 23 July, RG 280, box 495, case 199–2114, Beaumont Mfg. Co. For the actual curtailments and wage cuts, see the Una *News-Review,* 8, 15 April, 13 May 1938.

15. D. Yates Heafner to J. R. Steelman, 15 Oct. 1938, RG 280, box 506, case 199–2499, Beaumont Mfg. Co.

16. Preliminary report of Charles N. Feidelson, undated, and amended complaint, 25 Jan. 1939. Both in RG 25, entry 155, box 448, Beaumont Mfg. Co. See also D. Yates Heafner to J. R. Steelman, 15 Oct., 19 Nov. (quotation), 10 Nov. 1938 (telegram). All in RG 280, box 506, case 199–2499, Beaumont Mfg. Co., and the Una *News-Review,* 7, 21 Oct., 18 Nov. 1938.

17. Preliminary report of Charles N. Feidelson, undated, and Thomas I. Emerson to Nathan Witt, 1 (quotation), 8 Aug. 1939. All in RG 25, entry 155, box 448, Beaumont Mfg. Co. folders. Attorney Emerson maintained that Jennings and his associates had bargained in good faith until the 4 January meeting, when TWOC negotiators "reopened several questions already settled" and demanded that its new proposal be "accepted or rejected *without modification, alteration or revision.*" Although federal mediators were able to convene a few more meetings, neither an affronted Jennings nor adamant TWOC officials were willing to talk further.

18. Of twenty-one alleged discriminatory discharges, an NLRB investigation found that ten of the affected individuals did not want their cases prosecuted, and none of the remaining cases involved local union officers. Only six, in the NLRB's view, held possible merit. Even so, an NRLB agent was able to get Dudley Jennings to agree to reinstatement in nine of the eleven pending cases. Textile Workers Organizing Committee leaders rejected this settlement, further enraging the NLRB. Thomas I. Emerson to Nathan Witt, 8 Aug. 1939; William E. Spencer to Charles N. Feidelson, 26 Oct. 1939; Warren Woods to Beatrice M. Stern, 16 Nov. 1939; Charles N. Feidelson to Beatrice M. Stern, 5 Dec. 1939, RG 25, entry 155, box 448, Beaumont Mfg. Co. file.

19. By the spring of 1939, both AFL and CIO partisans were far outnumbered by prounion workers who wanted nothing to do with either union. In March, a four-member committee—three of them activists dating back to the early 1930s—began circulating petitions to form an independent union. The NLRB viewed this as the first genuinely independent effort to emanate from the South since the passage of the Wagner Act. According to NLRB regional director Charles Feidelson, "Their reaction against the tactics used by both AFofL and CIO groups has been due almost enirely to the stupid strategies adopted by local leaders of the nation-

ally affiliated labor organizations." Preliminary report of Charles N. Feidelson, undated, RG 25, entry 155, box 448, Beaumont Mfg. Co. folders. The NLRB ultimately decided not to hold a new representation election at Beaumont, however, given other aspects of the devolving situation.

20. During this period, the Beaumont local did function erratically, obtaining help from either the AFL or the CIO as opportunities arose (as revealed in the daily organizing reports of TWUA representative Don McKee). For the final switch back to the UTWA, see D. Yates Heafner report, 31 Jan. 1942, RG 280, box 946, case 196–9397, Beaumont Mfg. Co.

21. Preliminary report of Charles N. Feidelson, undated, RG 25, entry 155, box 448, Beaumont Mfg. Co. folders.

22. As early as March 1937, Local 2070 treasurer G. Walter Moore wrote to Washington requesting "any information pertaining to the C.I.O. which I can teach the workers here." Within months, he and the local's other officers were on the TWOC staff. In the meantime, Tucapau's case before the NLRB continued to grind on without any sign of resolution. Moore's family was evicted from their village home while Moore himself was organizing for TWOC in Georgia. G. Walter Moore to Committee for Industrial Organization [sic], 26 March 1937, and C. L. Gibson to G.W. Moore, 3 Aug. 1937. Both in Moore Papers.

23. G. Walter Moore to R. R. Lawrence, 27 Aug. 1938, Moore Papers. In a parting jab, Moore reproved Lawrence and other TWOC representatives for what Moore viewed as their disconnection from what was left of the southern textile union movement: "In case you do not know where Tucapau is, just come to Spartanburg and the committee will be glad to meet you there."

24. G. Walter Moore to Isabelle M. Plunkett, 1 Dec. 1938, Moore Papers. TWOC Carolinas director Seth P. Brewer denied that any such behind-the-scenes agreement had been struck, but Plunkett herself admitted that Brewer had been meeting with the NLRB on all pending South Carolina cases independently of the locals involved. Isabelle M. Plunkett to Walter Moore, 2 Dec. 1938, and S. P. Brewer to Walter Moore, 5 Dec. 1938. Both in Moore Papers.

25. G. Walter Moore to John L. Lewis, 1 Dec. 1938, Moore Papers. In another letter to Lewis, rank-and-file workers J. L. McQueen and Scott B. Sudduth charged that Tucapau's case had been "constantly deferred in favor of younger cases. . . . We were unable to get any information or any satisfaction as to when or if ever we will get a hearing even tho we have been locked out nearly two years. We do not get any satisfaction from the Atlanta Board or from the T.W.O.C. Office, representatives of the T.W.O.C. do not co-operate or even recognize our local T.W.O.C. office or officials, but are constantly in conference with the mill Officials dickering for a settlement without conferring with our local T.W.O.C. officials or our Shop Committee." J. L. McQueen and S. B. Sudduth to John L. Lewis, 1 Dec. 1938, TWUA Papers (Mss. 367), box 67.

26. Although Seth P. Brewer officially protested the NLRB's final decision in the

strongest language, the feeling persisted in Tucapau that somehow TWOC was at least partly responsible for the outcome. In April 1939, Cloyd Gibson—still president of the Tucapau local and still working as a TWOC organizer—protested to TWOC attorney John Abt that "there seems to be something very fishy about this whole affair. . . . We cannot understand how Montgomery got the 'Ship Hand' over the Board in such a way that he could dictate the terms of settlement in these three cases." (Gibson was referring not only to the Startex case, as the old Tucapau case had been restyled, but also to the equally disagreeable settlements handed down for Spartan Mills and Gaffney Manufacturing.) "If he gets by with this," he continued, "it will set a precedent by which all other manufacturers against whom Labor Board cases are pending can dictate to the Board the terms under which they can settle. It will also give us a set-back in organizing the workers since they will know that the companys can fire as many as they please and then name the ones to return to work." S. P. Brewer to Gerhard P. Van Arkel, 17 Feb., 3 March 1939, and C. L. Gibson to John Abt, 5 April 1939. All in Moore Papers.

27. Although Janet Irons has cogently summarized southern textile workers' disenchantment with the CIO ("Testing the New Deal," 536–40), and Paul Richards has briefly noted the UTWA-AFL's resurrection ("History of the Textile Workers Union of America," 62–63, 78–80), no history of the new UTWA or the SCTF exists. The event was well covered from the CIO perspective in the *Industrial Leader* (23 Dec. 1938 and 20 Jan., 3, 10, 17 Feb., and 21 April 1939) and from a carefully nonpartisan, local perspective in the Una *News-Review* (27 Jan., 3, 17, 24 Feb., 3, and 17 March 1939). Southerners were key players at every step. Spartanburg's Furman Garrett and Gordon Chastain were even present at a secret Washington meeting on 19 January outlining the new organization's plans to combat the CIO. See "confidential" memorandum, 21 Jan. 1939, and Clarence H. Williams to John R. Steelman, 30 Jan. 1939, RG 280, box 122, file 195–855, UTWA general file. Back in Spartanburg County, the CIO was finished by late 1939, all its locals either having defected (Tucapau, Spartan, and Fairmont) or become incapacitated (Beaumont and Inman Mills). Organizing drives at other plants disintegrated. Only at Clifton No. 1 and No. 2 did the CIO retain a presence, largely due to local union president H. M. Branch's personal friendship with TWOC leaders. See CIO organizer Don McKee's reports, 1939–40, McKee Papers.

28. Such sentiments were not new. Southern dissatisfaction with national union policies had surfaced in mid-1936 and again in mid-1937. UTWA Convention Proceedings, 1936, 77, and UTWA Executive Council minutes, 12 Sept. 1935, UTWA Papers, box 674, folder 5; Una *News-Review,* 19 Feb. 1937.

29. Francis J. Gorman to All Unions, 21 Dec. 1938, UTWA Papers, box 1868, folder 10. The AFL's George Googe added a month later, "The purpose of this Federation is to give cotton textile workers in the South democratic self-rule for the first time in history." Undated press release [Jan. 1939], UTWA Papers, box 1868, folder 10.

30. Clarence H. Williams to John R. Steelman, 30 Jan. 1939, RG 280, box 122, file 195-855, UTWA general file.

31. SCTF pamphlet, "Democracy in Practice—Not Only in Words!" RG 280, box 122, file 195-855, UTWA general file. Organizer Gordon Chastain echoed Pollard's statement in comments made to the local labor press in Spartanburg. The SFTW would be " 'a Southern cotton workers organization for Southerners.' " Una *News-Review*, 27 Jan. 1939.

32. United Textile Workers of America, *Special Convention Proceedings* (Washington, 1939), and handwritten account of the convention by Fall River delegate (and TWUA-CIO mole) John Ronfield. Both in TWUA Papers (Mss. 367), box 67. The Spartanburg delegates who represented non- or barely existent locals were all veterans of earlier struggles and out of work. Paul Stephens of Spartan Mills represented Local 1908 of Cherokee Falls (in neighboring Cherokee County), and former Saxon activists E. M. Sisk, J. Monroe Mills, and Annie Laura West claimed to represent Locals 1936–Powell Knitting, 1836–Valley Falls, and 21998 (plant unknown). Credentials Report, *Special Convention Proceedings,* 53–56. The Southern Cotton Textile Federation was showcased on the third day of the convention (69).

33. G. Walter Moore to Sidney Hillman, 28 Dec. 1938, TWUA Papers (Mss. 367), box 67. There was some truth to such charges. As Paul Richards has noted, "Formed at the top," the Textile Workers Organizing Committee resembled the CIO in steel (SWOC) more than it did the union in the electrical or automobile industries, "where action at the membership level preceded organization." Richards, "History of the Textile Workers Union of America," 38.

34. The owners of Drayton and Whitney had already begun the sale of their residential holdings to workers; the war caught them off-guard, because a substantial minority of village residents no longer worked for the mills. Both plants built a few new wartime houses, as did a few of the larger rural mills such as Tucapau and Pacolet. Much of the new housing, however, was rated at the supervisory level, because the influx of new workers heightened the need for mills to attract and keep trained section hands and overseers. Only Beaumont Mill substantially increased basic worker housing during the war.

35. Information on these stoppages is drawn from the case files of the Federal Mediation and Conciliation Service and may underestimate the actual number of stoppages. For Clifton, see RG 280, box 8, case 202–3; box 84, case 205–1213; box 570, cases 199–4909 and 199–4909–1; box 582, case 199–5445; box 642, case 199–7886; box 648, case 199–8193; box 657, case 199–8662; and box 743, case 196–1942. For Startex, see RG 280, box 54, case 205–360; box 84, case 205–1216; box 659, case 199–8785; box 822, case 209–6404; and box 1062, case 300–9457. For Inman Mills, see RG 280, box 600, case 199–6079; box 987, case 300–5189 (also related files, box 1032, case 300–7734, and box 11, case 202–395); and box 1368, case 442–118. For Beaumont, see RG 280, box 718, case 209–1707; and box 809, case 209–5785. For

Spartan, see RG 280, box 656, case 199–8603; and box 1685, case 452–1016. For Fairmont, see RG 280, box 1005, case 300–6223.

36. Doffers at Whitney walked out in September 1940 in protest of changes in their doffing assignments and kept that mill closed for three days. In August 1941, quiller-tenders in Drayton's rayon department staged a brief stoppage to protest workloads; after repeated delays in obtaining government-sponsored time studies, they shut the entire mill down for a day in January 1942. Also in August 1941, a small group of finishing plant workers unhappy with their pay scale precipitated a full-scale, although brief, strike at Lyman. And in early 1944 doffers at Arcadia struck for a week to protest workloads and job assignments. William Fred Ponder to W. Rhett Harley, 21 Sept. 1940, and other documents, RG 280, box 774, case 196–3161, Whitney Mfg. Co.; report of field exmainer Joseph D. Gould, 9 June 1942, RG 25, entry 155, box 2580, Drayton Mills; documents in RG 280, box 626, case 199–7175, Pacific Mills; RG 280, box 1141, case 301–4119, Mayfair Cotton Mills; RG 280, box 1204, case 301–7943, Mayfair Mills; RG 280, box 1232, case 301–9690, Mayfair Mills.

37. The CIO attempted to capitalize on the Lyman strike, and the AFL at Drayton, both to no avail. The sordid story of the collapse of the UTWA's Drayton campaign is related in RG 25, entry 155, box 2580, Drayton Mills.

38. This history is most concisely given in the company brief filed by lawyer L. W. Perrin, 9 June 1945, in a later NLRB election case. See RG 25, entry 155, box 4268, Inman Mills.

39. In early 1943, both the company and the union agreed to a series of government-sponsored time studies, but even after the company and Local 1935's leaders affirmed the results of these studies, the affected doffers rebelled at their revised work assignments. Twelve refused to comply on the spot and were summarily discharged. The remaining doffers walked out in solidarity, shutting down the entire plant from 12 to 20 April 1943. Federal conciliators convinced the doffers to return to work pending new time studies by a new technician. When he arrived at Inman on the evening of 5 May, he found that the doffers had struck again earlier in the afternoon to protest his tardiness. The doffers found the results of this second round of studies equally objectionable. This time, they followed their contract and sent the matter to arbitration, but arbitration was a slow process, and on 1 June the doffers struck for a third time, demanding immediate adjustments in their workloads. The War Labor Board ultimately adjusted the matter, and all the doffers were reinstated, although five cardroom employers who struck in sympathy during the third walkout were permanently discharged. RG 280, box 905, case 196–7837; box 9, case 202–279; box 883, case 209–9452; box 987, case 300–5189; and box 1032, case 300–7734. All Inman Mills.

40. Events reviewed in report of the Fourth Regional War Labor Board, 9 May 1944, copy found in Cherokee-Spartanburg Joint Board Papers, box 278.

41. Report of the Fourth Regional War Labor Board, 9 May 1944; see also RG 280, box 1368, case 442–118, Inman Mills.

42. Report of the Fourth Regional War Labor Board, 9 May 1944.

43. Annie Laura West to Francis Gorman, 18 April 1944, UTWA Papers, box 385, folder 321.

44. Handwritten minutes of Cherokee-Spartanburg Joint Board's 12 Nov. 1944 meeting; list of members of organizing committee, Jan. 1945; and transcript of NLRB election hearing, 31 May 1945. All in the Cherokee-Spartanburg Joint Board Papers, box 278, as is C. D. Puckett to NLRB, 25 July 1945.

45. During the TWUA drive, the UTWA had distributed leaflets in the mill village to remind workers that "the local C.I.O. leaders in your plant are the same ones who led you out on strike some time ago and lost for you your seniority rights, among other things, that the International Union had won for you. . . . Shelton and his gang," the UTWA concluded, were "Union Judases." In the election of 28 August, however, the UTWA received only thirteen votes, revealing how closely Inman's union movement was tied to its local leadership. Unsigned [UTWA] to "Textile Worker," 14 Aug. 1945, Cherokee-Spartanburg Joint Board Papers, box 278; RG 25, entry 155, box 4268, Inman Mills.

46. Minutes of CSJB meetings, 10 May, 13 Sept. 1947, Cherokee-Spartanburg Joint Board Papers, box 273; report of Charles D. Puckett, 1 Oct. 1947, TWUA Papers (Mss. 129A), series 2A, box 4, Cherokee-Spartanburg Joint Board Manager Reports

47. In the fall of 1947, a group of Inman unionists led by the officers of TWUA Local 731 even applied for a UTWA charter without the knowledge of the CIO. Cherokee-Spartanburg Joint Board minutes, 13, 27 Sept., 11 Oct. 1947, 13 Nov. 1948; and report of Charles D. Puckett, 14 Nov. Both in TWUA Papers (Mss. 129A), series 2A, box 4, Cherokee-Spartanburg Joint Board Manager Reports. See also John W. Pollard to Lloyd Kleinert, 10 Nov. 1947, UTWA Papers, box 420, folder 933.

48. "I am not at all proud of this settlement," the TWUA's Julius Fry admitted, "however, with all the circumstances, it is my considered judgment that we did the best we could." AFL partisans in the local spread word that "the Contract was made with the National Union and that the Local Membership had no voice or vote on the matter." Julius R. Fry to Roy R. Lawrence, 12 Dec. 1947, Cherokee-Spartanburg Joint Board Papers, box 277; report of C. D. Puckett, 1 Oct. 1947, TWUA Papers (Mss. 129A), series 2A, box 4, Cherokee-Spartanburg Joint Board Manager Reports.

49. Report of E. L. Smith, 14 June 1949, TWUA Papers (Mss. 129A), series 2A, box 11.

50. J. W. Kelly, memorandum to file, 1 Nov. 1950; William Pollock to Charles Auslander, 7 Dec. 1950; Charles Auslander to Pollock, 19 Jan 1951; and Charles Auslander to Wilbur R. Samuels, 26 Jan. 1951. All in TWUA South Carolina State Director's Papers, box 320. In 1953 the UTWA attempted a return to Inman but was only able to sign about 150 of the plant's eight hundred workers. C. H. Pearson to Anthony Valente, 2 April 1953, UTWA Papers, box 420, folder 933.

51. Of course, as the internal histories of the Saxon, Startex, and Spartan cases showed, the Wagner Act's protections were thin indeed and often outright illusory. As Colin Gordon has noted, "Taft-Hartley was not so much a retreat from Wagner as it was an evaporation of the circumstances (depression and war) under which concessions made sense to business." In short, it was "a clarification of the conservative, pragmatic unionism that business had always expected from New Deal labor policy." *New Deals*, 302.

52. Operation Dixie's tragic story is told in Griffith, *The Crisis of American Labor*, supplemented by Zieger, *The CIO*, 227–41. Griffith's account is primarily thematic and builds more on the stories of organizers than of workers; she does, however, provide an excruciating case study of how the TWUA-CIO, upon whom the fate of Operation Dixie necessarily came to rest, failed at the Kannapolis-based Cannon Mills chain (46–61). As Griffith rightly concludes, "For American labor, Operation Dixie was, quite simply, a moment of high tragedy from which it has yet to fully recover" (176).

53. The TWUA lost Arcadia by a vote of 200-521 on 28 February 1946 and Fairforest Finishing by a vote of 159-375 on 14 November 1946. The Saxon campaign stalled because by the mid-1940s most of the Saxon community's leaders—including many of old Local 1882's officers—no longer worked inside Saxon mill. The financially troubled Cowpens Mill reopened twice in the late 1940s. The first time, it was almost immediately organized by the TWUA, whose campaign disintegrated in early 1947 after the company fired the union's key committee person; in early 1948 the TWUA's drive collapsed days before an election, when managers began crating up machinery for supposed shipment to South America. The Lyman and Arkwright campaigns stalled early.

For Arcadia, the case file is missing from NLRB records but see election card in present-day UNITE office files. Also see Cherokee-Spartanburg Joint Board minutes, 26 Jan. 1947, Cherokee-Spartanburg Joint Board Papers, box 273. For Fairforest, see RG 25, entry 155, box 4676, Fairforest Finishing Co. Also see Franz Daniel's weekly organizing reports, TWUA Papers (Mss. 129A), series 2A, box 4. For Arkwright, see membership lists and other related documents in Cherokee-Spartanburg Joint Board Papers, box 273 (first and second folders). For Saxon, see Rev. John B. Isom's diary entries for 1946, Isom Papers. For Lyman, see weekly reports of TWUA South Carolina state director Franz Daniel for 1946, TWUA Papers (Mss. 129A), series 2A, box 4. Also see weekly reports of State Director Charles Auslander (esp. 11 Nov. 1949, 21 March, 24 May, 24 Aug., 26 Oct. 1950, 16 Feb., 3 April 1951), TWUA Papers (Mss. 129A), series 2A, box 11. For Cowpens Mill (Leading Embroidery Co. and/or Linda Cotton Mills), see reports of Franz E. Daniel, 30 Aug. 1946, 31 May 1947, TWUA Papers (Mss. 129A), series 2A, box 4; reports of Cherokee-Spartanburg Joint Board manager E. L. Smith, 14 June, 14 July, 8 Sept. 1949, TWUA Papers (Mss. 129A), series 2A, box 11; and Robert S. Cahoon to Franz Daniel and Charles Auslander, 7 Oct. 1949, and Charles Auslander to Solomon Barkin, 21 Oct. 1949, TWUA South Carolina State Director's Papers, box 320.

54. Reports of Cherokee-Spartanburg Joint Board director C. D. Puckett, 6 Jan., 8 Feb., 11 March, 8 May, 1 July, and 1 Sept. 1947, TWUA Papers (Mss. 129A), series 2A, box 4; reports of Franz E. Daniel, TWUA Papers (Mss. 129A), series 2A, box 4 (especially report for 19 Aug. 1947); USFMCS cases 474–1059 and 474–1771, RG 280, boxes 2210 and 2222; Franz E. Daniel to Clay Fulks, 3 April 1947, Operation Dixie Papers (microfilm edition), series 18, frame 45; and weekly reports of Cherokee-Spartanburg Joint Board manager M. Wade Lynch, 10 March, 10 April, 9 May, 9 June, 12 Aug. 1951, TWUA Papers (Mss. 129A), series 2A, box 11. For an excellent parallel account of the TWUA's Operation Dixie failure in a comparable small-town southern mill, see Brattain, " 'A Town as Small as That.' "

55. Jesse B. Smith to George Baldanzi, 11 Dec. 1946, ODA 16:11.

56. James A. Chapman to Stanley W. Converse, 18 April 1949, also enclosures and accompanying news clippings, Clifton Mfg. Co. Papers, series 6, box 7, folder 93.

57. During this period a weak American Federation of Hosiery Workers local did exist at Powell Knitting, but it kept aloof from the overall textile scene and had no known relations with either the UTWA or the TWUA.

CHAPTER 8: LAST STAND

1. The Textile Workers Organizing Committee first petitioned for an election in late 1937, officially claiming 61 percent of the workers at all three Clifton mills. The NLRB's Charles N. Feidelson objected, noting the union had "a substantial majority in Plant No. 2, a slight majority in Plant No. 1, and only a few members in Plant No. 3." On 11 April 1938 TWOC filed an amended petition covering plants No. 1 and No. 2 only. That satisfied Feidelson, but predictable procedural delays ensued, aggravated by Clifton company president J. Choice Evins, who refused to sanction any election. RG 280, box 492, case 199–1978; box 506, case 199–250; and box 2, case 202–9, all Clifton Mfg. Co.; RG 25, entry 155, box 543, six Clifton Mfg. Co. folders. The Feidelson quotation is from Charles N. Feidelson to Nathan Witt, 7 July 1938, in second folder.

2. Workers' actions—only some of which made it into formal labor-management records—included a two-day stoppage in No. 2's weave room in January 1940 over an "accumulation of controversial issues centering on promotion," prompting a lockout on the company's part and a threatened strike of all three plants on the union's, as well as a one-day strike by the same workers in February to enforce the promises made by the company during the January shutdown. RG 280, box 570, cases 199–4909 and 199–4909–1, Clifton Mfg. Co.; *Industrial Leader,* 12 Jan., 1 March 1940.

3. Although the weavers' grievances that actually provoked this strike were real,

much more was involved: "The main obstacle seems to be the company's reluctance to sign a contract. Apparently this group of manufacturers in this section have an understanding that they won't enter into any contractual relations or sign with any of the organizations. None of them wants to be the one to make the first move." RG 280, box 743, case 196–1942, Clifton Mfg. Co. No. 2, especially Paul R. Christopher to John R. Steelman, 20 April 1940, and memorandum to file, W.C.T. from telephone conversation with Daniel H. Taft, 25 May 1940 (quotation).

4. RG 280, box 832, cases 196–5146 and 196–A–5146, Clifton Mfg. Co.; *Industrial Leader,* 11 April 1941.

5. RG 280, box 872, case 196–6546, Clifton Mfg. Co.; *Industrial Leader,* 17 Dec. 1941.

6. RG 280, box 648, case 199–8193, Clifton Mfg. Co. No. 3; *Industrial Leader,* 10, 31 July 1942.

7. Six stoppages at No. 2 involved doffers (April and September 1942), slashers (June 1942), and battery hands (December 1943 and twice in January 1944); one at No. 1 involved doffers and spinners (December 1943); and one at No. 3 involved the carding department (October 1944). RG 280, box 642, case 199–7886; box 84, case 205–1213; box 657, case 199–8662. See also reports of Charles D. Puckett, 20–22 Dec. 1943, and 8, 20–21 Jan. 1944, and Cherokee-Spartanburg Joint Board minutes, 8 Jan., 14 Oct. 1944. All in Cherokee-Spartanburg Joint Board Papers, box 273.

8. RG 280: box 91, case 205–1457; box 90, case 205–1434; box 8, case 202–203; box 91, case 205–1476; box 11, case 202–351; box 1003, case 300–6085; box 121, case 205–2468; box 132, case 205–2807; box 117, case 205–2352; box 20, cases 202–711 and 202–712; box 171, case 205–4071; and box 179, case 205–4370; all Clifton Mfg. Co.

9. Earl L. Smith to R. R. Lawrence, 16 Nov. 1942, RG 280, box 169, case 195–2076, Clifton Mfg. Co.

10. "When we try to meet with them the only ones our committees and Stewards can get to see is the Overseers and Plant Superintendents, and they never have authority enough to settle any Grievances, then when we want a conference with Mr. Stanley Converse . . . , he always is too busy to meet with us this week, we will have to wait until next week, then next week he will have to be gone off on business, we will meet next week, then next week probably if we can get to see him to arrange a conference with him he will say that the company has a policy of this or that, or that we will have to give him two or three weeks to check into the matter, and after the two or three weeks have gone by and we finally run him down again he has been so busy that he has not had time to check yet but that he will look into it in a few days and let us hear from him. So it is just one run around after another and we never get anything settled." E. L. Smith to J. R. Steelman, 4 Feb. 1943 (quotations), and cover letter of same date to Emil Rieve. Both in RG 280, box 950, case 300–3051, Clifton Mfg. Co.

11. Among the most active were R. S. Huskey, T. N. Hicks, Aron J. and N. A. Mc-

Connell, George B. Adair, P. H. Hopper, E. D. Lovelace, Gary Coggins, Paul and Will White, Dexter Fowler, Elbert Thornton, Furman Mabry, Scoval Baker, Ola Bagwell, Otis Seals, M. L. Chastain, Chester Bible, and Joe Barber.

12. Cherokee-Spartanburg Joint Board minutes, 11 Nov. 1944, Cherokee-Spartanburg Joint Board Papers, box 273.

13. Reports of Cherokee-Spartanburg Joint Board manager E. L. Smith, 14 June 1949 (includes quotation), 14 July, 8 Sept. 1949, TWUA Papers (Mss. 129A), series 2A, box 11.

14. As TWUA state director Charles Auslander later noted, "There isn't any question that . . . the company, backed up by the employers in the state, [is] . . . hell bent on eliminating us." No incriminating correspondence survives between James A. Chapman and Stanley Converse, but Chapman did keep Converse abreast of the TWUA situation at Inman Mills throughout 1949. During the Clifton strike, Converse apparently kept both industrialists and politicians in South Carolina informed. On the day before Converse attempted to reopen the mills in January 1950, for example, construction magnate Charles E. Daniel of Greenville noted in a private letter (a copy of which also went to South Carolina Senator Strom Thurmond) that Spartanburg County would be "throwing out the last C.I.O. unit tomorrow." Charles Auslander to William Pollock, 11 May 1950, TWUA Papers (Mss. 396), box 68; James A. Chapman to Stanley W. Converse, 18 April 1949, also enclosures and accompanying newsclippings, Clifton Mfg. Co. Papers, series 6, box 7, folder 93; copy of letter, Charles E. Daniel to W. Erskine Gallant, 23 Jan. 1950, Clifton Mfg. Co. Papers, series 6, box 9, folder 125.

15. The best-documented struggle during the period immediately before the strike concerned the No. 2 battery-fillers, which in many ways paralleled that of the No. 3 loom-fixers. In December 1948, the company—having previously notified the union—effected a major reorganization of work in No. 2's weave room. As part of this reorganization, the task of cleaning grates and harnesses was made the exclusive responsibility of two former battery-fillers (a demotion), with consequent redistribution of the remaining work. That seemed fair enough to weaving overseer C. W. Wooten and general manager T. I. Stafford. It did not, however, suit the affected battery-fillers. On the day the change was announced, they followed the lead of ardent unionist Ruby Bagwell in refusing to begin the new assignments and spent the rest of the morning "in a huddle on the spare floor." When Wooten reminded them of their contractual obligations, "Ruby said she knew the contract and [knew] they were supposed to try them for thirty days, but that if they tried them they would just be stuck with them. . . . That if [a] job was heavy, we wouldn't change—[we] only changed when jobs showed light." Bagwell charged that the company's time studies always seemed to prevail in the company's favor; that filing "complaints didn't do any good"—"it would be six months before anything was completed on them." Arbitration was slow and worthless. In other words, the mechanics of contractual

relations had effectively broken down, at least in Ruby Bagwell's opinion, and there was nothing left but for the battery-fillers to take matters into their own hands. After some private discussion, they decided to work only their old jobs. Later, Local 325 forced them to try the new ones, whereupon they filed complaints alleging excessive workload. When the company announced results of its own tests in May, Bagwell's fears were realized. The company reported that the battery-fillers were, on average, filling 551 bobbins per hour compared with the company's official standard of six hundred per hour—their jobs were "underloaded." Bagwell's protests—that the poor performances were due to some jobs requiring as many as three different kinds of filling carried up and down as many as three different narrow, uneven alleyways—went unheeded. After a section hand complained "that the seconds were too high," management put more of the cleanup back onto the remaining overburdened battery-fillers, who, ever more incensed, filed yet another complaint. All these allegations were still wending their way through contractual grievance procedures at the time of the strike. C. W. Wooten memoranda, 14 Sept., 22 Nov. 1948; handwritten report of T. I. Stafford, 6 Nov. 1948; C. W. Wooten to T. I. Stafford, 20 Jan. 1949; complaints filed by Gladys M. Sprouse, 25 Jan. 1949, and Ruby Bagwell, 10 Feb. 1949; memorandum, G. B. Greene to C. W. Wooten, 25 May 1949. All in Clifton Mfg. Co. Papers, series 6, box 6, folder 84.

16. The bulk of an internal understanding of the Clifton strike comes from memoranda kept by company supervisors whose names I will subsequently abbreviate as CWW (C. W. Wooten), PHD (P. H. Dickson), WMF (William M. Foster), and TIS (Thomas I. Stafford).

17. Affidavit of H. B. Davis, 28 May 1948, Clifton Mfg. Co. Papers, series 6, box 7, folder 94. The grievance was formally filed on 31 May 1948. Clifton Mfg. Co. Papers, series 6, box 9, folder 123.

18. H. B. Davis note, 29 May 1948, added to affidavit of 28 May 1948, Clifton Mfg. Co. Papers, series 6, box 7, folder 94; shop committee meeting minutes, 7, 17 June 1948, Clifton Mfg. Co. Papers, series 6, box 9, folder 125.

19. Shop committee meeting minutes, 30 June 1948, Clifton Mfg. Co. Papers, series 6, box 9, folder 125.

20. TIS memorandum, 17 Nov. 1949, Clifton Papers, series 6, box 9, folder 123; opinions and orders of arbitrator Paul N. Guthrie, 17 May 1949, TWUA South Carolina State Director's Papers, Clifton Mfg. Co. folder 2, box 319. Guthrie declined to give precise counsel as to how the new jobs should have been reconfigured.

21. Summarized in TIS memorandum, 17 Nov. 1949, Clifton Mfg. Co. Papers, series 6, box 9, folder 123. In late August, TWUA representative E. L. Smith barely headed off a wildcat strike. He "stressed the fact that the only way a job could be studied to determine the workload was while the job was still running" but noted, "For a number of years, the loomfixers have been fed up with checking" and remained unreconciled. E. L. Smith to Charles Auslander, 24 Aug. 1949, TWUA

South Carolina State Director's Papers, Clifton Mfg. Co. folder 2, box 319. For an excellent summary of the loom-fixers' grievances and the opening days of the stoppage in their own words, see W. E. Lands and E. L. Smith to Clifton Mfg. Co., 11 Nov. 1949, TWUA South Carolina State Director's Papers, Clifton Mfg. Co. folder 2, box 319.

22. PHD memorandum, 31 Oct. 1949, Clifton Mfg. Co. Papers, series 6, box 9, folder 126. On each shift, weaving supervisors made a personal canvass of the loom-fixers. Grady Parris said "he was not going to kill hisself" and would not fix on more than ninety-three looms. Samuel Fowler said "so far as he was concerned he liked the jobs alright as last week but the most of the other fixers was fixing on ninety-three and he felt like they ought to stick together on this thing." Creston Hollifield said "he did not want to be a Black Ball—it would make him feel like a fool." Others indicated union solidarity by referring bosses to shop stewards. Within a few days, the supervisors at No. 3 knew precisely which loom-fixers were antiunion, which fully supported the strike, and which were wavering. Unfortunately for the company, the majority on all three shifts had cast their lot with the union. J. W. Coggins memorandum, 31 Oct. 1949, Clifton Mfg. Co. Papers, series 6, box 9, folder 126.

23. Looms were designed to stop automatically when the apparatus sensed a mechanical problem. Although looms sometimes stopped because of simple mechanical problems that the weavers themselves could fix, any weaver who tried to unflag his or her own looms was sure to receive a personal visit from one of the loom-fixers. PHD memoranda, 1, 2, 3 Nov. 1949, and J. W. Coggins memorandum, 1 Nov. 1949, Clifton Mfg. Co. Papers, series 6, box 9, folder 126 (the fixers who are quoted were E. M. White and Horace Waddell, respectively).

24. PHD memoranda, 7, 8, 9 Nov. 1949, Clifton Mfg. Co. Papers, series 6, box 9, folder 126.

25. At No. 2, the stoppage actually began a shift early, during the last hours of 7 November. Some fixers stood around their work benches while others talked quietly in the old tying-in room. When supervisor W. M. Foster asked them what the trouble was, they replied that "there was no trouble . . . that the fixers were just not going to take down any more flags till they got the trouble straightened out at Converse." WMF memoranda, 7, 8 Nov. 1949, and T. W. Coggins memorandum, 7 Nov. 1949, Clifton Mfg. Co. Papers, series 6, box 9, folder 126.

26. "It has no paid Holidays, only $1\frac{1}{2}$ time pay if work is performed on six holidays, no reporting pay, no company paid insurance, no use of bulletin boards in plants, a very bad workload clause, no guaranteed wage scale and many other things are not in it that should be." Report of Cherokee-Spartanburg Joint Board manager Earl L. Smith, 8 Dec. 1949, TWUA Papers (Mss. 129A), series 2A, box 11.

27. Report of S.C. State Director Charles Auslander, 27 Dec. 1949, TWUA Papers (Mss. 129A), series 2A, box 11.

28. Charles Auslander to William Pollock, 8 Dec. 1949, TWUA South Carolina State Director's Papers, Clifton Mfg. Co. folder 2, box 319.

29. For instance, *Textile Labor,* the official TWUA publication, did not even mention the Clifton situation until 17 December, more than a month after what the TWUA labeled a "lockout" had begun. Throughout the strike, *Textile Labor* gave the Cliftons only cursory attention, especially in comparison to its coverage of other, more sanctioned conflicts elsewhere in the South. *Textile Labor,* 17 Dec 1949, 7, 21 Jan, 4, 18 Feb, 13 May 1950. In fact, communication between Local 325 and TWUA officials was minimal throughout the strike, especially during its early stages. Despite warnings sounded by local TWUA representative E. L. Smith during the summer and early fall, the loom-fixers' actions took TWUA leaders completely by surprise. As late as mid–November, neither Local 325 nor the company had officially informed the TWUA that anything out of the ordinary was happening. "We are sitting tight awaiting developments," a perplexed Charles Auslander told his TWUA superiors on 11 November. Reports of Cherokee-Spartanburg Joint Board manager E. L. Smith, 14 June, 14 July, 8 Sept. 1949, and Auslander's report of 11 Nov. 1949. All in TWUA Papers (Mss. 129A), series 2A, box 11. See also E. L. Smith to Charles Auslander, 24 Aug. 1949, TWUA South Carolina State Director's Papers, Clifton Mfg. Co. folder 2, box 319.

30. Report of Cherokee-Spartanburg Joint Board Manager E. L. Smith, 30 Jan. 1950, TWUA Papers (Mss. 129A), series 2A, box 11. Concerning the problems of financing the strike (a major burden for the already struggling TWUA), see report of Cherokee-Spartanburg Joint Board manager E. L. Smith, 30 Jan. 1950, TWUA Papers (Mss. 129A), series 2A, box 11; also see Charles Auslander to Wilbur R. Samuels, 19 Jan. 1950, and to William Pollock, 24 March 1950, TWUA Papers (Mss. 396), box 68.

31. Report of S.C. State Director Charles Auslander, 11 Nov. 1949, TWUA Papers (Mss. 129A), series 2A, box 11.

32. Company memoranda, 10, 21 Jan. 1950, Clifton Mfg. Co. Papers, series 6, box 9, folder 125.

33. The context was specifically local. As Mary Wingerd notes in her study of the Cooleemee, N.C., mill village, "Community encompassed only a certain category of worker and its meaning had real geographical limits" even before the coming of the union. "Partially because of Cooleemee's isolation, partly in response to Erwin's specific management style, but to a great degree because of the particular way women and men chose to characterize themselves as workers, their identity was inseparable from the specific context of Cooleemee." Thus, the Cooleemee TWUA local "was not to be an oppositional union in the classic sense of other CIO unions that formed in the same period; nor was it a company union. It was in fact a hybrid of the two" and rooted in all the ambiguities of mill-village life—an "attempt to craft a new form of defense without discarding the effective elements of former custom."

Although Clifton workers had labored under a less-consciously paternalistic employer and by the 1940s possessed considerable more experience with unionism than their Cooleemee counterparts, Local 325 operated in a similar way—at least as long as the Clifton Manufacturing Company agreed to abide by what workers viewed as the traditional rules of the game. When TWUA officials attempted to involve themselves in the Clifton strike, they found themselves mystified by this particular flavor of unionism. Charles Auslander at one point even damned Local 325 as "a glorified company-union set-up," indicating how little he actually understood about life and labor in the Cliftons. Wingerd, "Rethinking Paternalism," 7, 30, 31; report of S.C. State Director Charles Auslander, 27 Dec. 1949, TWUA Papers (Mss. 129A), series 2A, box 11.

34. For the most part, this involved the phrase "yellow scab" or its variants: "corruptive scab," "yellow bastard," and "yellow two-faced skunk." Examples all from the Clifton Mfg. Co. Papers, series 6: picket cat-calls, 31 Jan., 10, 14 Feb. 1950, box 7, folder 91; J. H. Mason memorandum, 26 Jan. 1950, box 10, folder 129; WMF memoranda, 16 Jan., 8, 14 Feb. 1950 box 10, folder 129.

35. The topic is explored more fully in the work of Jacquelyn Dowd Hall, Joel Williams, and Martha Hodes. See especially Hall, "The Mind That Burns in Each Body," 71.

36. Undated, unsigned memorandum (concerning Junior Benton), and unsigned memorandum (concerning what Melvin Frady hollered at S. T. Guest) of 25 Jan. 1950. Both in Clifton Mfg. Co. Papers, series 6, box 10, folder 129.

37. WMF memorandum, 30 Jan. 1950, Clifton Mfg. Co. Papers, series 6, box 10, folder 129.

38. WMF memorandum, 27 Jan. 1950, Clifton Mfg. Co. Papers, series 6, box 9, folder 127 (Bagwell); CWW memorandum, 3 Feb. 1950, Clifton Mfg. Co. Papers, series 6, box 7, folder 95 (Justice).

39. Unsigned memorandum, 16 Feb. 1950, Clifton Mfg. Co. Papers, series 6, box 10, folder 129. A similar incident involved three male strikers who "had a dog at the lower gate and were going through all kinds of vulgar motions with the dog for the benefit of some spinners who were eating their lunch on [the] spare floor near [the] upper end windows." WMF memorandum, 27 Jan. 1950, Clifton Private Papers.

40. Picket cat-calls, 2 Feb. 1950, Clifton Mfg. Co. Papers, series 6, box 7, folder 91.

41. Interview with Furman Mabry and Louise Mabry.

42. WMF memorandum, 12 April 1950, Clifton Mfg. Co. Papers, series 6, box 10, folder 129.

43. Picket cat-calls (concerning Frances Bradley Rogers), 2 Feb. 1950, Clifton Mfg. Co. Papers, series 6, box 7, folder 91.

44. Viola Mason reports, 17, 25 Feb. 1950, Clifton Mfg. Co. Papers, series 6, box 7, folder 91.

45. Examples in CWW memoranda of 10, 16, 23, 24 Jan. 1950 (all concerning automotive charivaris at No. 2), Clifton Mfg. Co. Papers, series 6, box 7, folder 95.

Many of Clifton's residents had emigrated to Spartanburg from Appalachia, where they would have known the old-fashioned charivari (or shivaree) as a long-standing method of enforcing community moral standards. More traditional charivaris also occurred during the strike. When strikebreaker Ralph Henard tried to spend an evening visiting in late February, unionists made a continual disturbance on a neighboring porch to protest. Another strikebreaker, Anabel Hughes, reported that her neighbors had embarked on a campaign of beating pots and pans continuously during the evening hours. W. H. Adair reported that the teenaged daughter of striker Deseree Hembree drove by his house five times in one day, "holloring and beating on [a] bucket." WMF memorandum, 1 March 1950, Clifton Mfg. Co. Papers, series 6, box 10, folder 129; CWW memorandum, 3 March 1950, Clifton Mfg. Co. Papers, series 6, box 7, folder 95.

46. One such nocturnal caravan visited the homes of Reverend Shealy and Principal Frick, as well as the Clifton school and Shealy's Presbyterian church. On a few occasions, cars bearing loudspeakers fanned out into the surrounding countryside to harass outlying strikebreakers, but those efforts ceased after the Cherokee County sheriff's department threatened full prosecution of those responsible. WMF memorandum, 12 Jan. 1950, Clifton Mfg. Co. Papers, series 6, box 10, folder 129; *Spartanburg Herald*, 17 Feb. 1950.

47. One evening in January when strikebreaker Virginia Courtney was driving through No. 1, she found the turn onto Glendale Line blocked by a striker's parked truck; she was forced to drive completely around the village in order to get back home. WMF memorandum, 19 Jan. 1950, Clifton Mfg. Co. Papers, series 6, box 10, folder 129; see also WMF memorandum of 24 Jan. 1950 for a similar impromptu blockade.

48. WMF memorandum, 4 Jan. 1950, Clifton Mfg. Co. Papers, series 6, box 10, folder 129.

49. Barber worried about the health of his elderly parents, whose antiunion sentiments were well known. "This thing is almost five months old and their nerves are shot. . . . My father has a bad heart and he has lost several pounds of weight worrying about this. My mother is just a bundle of nerves." Yet Barber indirectly acknowledged that, at least for the moment, the Sealses had the upper hand. He begged T. I. Stafford not to let the Sealses (or anyone else) know who had complained, "because they would make it worse." J. E. Barber to TIS, 20 March 1950, and WMF memorandum, 27 Jan. 1950. Both in Clifton Private Papers.

50. For an example, see WMF memorandum, 1 Feb. 1950, Clifton Mfg. Co. Papers, series 6, box 10, folder 129.

51. WMF memorandum, 17 Feb. 1950, Clifton Mfg. Co. Papers, series 6, box 10, folder 129.

52. "Striking Is a Family Affair," broadside in Clifton Private Papers. The two children in the accompanying illustration held signs reading "Me Too" and "Stick to it, Pop."

53. CWW memorandum (W. H. Adair testimony), 2 March 1950, Clifton Mfg. Co. Papers, series 6, box 7, folder 95; unsigned handwritten memoranda, 6 April 1950, Clifton Private Papers; WMF memorandum (concerning Stacy Powell), 9 March 1950, and typed unsigned memorandum, 2 Feb. 1950, Clifton Mfg. Co. Papers, series 6, box 10, folder 129.

54. R. D. Shropshier, Sr., to Stanley Converse, 26 Jan. 1950, Clifton Mfg. Co. Papers, series 6, box 10, folder 129.

55. Picket cat-calls, 31 Jan. 1950, Clifton Mfg. Co. Papers, series 6, box 7, folder 91.

56. Summarized in Mary Carr memorandum, 7 Feb. 1950, Clifton Mfg. Co. Papers, series 6, box 7, folder 91.

57. At least thirteen black workers at all three mills did obey the initial strike call. Whether they stayed away in support of the union or because they feared the outcome of crossing the picket line is unknown, but they all later went back to work under pressure from the company. Interview with Anderson Gray; typed company memorandum, 9 Dec. 1949, Clifton Private Papers.

58. WMF memoranda, 23 Jan. (quotation), 8 Feb. 1950, Clifton Mfg. Co. Papers, series 6, box 10, folder 129; CWW memorandum, 10 March 1950, Clifton Mfg. Co. Papers, series 6, box 7, folder 95.

59. WMF memoranda (concerning "Mr. Thomas" and Hopper's Garage), 9 Jan. 1950, and E. S. Davis typed memorandum (concerning Twin States Foundry), 15 Feb. 1950, Clifton Mfg. Co. Papers, series 6, box 10, folder 129. In the last instance, pickets told a would-be delivery man from Twin States Foundry that "they would make it hard on his company when they returned to work" by saying "'that your castings and material is no good and make so many complaints that the company will have to quit using your stuff.'" The driver turned back but later made his delivery after consultation with Clifton company officials.

60. In Cooleemee as at the Cliftons, the company "filled its low-level management positions almost exclusively from the ranks of the local workforce." In times of social stress (such as a strike), "a single family might find itself with members on both sides of a labor dispute, further complicating loyalties and obligations." Wingerd, "Rethinking Paternalism," 20.

61. Typed company memorandum, 9 Dec. 1949, Clifton Private Papers (for those who stayed out). Supervisor Belton Coggins had been a union supporter for years; his brother Gary remained active in Local 325 and even served a term as president. In 1949, however, Belton Coggins was caught, classified as a foreman in the No. 1 machine shop. "He had to work—he didn't have no other choice, see, because he was a bossman," his wife later recalled; he "like to lost his job, because he believed in it." His wife, herself a former mill worker, operated a beauty shop in the No. 1 community building at the time of the strike. Every day she witnessed the verbal (and sometimes physical) melees that occurred at the plant gate. Her only consolation was that the pickets, many of whom had known her and her husband all their lives, also

knew their true feelings and kept the barrages aimed at Belton to a minimum. "The biggest part of them that was out there knew that he was for them," not only just "rooting for them" but also surreptitiously providing food for some striking families. Interview with Marie Coggins.

62. John Roland Brown was master mechanic at the No. 2 machine shop. He did not strike because he "couldn't—I didn't come under the contract." Helen Brown was another story. As she recalled, "I had a job that come under the contract. I stayed out about two months. And John Roland had to work because he didn't come under the contract. . . . The ones that was staying out, some of them just made it real hard on me . . . on account of him, and so I just stood it as long as I could. And they really hurt me, all the yelling." One day as she drove down to the mill to pick her husband up from work the abuse proved too much and she decided to cross. She later blamed the union for her decision, which she painted in economic as well as psychological terms: "They was causing it—they'd already been calling me everything under the sun. And I wasn't getting any money on that." Helen Brown received the harsher condemnation, roundly vilified by her neighbors and memorialized for half a century thereafter as the first production worker to break ranks at No. 2. Interview with John Roland Brown and Helen (Cash) Brown; other private conversations with Clifton residents.

63. Picket cat-calls, 3 Feb. 1950, Clifton Mfg. Co. Papers, series 6, box 7, folder 91.

64. Picket cat-calls, 13 Feb. 1950, Clifton Mfg. Co. Papers, series 6, box 7, folder 91.

65. WMF memoranda, 3 Feb. 1950 (concerning Eulys Willis) and 13 Feb. 1950 (concerning Joe Parris), Clifton Mfg. Co. Papers, series 6, box 10, folder 129. See also CWW memorandum (concerning John McCarley), 10 March 1950, Clifton Mfg. Co. Papers, series 6, box 7, folder 95.

66. CWW memorandum, 30 Jan. 1950, Clifton Mfg. Co. Papers, series 6, box 9, folder 127.

67. Interview with George McCarley.

68. The TWUA later instructed its members to cease filing such charges and withdrew those pending; those filed by strikebreakers were almost all withdrawn or ultimately dismissed. Charles Auslander, blind note to Robert S. Cahoon on letter, and C. Yates Brown to Charlie Auslander, 19 May 1950, TWUA South Carolina State Director's Papers, Clifton Mfg. Co. folder 1, box 318.

69. For example, the company later charged five strikers with having set up "an organized and consistent campaign of terrorizing scabs at points remote from the plant, especially in Spartanburg." See handwritten note of Charles Auslander, 28 July 1950, and Robert S. Cahoon, blind note to Auslander on a copy of a letter to Stanley Converse, undated. Both in TWUA South Carolina State Director's Papers, Clifton Mfg. Co. folder 1, box 318.

70. WMF memorandum, 29 March 1950, Clifton Mfg. Co. Papers, series 6, box 9, folder 129.

71. WMF memorandum, 27 Jan. 1950, and see also Elbert Hughes memorandum, 27 Jan. 1950 (concerning striker Minus Revels attempting to get three women not to report back to work). Both in Clifton Mfg. Co. Papers, series 6, box 9, folder 129.

72. Unsigned memorandum, 16 Feb. 1950, Clifton Mfg. Co. Papers, series 6, box 9, folder 129.

73. WMF memorandum, 7 Feb. 1950, Clifton Mfg. Co. Papers, series 6, box 9, folder 129.

74. TIS memoranda, 22 Feb. 1950, Clifton Mfg. Co. Papers, series 6, box 9, folder 129.

75. These back-to-work notices, with the employees' responses typed on the reverse are found in Clifton Mfg. Co. Papers, series 6, box 10, folder 124.

76. Report of S.C. State Director Charles Auslander, 27 Dec. 1949, TWUA Papers (Mss. 129A), series 2A, box 11.

77. Report of S.C. State Director Charles Auslander, 21 March 1950, TWUA Papers (Mss. 129A), series 2A, box 11; Charles Auslander to William Pollock, 24 March 1950, TWUA South Carolina State Director's Papers, Clifton Mfg. Co. folder 2, box 319.

78. As an exhausted Charles Auslander noted, "We failed to make any gains other than an agreement on a permanent arbitration set-up in place of the A.A.A. We had to take a very obnoxious no-strike clause and were forced to accept a revocable check-off in place of the irrevocable one that we held before," all in order to side-step the company's obvious plan of "deliberately trying to break our union." "We came as close as humanly possible to having no agreement at all," negotiator Robert Calhoon admitted. Report of S.C. State Director Charles Auslander, 24 May 1950, TWUA Papers (Mss. 129A), series 2A, box 11; Robert S. Cahoon to Stanley Converse, 19 April 1950, blind note to Auslander, and Charles Auslander to William Pollock, 11 May 1950. Both in TWUA South Carolina State Director's Papers, Clifton Mfg. Co. folder 2, box 319.

79. The campaign for full reinstatement of strikers (an interesting story in itself) is related in the following documents, all found in TWUA South Carolina State Director's Papers, Clifton Mfg. Co. folder 1, box 318: Robert S. Cahoon, affidavit to arbitrator William M. Hepburn, 26 May 1950; opinion and award of arbitrator William M. Hepburn, 21 June 1950; Charles Auslander to Stanley W. Converse, 12 July 1950; memorandum, 6 July 1950, Charles Auslander to Stanley W. Converse, 12 July 1950; and Robert S. Cahoon to Charles Auslander et al., 4 Dec. 1950.

80. In his fine dissection of the 1939 strike at Crown Cotton Mills of Dalton, Georgia, Douglas Flamming has made similar observations. In the wake of the strike, antiunion workers actually filed suit against the state for compensation of wages lost while the mill was on strike. As Flamming notes, "The suit became a symbol for a community divided." These antiunion workers argued in their brief that they constituted a separate group within the Crown villages, "a class diametrically opposed to the union workers and the strike. . . . The millhands' own culture was geared more toward mutual interdependence than individualism, but the

tradition of unity could cut two ways. It could nourish a vibrant community of workers and contribute to successful unionization, but it could also lead to severe polarization within the mill village." *Creating the Modern South,* 228–29.

81. Interviews with Mary Carr, Betty (Hughes) Carr, and Ruth Barber.

82. Interview with Delbert Willis and Nell Willis.

83. Picket cat-calls, 10, 13 Feb. 1950, Clifton Mfg. Co. Papers, series 6, box 7, folder 91.

84. Interviews with Elbert Stapleton and Georgia Seals.

85. Interview with Pauline Bible.

86. On the eve of the strike, E. L. Smith had estimated the union's membership at more than 90 percent; by the fall of 1950, it had fallen to 64 percent. Local 325 continued to hold more or less a majority at the Cliftons until the day that No. 3 closed its doors in 1972, but attendance at meetings declined dramatically. E. L. Smith report, 14 June 1949, and Paul B. Faucette report, 24 Oct. 1950. Both in TWUA Papers (Mss. 129A), series 2A, box 11. Interviews with Furman Mabry and Ruth Barber.

87. Ibera Holt, in interview with Georgia Seals and Ibera Holt.

CHAPTER 9: HOPE, FEAR, AND THE RISKS OF PUBLIC LIFE

1. Interview with Kathryn Mabry Holden. For the Clifton flood, see Hembree and Moore, *A Place Called Clifton,* 78–95. The fact of the flood's lingering impact on Clifton's collective consciousness is evident in interviews with Delbert Lewis, Nell Lewis, M. A. Worley, Kathryn Mabry Holden, John Roland Brown, and Helen (Cash) Brown.

2. Interview with A. Beatrice Norton.

3. Interviews with Ruby Bevill (all quotations), Polly Foster, and Fred Jewell.

4. Ibid.

5. "That was one of our (I say) laws, when we joined our union, that [when] it was over and finished, not to dig it back up." Interview with A. Beatrice Norton.

6. Ibid. Norton's involvement with the Brown Lung Association included a successful local campaign to get the Spartanburg County commissioners to declare a special Brown Lung Week and a trip to Washington, D.C., to hear the BLA's case argued before the Supreme Court. In late 1980 her thoughts were still centered on events forty-five years earlier. Asked what she wanted for Christmas, she replied, "To be alive to see justice for everyone, and a clean and safe workplace for those still in the mills." Spartanburg *Brown Lung News,* Nov.–Dec. 1980, Brown Lung Association Papers (Mss. 4463), folder 28; interview with A. Beatrice Norton. Although Norton's case may have been exceptional, evidence suggests otherwise. Grover and Alice Hardin, who led the antibyssinosis fight in neighboring Greenville, had also been leaders in Greenville's lone organized mill—Woodside—during the 1930s and 1940s. Their story, as told by Allen Tullos in *Habits of Industry,* 255–84, documents their BLA

involvement but barely mentions their earlier union activity (275–76). Equally disappointing is Botsch, *Organizing the Breathless*, which gives virtually no attention to the backgrounds of local BLA leaders.

7. Berry, "A Poem of Difficult Hope," 62.

8. Flannery O'Connor observed as much in a 1957 response to a *Life* magazine editorial entitled "Who Speaks for America Today?" The gist of the editorial "was that in the last ten years this country had enjoyed an unparalleled prosperity, that it had come nearer to producing a classless society than any other nation, and that it was the most powerful country in the world, but that our novelists were writing as if they lived in packing boxes on the edge of the dump while they awaited admission to the poorhouse." The editors of *Life* requested a more uplifting American literature, one more in accord with the prosperous, powerful nation purveyed by the prevailing political culture and emphasizing "the joy of life itself," or at least the manifestation of joy generally associated with the American dream. Instead, as O'Connor wryly noted, the American writer increasingly suspected "some ugly correlation between our unparalleled prosperity and the stridency of these demands for a literature that shows us the joy of life. He may at least be permitted to ask if these screams for joy would be quite so piercing if joy were really more abundant in our prosperous society." *Mystery and Manners,* 25–26, 30.

9. Interview with Laurin B. Goolsby and Phoebe Goolsby (emphasis added).

10. On the ethical underpinnings of struggle, I am indebted to Hallie, *Lest Innocent Blood Be Shed.*

11. Joe Brooks of Thomasville, N.C., quoted in Waldrep, "Toward a Genealogy of Fear."

12. Unfortunately, the historiography of working-class America has been as much cause as symptom in perpetuating these twin unhelpful modes of analysis. Most present-day labor history views workers' struggles through decidedly rose-colored glasses. As George Lipsitz has noted, "A school of labor history where workers never suffer defeats does not help us understand the very real problems that actual workers have faced in the past and are facing in the present." Literature not falling into this category generally swings to the other extreme, or, in Lipsitz's words, "writes pessimism in the present back into the past." Neither approach, as Lipsitz observes, is helpful to either working-class people or the nation at large. *Rainbow at Midnight,* 8–9.

13. King, *Why We Can't Wait,* 40.

14. Ibid., 30. King's ethical understandings of struggle were, of course, largely underwritten by both his Christianity and a generalized conception of fairness and responsibility. As he put it in his letter from the Birmingham jail, "One who breaks an unjust law must do so openly, lovingly, *and with a willingness to accept the penalty*" (King, *Why We Can't Wait,* 83, emphasis added). Robert Moses, the other great tactician of the movement, drew his understanding of struggle less from the Bible than from the writings of Albert Camus. As his biographer has explained, Moses's

ethics were purer than King's, for whom the maneuverings of politics always held equal attraction. Yet in the abstract they thought alike. As Moses put it in a SNCC speech following the murders of three civil rights workers near Philadelphia, Mississippi, in 1963, "In our country we have some real evil, and the attempt to do something about it involves enormous effort . . . and therefore tremendous risks." Even after the enormous disappointment of the 1964 Democratic convention in Atlantic City—at which Moses's Mississippi Freedom Democratic Party (MFDP) was denied seating—Moses continued to sound this theme of self-sacrifice. "Somebody may have to be ploughed under," he explained, echoing textile worker Joe Brooks's comment on Gastonia, "but, after all, that's what a revolution means." Burner, *And Gently He Shall Lead Them*, passim (quotations on 158, 193).

15. As "southerners," the textile workers might have fared better; after all, white southerners were rooted in a broader regional culture predicated upon the experience of defeat at Appomattox. But as "workers," as both the union and the federal administration that fed their hopes insisted on categorizing them, their chances were slim. As individual participants in mainstream American culture, and the American labor movement as an institutional construct firmly fixed within that same culture, they were ideological captives.

EPILOGUE

1. Hembree and Crocker, *Glendale*, 29.

2. Dan River initially promised to keep the mills running and even projected a major modernization effort. Perhaps the effort assumed intimidating proportions. After all, under Stanley Converse the Clifton company had been notorious for recycling its used machinery. (Converse himself, it was said, was occasionally spotted picking through company trash piles looking for salvageable spare parts.) Or perhaps Dan River's true goal, from the beginning, was simply to eliminate competition. As worker Jack Thornton declared, "Dan River had no intention of keeping these mills running. . . . They bought 'em to get 'em out of their market. . . . It was a tax write-off, an elimination." Overseer George McCarley claimed that he knew of Dan River's ultimate intentions early on in the new company's administration, but that he and other high-level officials were charged with silence, since premature knowledge of the closings "would just cause confusion." Interviews with George McCarley and Aaron Thornton.

3. Interviews with Mary Carr and Betty (Hughes) Carr.

4. Hembree and Moore, *A Place Called Clifton*, 73–77.

5. Georgia Seals, in interview with Georgia Seals and Ibera Holt.

6. Interviews with George Sprouse, Verdie Lee Sprouse, Aaron Thornton, Howard Croxdale, Abbie Lee Croxdale, Mary Carr, and Betty (Hughes) Carr.

7. Quotations, in order, from interviews with Pauline Bible, Ruth Barber, Ibera Holt, Aaron Thornton, and Vessie M. Bagwell.

8. Virtually all my Clifton interviews cover the ground of post-Clifton employment, especially those of Charlie Quinn, George Sprouse, Verdie Lee Sprouse, Mary Carr, and Betty (Hughes) Carr. At Arrow Automotive, Charlie Quinn "saw friends all over the plant." Collins and Aikman hired Betty Carr to take charge of their personnel work at Cowpens; she saw to it as a matter of personal mission that the new plant hired as many old Clifton workers as possible, although not those with questionable (including, sometimes, prounion) records.

9. Interviews of Kathryn Mabry Holden (concerning her brother Paul Mabry), George Sprouse, Verdie Lee Sprouse, Mary Carr, Betty (Hughes) Carr, and Georgia Seals and Ibera Holt. As Betty Carr explained, "People would come in, they were desperate—they didn't know which way to move or turn; some of them were just at the age that they knew they couldn't probably go anywhere else. Part of them didn't even have transportation to go anywhere else. And they would break down, grown people, and cry to you—even men."

10. Interview with Charlie Quinn. As Quinn explained, textile work by the 1960s was "a rut" that prevented workers from "trying to do better." "Most everybody that left Clifton got a better deal than what they had when they was at Clifton," he maintained, and others back his testimony. Interviews with George Sprouse, Verdie Lee Sprouse, John Roland Brown, Helen (Cash) Brown, Aaron McConnell, Etrulia McConnell, Aaron Thornton, and Georgia Seals and Ibera Holt.

11. Ibera Holt, in interview with Georgia Seals and Ibera Holt.

12. "You was always so anxious to read in the paper about somebody that you knew back then, or run into somebody on the street that you'd known and worked with all your life." Interview with Howard Croxdale and Abbie Lee Croxdale (quotation).

13. These themes are echoed by Douglas Flamming in his account of the demise of the Crown Cotton Mills community of Dalton, Georgia: "Without any sustaining force, without the mill or the union, the community of workers had no means of perpetuating itself." *Creating the Modern South,* 335.

Glossary

Battery-filler: Draper-style looms featured a round, barrel-like device, a "battery," which held spare bobbins of thread (quills). Battery-fillers moved up and down the weave-room aisles with a small wagon ("cheese truck") replacing the empty bobbins with full ones.

Doffer: "Doffing" was the job of removing full spindles of thread or bolts of cloth from the spinning or weaving machinery. "Warp doffers" carried the heavy warps (bolts of yarn) from the slashing department to drawing-in.

Drawing-in: The job of pulling the initial strands of yarn from a warp beam through the heddles and reeds of a loom harness, preparatory to weaving, was called "drawing-in." Before the mid-twentieth century, this process was done entirely by hand. Consequently, drawing-in was considered highly skilled work, because the production of patterned cloth required precise placement of the strands. Not to be confused with "tying-in," which followed drawing-in and involved the insertion of the prepared beam into the loom.

Overseer: A supervisor responsible for an entire department within a mill: carding, spinning, weaving, and finishing. Each mill's master mechanic and "outside boss" (over the village maintenance crews) were accorded honorary overseer status.

Pick clock: A device installed on looms (beginning in the 1920s) to gauge a weaver's productivity by counting the number of "picks" (shuttle passes) over a given shift.

Picker: Male workers who forced bales of raw cotton into the picker machine using sharpened sticks ("picker sticks"), preparatory to carding.

Quiller: "Quills" were a specific type of bobbin designed to fit into the shuttle of a Draper-style loom. A quiller operated the quiller machine, which wound yarn from cones or spindles onto bobbins. "Pouring up quills" meant removing empty bobbins from looms and reinserting them into the quiller machine.

Roving: The thick, rope-like mass of cotton fibers sent from the card room to the spinning room, where it was "laid up" above the spinning machinery in large coils—hence "roving haulers" or "laying up roving."

Second hand: A foreman, serving under an overseer. "Section hands" were assistant second hands responsible for a specific section of weaving or spinning machinery. Both were privately referred to by workers as "straw bosses."

Slasher: A worker who operated the slashing machinery, which joined multiple warp beams of yarn into a single, full-loom beam, preparatory to weaving.

Slubber: The final stage in the carding department. A slubber hand-operated the slubber machine, which received processed cotton from the cards and formed it into roving. The "speeder" was a device in the slubber machinery, often operated by a separate worker, which expelled the roving from the machinery in long coils.

Spare hand: A worker without a regularly assigned job who filled in for absent workers, often on a part-time basis. Spare hands were either new workers (waiting for a full-time job to open) or workers whose family duties prevented full-time employment. Large mills often kept a few spare hands ready on each shift at a central location known as the "spare floor."

Spinner: Anyone operating the spinning machinery, which was installed in long rows, each row having two "sides." Thus, a spinner responsible for "eight sides" was actually in charge of four long rows of machinery.

Spooler: A worker operating the spooler machinery, which wound yarn from spinning bobbins onto cones, which could then be used in the warper or quiller machines.

Warper: A worker operating the warper machine, which prepared warps (beams of yarn) for weaving by winding yarn onto empty cloth bolts.

Bibliography

INTERVIEWS

In its original conceptualization, this work involved hundreds of interviews—taped and untaped—in some thirteen southern localities in five states and covering eleven major industries. The present list includes all recorded interviews I conducted concerning Spartanburg County, S.C., and textile life and labor before 1950. Copies of these tapes remain in my possession. Although all ninety interviews listed were important in shaping my understanding of Spartanburg mill culture and the labor movement, I have chosen to limit citations in the text only to those I deemed especially relevant, marked in this bibliography with an asterisk (*).

Herman Bagwell*, 3 March 1993, Chesnee, S.C.
Vessie M. Bagwell*, 25 Feb. 1993, Clifton, S.C.
Ruth Barber*, 11 Feb. 1993, Clifton, S.C.
Ruby Bevill*, 30 June 1994, Spartanburg, S.C.
Pauline Bible*, 27 Feb. 1993, Clifton, S.C.
J. E. Blackwell and Lucille Blackwell, 1 March 1993, Startex, S.C.
Lydia V. Blackwell with Audrey Knight, 27 Oct. 1993, Spartanburg, S.C.
Rev. Doyle Brown, 17 Feb. 1993, near Fingerville, S.C.
James W. Brown, 8 July 1994, Pacolet Mills, S.C.
John Roland Brown and Helen (Cash) Brown*, 15 Feb. 1993, Clifton, S.C.
Virginia Brown, 7 July 1994, Drayton, S.C.
William A. Bryant*, 8 June 1994, Spartanburg, S.C.
Len W. Bryson, 1 July 1994, near Lyman, S.C.
Pettit Calvert and Vernie Calvert*, 13 Feb. 1993, Moore, S.C.
J. Luther Campbell*, 27 Feb. 1993, Arcadia, S.C.
Mary Carr and Betty (Hughes) Carr, 4 March 1993, Clifton, S.C.
Marie (Vaughn) Coggins*, 12 Feb. 1993, Clifton, S.C.
Rev. Clarence E. Crocker, 2 Dec. 1993, Glendale, S.C.
Howard Croxdale and Abbie Lee Croxdale*, 10 Feb. 1993, Spartanburg, S.C.

Laura Daugherty*, 30 Nov. 1993, Greenville, S.C.

Mozelle Dawkins, 23 Feb. 1993, Cowpens, S.C.

Jim Dawson, 12 Feb. 1993, Clifton, S.C.

Paul Dearybury and Virl Dearybury*, 17 Feb. 1993, Converse, S.C.

Jasper DeYoung and Mae DeYoung*, 4 March 1994, Duncan, S.C.

Robert W. Donnahoo*, 8 Aug. 1994, Moorestown, N.J.

Vivian Duncan*, 27 June 1994, Spartanburg, S.C.

Clayton Faulkner*, 18 Feb. 1993, Roebuck, S.C.

Bessie D. Foster, 29 Oct. 1993, Whitney, S.C.

Earl Foster and Juanita Foster, 26 Oct. 1993, Whitney, S.C.

Polly Foster*, 27 June 1994, Spartanburg, S.C.

Vernon Foster*, 5 July 1994, Spartanburg, S.C.

Millard C. Freeman*, 27 Oct. 1993, Startex, S.C.

Fred Gardner, 26 Feb. 1993, Cowpens, S.C.

Walter Garrett, 16 Feb. 1993, Converse, S.C.

Irene Gault, 7 July 1994, Drayton, S.C.

J. D. Gault, 6 July 1994, Drayton, S.C.

Mamie Gault, 27 June 1994, Spartanburg, S.C.

Laurin B. Goolsby and Phoebe Goolsby*, 28 June 1994, Spartanburg, S.C.

Anderson Gray*, 26 Oct. 1993, Cowpens, S.C.

Homer Lee Harrison*, 18 Feb. 1993, Spartanburg, S.C.

Ernest C. Hawkins*, 27 Oct. 1993, Spartanburg, S.C.

William Ned Hemphill, 8 July 1994, Pacolet Mills, S.C.

Ralph Henard, 1 March 1993, Clifton, S.C.

Kathryn Mabry Holden*, 9 Feb. 1993, Clifton, S.C.

Fred Jewell*, 27 June 1994, Spartanburg, S.C.

Hoyt Jones and Marie Jones*, 12 Feb. 1993, Clifton, S.C.

Marion J. Lindsay, 5 July 1994, Spartanburg, S.C.

Marie Littlejohn, 8 July 1994, Pacolet Mills, S.C.

Joe Love*, 25 Feb. 1993, Startex, S.C.

George McCarley*, 11 Feb. 1993, Clifton, S.C.

Aaron J. McConnell and Etrulia McConnell*, 4 March 1993, Clifton, S.C.

Mattie McGraw, 29 June 1994, Glendale, S.C.

Furman Mabry and Louise (Vaughn) Mabry*, 6, 9 Feb. 1993, Clifton, S.C.

Zelia Ann (Chapman) Mabry*, 11 Feb. 1993, Cowpens, S.C.

Thelma Mills, 27 June 1994, Spartanburg, S.C.

George W. Moore Jr.*, 4 March 1994, Wellford, S.C.

Marie Moore, 7 July 1994, Drayton, S.C.

J. D. Morgan, 8 July 1994, Pacolet Mills, S.C.

Emmett Mostiler and Pearl Mostiler, 22 Feb. 1993, Clifton, S.C.

Jerry Mostiler, 18 Feb. 1993, Clifton, S.C.

Anna Fay Neighbors, 1 July 1994, Spartanburg, S.C.
A. Beatrice Norton*, 29 June 1994, Spartanburg, S.C.
Chester Pack, 30 June 1994, Spartanburg, S.C.
Lewis V. "Buck" Petty, 15 Feb. 1993, Roebuck, S.C.
Brooks Pollard*, 4 March 1994, Spartanburg, S.C.
Mamie McAbee Pollard*, 6 July 1994, Spartanburg, S.C.
Irene Pruitt, 30 June 1994, Drayton, S.C.
Elbert J. Pye*, 6 July 1994, Spartanburg, S.C.
Charlie Quinn*, 19 Feb. 1993, Clifton, S.C.
Alvin Ravan, 24 Feb. 1993, Converse, S.C.
Charles Reid, 16 Feb. 1993, Converse, S.C.
Clement A. Riddle, 27 Oct. 1993, Spartanburg, S.C.
Ethelene Rogers, 8 July 1994, Pacolet Mills, S.C.
Evelyn Neal Satterfield*, 1 July 1994, Spartanburg, S.C.
Georgia Seals and Ibera Holt, with Carson Seals*, 23 Feb. 1993, Clifton, S.C.
Willie Mae Shepherd*, 2 Dec. 1993, Greenville, S.C.
Ruby Knuckles Smith, 6 July 1994, Pacolet Mills, S.C.
Edna Sprinkle and Pauline Smith, 24 Feb. 1993, Clifton, S.C.
George Sprouse and Virdie Lee Sprouse*, 17 Feb. 1993, Spartanburg, S.C.
Elbert Stapleton*, 2 March 1993, Clifton, S.C.
Paul O. Taylor*, 2 Dec. 1993, Spartanburg, S.C.
Ethel L. Thompson, 5 July 1994, Spartanburg, S.C.
Aaron "Jack" Thornton*, 10 Feb. 1993, Clifton, S.C.
Evelyn P. Toney, 26 Oct. 1993, Spartanburg, S.C.
Lonnie Tracy and Edith Tracy, 26 Feb., 2 March 1993, Cowpens, S.C.
Roy Turner, 30 June 1994, Spartanburg, S.C.
F. Vard Whitt, 26 Feb. 1993, Cowpens, S.C.
Delbert Willis and Nell Willis*, 12 Feb. 1993, Clifton, S.C.
W. Elmer Willis, 30 June 1994, Glendale, S.C.
M. A. "Knot" Worley*, 23 Feb. 1993, Clifton, S.C.

MANUSCRIPTS

National Archives, Washington and College Park:
    Federal Mediation and Conciliation Service (FMCS) Papers (RG 280)
    National Labor Relation Board (NLRB) Papers (RG 25)
    National Recovery Administration (NRA) Papers (RG 9)
Privately Held:
    Clifton strike miscellanea (Clifton Private Papers), held by anonymous source,
        Spartanburg, S.C.
    Rev. John Isom Papers, held by Mary-Elizabeth Isom, Chicago

Don McKee organizing reports, held by Don McKee, Maplewood, N.J.
G. Walter Moore, Sr., Papers, held by George W. Moore, Jr., Wellford, S.C.
Southern Historical Collection, Wilson Library, UNC–Chapel Hill:
  Brown Lung Association Papers (Mss. 4463)
Southern Labor Archives, Georgia State University, Atlanta:
  United Textile Workers of America (UTWA) Papers
Special Collections, Clemson University, Clemson:
  Clifton Manufacturing Company Papers (Clifton Papers)
Special Collections, Perkins Library, Duke University, Durham, N.C.:
  CIO Southern Organizing Drive Papers (a.k.a. Operation Dixie Papers)
  TWUA Cherokee-Spartanburg Joint Board Papers
  TWUA South Carolina State Director's Papers (a.k.a. Auslander Papers)
State Historical Society of Wisconsin (SHSW), Madison:
  Textile Workers Union of America (TWUA) Papers

PERIODICALS

Spartanburg Herald; Spartanburg Journal; Textile Labor; Textile Labor Banner; The Textile Worker; Una *News-Review;* Winston-Salem *Industrial Leader*

BOOKS, ARTICLES, AND THESES

Beatty, Bess. "Textile Labor in the North Carolina Piedmont: Mill Owner Images and Mill Worker Responses, 1830–1900." *Labor History* 25 (Fall 1984): 485–503.

Berry, Wendell. "A Poem of Difficult Hope." In *What Are People For?* 58–63. San Francisco: North Point Press, 1990.

Botsch, Robert E. *Organizing the Breathless: Cotton Dust, Southern Politics, and the Brown Lung Association.* Lexington: University Press of Kentucky, 1993.

Brattain, Michelle. "'A Town as Small as That': Tallapoosa, Georgia, and Operation Dixie, 1945–1950." *Georgia Historical Quarterly* 81 (Summer 1997): 395–425.

Burner, Eric. *And Gently He Shall Lead Them: Robert Parris Moses and Civil Rights in Mississippi.* New York: New York University Press, 1994.

Camak, David English. *Human Gold from Southern Mill Hills.* N.p.: Parthenon Press, 1960.

Carlton, David L. *Mill and Town in South Carolina, 1880–1920.* Baton Rouge: Louisiana State University Press, 1982.

Carpenter, JoAnn Deakin. "Olin D. Johnston, the New Deal and the Politics of Class in South Carolina, 1934–1938." Ph.D. diss., Emory University, 1987.

Cobb, James C. *Industrialization and Southern Society, 1877–1984.* Lexington: University Press of Kentucky, 1984.

Cohen, Lizabeth. *Making a New Deal: Industrial Workers in Chicago, 1919–1939*. New York: Cambridge University Press, 1990.

DeNatale, Douglas. "Bynum: The Coming of Mill Village Life to a North Carolina County." Ph.D. diss., University of Pennsylvania, 1985.

Dozier, Katharine. *The Pictured Story of the Community Activities, Pacolet Manufacturing Company, Spartanburg, South Carolina, 1882–1927*. N.p.: privately printed, 1927.

Eller, Ronald D. *Miners, Millhands, and Mountaineers: Industrialization of the Appalachian South, 1880–1930*. Knoxville: University of Tennessee Press, 1982.

Flamming, Douglas. *Creating the Modern South: Millhands and Managers in Dalton, Georgia, 1884–1984*. Chapel Hill: University of North Carolina Press, 1992.

Gerstle, Gary. *Working-Class Americanism: The Politics of Labor in a Textile City, 1914–1960*. New York: Cambridge University Press, 1989.

Gordon, Colin. *New Deals: Business, Labor, and Politics in America, 1920–1935*. New York: Cambridge University Press, 1994.

Grantham, Dewey U. *Southern Progressivism: The Reconciliation of Progress and Tradition*. Knoxville: University of Tennessee Press, 1983.

Griffin, Richard W., and Diffie W. Standard. "The Cotton Textile Industry in Ante-Bellum North Carolina." *North Carolina Historical Review* 34 (January and April 1957): 15–35 , 131–64.

Griffith, Barbara S. *The Crisis of American Labor: Operation Dixie and the Defeat of the CIO*. Philadelphia: Temple University Press, 1988.

Hall, Jacquelyn Dowd. "The Mind That Burns in Each Body: Women, Rape, and Racial Violence." *Southern Exposure* 12 (Nov.–Dec. 1984): 61–71.

Hall, Jacquelyn Dowd, James Leloudis, Robert Korstad, Mary Murphy, Lu Ann Jones, and Christopher B. Daly. *Like a Family: The Making of a Southern Cotton Mill World*. Chapel Hill: University of North Carolina Press, 1987.

Hallie, Philip. *Lest Innocent Blood Be Shed: The Story of Le Chambon and How Goodness Happened There*. New York: Harper and Row, 1979.

Hembree, Michael, and Paul Crocker. *Glendale: A Pictorial History*. N.p.: privately printed, 1994.

Hembree, Michael, and David Moore. *Clifton: A River of Memories*. Clinton, S.C.: Jacobs Press, 1988.

———. *A Place Called Clifton: A Pictorial History of Clifton, South Carolina*. Clinton, S.C.: Jacobs Press, 1987.

Hodges, James A. *New Deal Labor Policy and the Southern Cotton Textile Industry, 1933–1941*. Knoxville: University of Tennessee Press, 1986.

Huss, John E. *Senator for the South: A Biography of Olin D. Johnston*. Garden City: Doubleday, 1961.

Irons, Janet Christine. "Testing the New Deal: The General Textile Strike of 1934." Ph.D. diss., Duke University, 1988. Published as *Testing the New Deal: The Gen-*

eral Textile Strike of 1934 in the American South. Urbana: University of Illinois Press, 2000. (Quotations in text are taken from the dissertation.)

Kelley, Robin D. G. *Hammer and Hoe: Alabama Communists during the Great Depression.* Chapel Hill: University of North Carolina Press, 1990.

King, Martin Luther, Jr. *Why We Can't Wait.* New York: New American Library, 1964.

Kohn, August. *The Cotton Mills of South Carolina.* Columbia: South Carolina Department of Agriculture, Commerce, and Immigration, 1907.

Lander, Ernest M., Jr. *The Textile Industry in Ante-Bellum South Carolina.* Baton Rouge: Louisiana State University Press, 1987.

Lipsitz, George. *Rainbow at Midnight: Labor and Culture in the 1940s.* Urbana: University of Illinois Press, 1994.

MacDonald, Lois. *Southern Mill Hills.* New York: Hillman Brothers, 1928.

McLaurin, Melton Alonza. *Paternalism and Protest: Southern Cotton Mill Workers and Organized Labor, 1875–1905.* Westport, CT: Greenwood Publishing Corp., 1971.

Mitchell, Broadus. *The Rise of Cotton Mills in the South.* Baltimore: Johns Hopkins University Press, 1921.

Mitchell, George Sinclair. *Textile Unionism in the South.* Chapel Hill: University of North Carolina Press, 1931.

O'Connor, Flannery. *Mystery and Manners.* New York: Farrar, Straus and Giroux, 1969.

Perry, Thomas K. *Textile League Baseball: South Carolina's Mill Teams, 1880–1955.* Jefferson, N.C.: McFarland, 1993.

Pope, Liston. *Millhands and Preachers: A Study of Gastonia.* New Haven: Yale University Press, 1942.

Potwin, Marjorie A. *Cotton Mill People of the Piedmont: A Study in Social Change.* New York: Columbia University Press, 1927.

Rhyne, Jennings J. *Some Southern Cotton Mill Workers and Their Villages.* Chapel Hill: University of North Carolina Press, 1930.

Richards, Paul David. "The History of the Textile Workers Union of America, CIO, in the South, 1937 to 1945." Ph.D. diss., University of Wisconsin-Madison, 1978.

Rich, Adrienne. Introduction. In *The Best American Poetry 1996.* New York: Scribners, 1996.

Selby, John G. "Industrial Growth and Worker Protest in a New South City: High Point, North Carolina, 1859–1959." Ph.D. diss., University of North Carolina, 1984.

Shifflett, Crandall A. *Coal Towns: Life, Work, and Culture in Company Towns.* Knoxville: University of Tennessee Press, 1984.

Simon, Bryant. "A Fabric of Defeat: The Politics of South Carolina Textile Workers in State and Nation, 1920–1938." Ph.D. diss., University of North Carolina, 1992.

Simon, Bryant. "Rethinking Why There Are So Few Unions in the South." *Georgia Historical Quarterly* 81 (Summer 1997): 465–84.

— Thompson, Holland. *From the Cotton Field to the Cotton Mill: A Study of the Industrial Transition in North Carolina.* New York: Macmillan, 1906.

Thompson, W. W., Jr. "A Managerial History of a Cotton Textile Firm: Spartan Mills, 1888–1958." Ph.D. diss., University of Alabama, 1960.

Tippett, Tom. *When Southern Labor Stirs.* New York: Jonathan Cape and Harrison Smith, 1931.

Tullos, Allen. *Habits of Industry: White Culture and the Transformation of the Carolina Piedmont.* Chapel Hill: University of North Carolina Press, 1989.

Waldrep, G. C. III. "Toward a Genealogy of Fear: The Legacy of the United Furniture Workers of America, CIO, in North Carolina." Unpublished paper.

— West, Annie Laura. "Southern Cotton Mills: 1850 and Now." *Una News-Review,* 11 Dec. 1936.

Wingerd, Mary. "Rethinking Paternalism: Power and Parochialism in a Southern Mill Village." *Journal of American History,* forthcoming.

Zahavi, Gerald. *Workers, Managers, and Welfare Capitalism: The Shoeworkers and Tanners of Endicott Johnson, 1890–1950.* Urbana: University of Illinois Press, 1988.

Zieger, Robert H. *The CIO, 1935–1955.* Chapel Hill: University of North Carolina Press, 1995.

Index

G. C. WALDREP III currently lives in the New Order Amish settlement at Yanceyville, North Carolina, where he has worked as a baker, teacher, and window-maker.

The Working Class in American History

Typeset in 9/13 ITC Stone Serif
with Futura display
Designed by Paula Newcomb
Composed by Celia Shapland
for the University of Illinois Press
Manufactured by Cushing-Malloy, Inc.

University of Illinois Press
1325 South Oak Street
Champaign, IL 61820-6903
www.press.uillinois.edu